A NEW ERA IN THE INDIAN POLITY

A NEW ERA IN THE INDIAN POLITY

A STUDY OF ATAL BIHARI VAJPAYEE AND THE BJP

G.N.S. RAGHAVAN
in association with
SESHADRI CHARI

GYAN PUBLISHING HOUSE
New Delhi 110 002

A New Era in the Indian Polity
A Study of Atal Bihari Vajpayee and the BJP
(Politics, History, Current Affairs, Biography)
ISBN: 81-212-0539-5

Published in 1996 in India by Gyan Publishing House
5 Ansari Road, New Delhi - 110002

Laser Typeset at Akshar, Delhi.
Printed at Mehra Offset Press, Delhi.

Contents

Preface

Like many Indians who grew up in the middle of the 20th century, I was influenced by the Gandhi-Nehru-Marx hagiology, and the corresponding Savarkar-Patel-RSS demonology promoted by the post-independence intellectual establishment. This establishment has flourished on state funding, and is exemplified by such institutions as the National Council of Educational Research & Training (some of its school textbooks used to extol the USSR till its collapse); the universities that have proliferated since independence; and the Nehru Memorial Museum & Library. As autonomous bodies, they need not have been subservient. But most of our intellectual elite have chosen to be conformist, like the sages of the Kaurava court and, in recent times, Soviet Academicians.

From the late 1980s, while working on a full-length biography of M. Asaf Ali, I became aware of an ominous similarity between certain trends in free India and the policies of religious minorityism and caste antagonism pursued by British colonialists. Depressed sections of Indian society became conversion fodder for invasive proselytisers, Muslim and Christian, augmenting the changes of faith effected at the point of the sword. The religious minorities thus created were utilised by the British rulers to weaken the national movement. By a supreme irony, Gandhiji unwittingly strengthened Muslim separatism through his espousal of the Khilafat cause which legitimised pan-Islamism. Tragically, religious minorityism has been kept alive in post-partition India by vote-seeking politicians in the name of secularism, so that loneliness continues to be the lot of the nationalist Muslim.

A second prong of British policy was to patronise loyalist elements in the upper crust of the Depressed Classes (later termed

Scheduled Castes) and non-Brahmin leaders of castes that were socially, even if not economically, backward. This was in order to counter the Congress which was in the beginning led by persons from the forward castes who had been the first to take to modern education. Caste conflict, too, has been kept alive after independence in the name of social justice. The Congress as well as several competing parties have found in the creamy layer of the Scheduled Castes, Scheduled Tribes and Other Backward Classes the key to vote banks. In the absence of universalisation of education and eradication of poverty, the vast majority of these social groups remain—like the non-creamy layers of the rest of the population— sunk in illiteracy and want.

Against this background I began to study the political philosophy and programme of the Bharatiya Janata Party. Much of it I found attractive: the emphasis on priority attention to the poorest in Deen Dayal Upadhyaya's exposition of Integral Humanism, which resonates with Gandhian Antyodaya; Atal Bihari Vajpayee's criticism of the Maruti car as a symbol of elitism; and the emphasis in the BJP's manifestos on applying protective discrimination in favour of the backward social groups in such a way as to benefit primarily the poorest among them.

Recent events have shown that the BJP needs to be on guard against power-seekers in its own ranks. It has also to resist the temptation of competitive parochialism on issues like inter-State sharing of river waters. At the same it has to be sensitive to regional susceptibilities in the matter of the three-language formula. Above all, on the subject of secularism, it is time for the BJP to ask that *sarva dharma sama bhaava*, a definition readily accepted by Hindus, be affirmed also by political and religious leaders of other religious communities. One way to promote inter-religious ecumenism is to make compulsory, at all stages of education, instruction in the humane values common to all religions at their best. This was advocated long back, in 1949, by the Radhakrishnan Commission on Education. It was also urged repeatedly by Maulana Azad as free India's first Education Minister. A non-official resolution on the subject in Parliament will put to the test all political parties and individuals who profess secularism.

A related suggestion made in this book is symbolic renaming

of the Babar and Aurangzeb roads in the national capital for honouring, instead, Sarmad the Sufi mystic (put to death by Aurangzeb) who was happy to be in "the garden of Sri Rama and Laxman", and Dara Shikoh (brother, and another victim, of Aurangzeb) who reverently studied the Upanishads and translated them into Persian.

In an earlier book, *Development and Communication in India: Elitist Growth and Mass Deprivation*, while suggesting that socially concerned men and women of goodwill, whatever their political inclination, should join hands and work together at the grassroots, I said: "The two Communist parties and the BJP between them have the largest potential stock of constructive workers. This is because they have committed cadres, in contrast to the hired crowds of supporters whom the other parties mobilise from time to time. Yet it is the Communist and BJP workers who are most bitterly opposed to each other, in hostility which is gleefully encouraged by the forces of the status quo." It is my hope that the present work may serve in some measure to diminish political untouchability by promoting sympathetic understanding of the BJP among that section of the intelligentsia which has been mistrustful of it.

Associated closely with me in the planning and preparation of this book is Seshadri Chari, editor of *Organiser* weekly. He provided me with valuable information and insights. I am also thankful to the contributors to the first part of the book for agreeing to the inclusion of extracts from their works. The personality that emerges from the pen portraits of Atal Bihari Vajpayee and his own articulation of his views is of a leader comparable to Jawaharlal Nehru in the early years of independence. It may be given to the BJP under Vajpayee's leadership to rectify socially divisive policies and to correct the elitist course of economic development, thereby demonstrating to the world that there is an alternative to the Stalinist and World Bank models.

If the BJP can rise to the challenge at the close of an unhappy millennium of subjection to foreign rule, culminating in partition and in a half-century of misrule by Congressmen and ex-Congressmen, the party can lead India into a happier millennium. It can launch a new era in the polity by completing the process of recovery of national identity, and help to fulfil the destiny of the world's largest democracy which is home to the oldest living civilisation.

New Delhi G.N.S. RAGHAVAN
23rd August 1996

PART I

THE MAN AND HIS VISION

CHAPTER 1

Recollections of an Associate

N.M. GHATATE*

Shri Atal Bihari Vajpayee has been on the central stage of national politics for a period longer than any other leader since independence. His parliamentary career commenced in 1957 and for four decades he has been influencing the politics of India both from inside and outside the Parliament. His every public utterance is news and his speeches are listened to with attention by his friends and foes alike. If his inimitable oratory, repartee and humour capture the hearts of the people, his tolerance, width of vision and reasoning based on facts and figures influence their minds. In Parliament he has spoken with authority on almost all aspects of Indian life—whether it is international affairs or agriculture, defence or social reforms, industry or education, Five-year Plans or Centre-State relations.

Shri Vajpayee does not mince words when criticism is due or warning necessary. But his criticism does not hurt any one. He has never hesitated to support a rival's point of view when situation demanded. His approach is constructive and persuasive, always emphasizing what is in the best national interest. His contribution in enhancing the standard of debates and maintaining the decorum and dignity of Parliament is second to none. In recognition of

* Dr. N.M. Ghatate is a senior advocate of the Supreme Court and the author of several books on law and on current affairs. He is a member of the national executive of the BJP.

his services to the country Shri Vajpayee was in 1992 awarded Padma Vibhushan by the President of India. In 1994, the then Prime Minister P.V. Narasimha Rao decorated him as the Best Parliamentarian.

Sense of Humour

Shri Vajpayee has his fingers on the pulse of the people and has an enviable knack of defusing tense situations by his humorous comments. His capacity to drive home a point and to inspire workers is unmatched.

The politician thinks of today while the statesman thinks of generations. Shri Vajpayee comes in the latter category. This fact repeatedly emerges from his speeches. On reading his speeches one is left with an impression that had his suggestions, warnings, and views been given the consideration they deserved, the country would not have been in such a grave political, economic and social crisis as it is today.

I have known Atalji since 1957—the year when he came to Parliament and I came to Delhi to study law. It was the beginning of a close and treasured relationship nearing four decades. As a man, he is intensely human, always willing to do his little bit to those who come for help. He speaks little but whatever he says touches the heart. To Atalji politics is a vehicle to serve his country and its people, whom he dearly loves. The underlying current of his thinking which surfaces in his speeches is that we have inherited a glorious civilization and we owe a duty to future generations to leave a better world.

No sooner did he come to Parliament in March 1957, his powerful oratory and thought-provoking speeches, ready wit and humour, mesmerized the House. In August 1957, Ananthasayanam Ayyangar addressed the students of Delhi University and when I asked him who is the best speaker in Parliament, he replied, "Shri Atal Bihari Vajpayee in Hindi and Prof. Hiren Mukherjee in English."

Foreign Affairs has been his favourite subject. Prime Minister Pandit Nehru was so moved by Atalji's speech in Hindi during a debate on the international situation that he chose to reply to the debate in Hindi instead of his usual English; and fully agreed with Atalji's statement that "to speak one requires voice but to keep silent one requires voice as well as brains." Panditji burst into peals of laughter when replying to his criticism of the Jana Sangh, Atalji said: "I know the Prime Minister does head-stand every day. I have no objection. But why does he see my Party upside down?"

After the death of Dr. Syama Prasad Mookerjee, a towering personality who founded the Jana Sangh, in the early fifties, Pandit Nehru remarked that the Jana Sangh is like a chicken without a head but still growing. The sixties saw a steady increase in its influence in all spheres, but the party suffered another set back. Pandit Deen Dayal Upadhyaya, President of Jana Sangh, died in mysterious circumstances. The party decided to choose Atalji as its new President. In his obituary speech he said: "Pandit Deen Dayalji lighted a lamp, we shall convert it into an inferno." This inspired the workers for the cause.

The seventies were a most eventful decade. In the Lok Sabha election of 1971, the Jana Sangh strength was reduced from 35 to 22. When I asked Atalji what was Prime Minister Indira Gandhi's reaction, he laughed and said, "Now she looks at us with a lot of affection and smiles."

During the 1971 Indo-Pak war Atalji toured the entire country helping to boost the morale of the people. On 16th December, 1971 when Bangladesh became independent Atalji went to Gwalior to address a public meeting and I was with him. Since he hailed from Gwalior and was elected to Parliament from there, the workers knew him intimately. Sheetala Sahai, who was then the MLA from Gwalior, said: "Now Indiraji will take full advantage of India's victory in the coming Assembly elections." He kept quiet then. But in the public meeting he warned the Congress: "Don't try to bake election bread on the funeral fire of our soldiers."

When the Government announced in Lok Sabha the cease fire decision, Atalji opposing the declaration said, "This is only a cease fire, not cessation of hostilities" and made a fiery speech. When Indira Gandhi met him in the lobby she remarked, "You already seemed to be gearing up for elections."

During Indira Gandhi's Emergency

For a year and a half, during the black days of Internal Emergency of 1975-76, his voice was not heard in Parliament as it was silenced by the Government which had, *mala fide*, detained him along with all Opposition leaders. Immediately after his arrest at Bangalore I went to see him. I was surprised to see him wearing jail clothes. I said: "Atalji what is all this?" He replied: "Now Indira Gandhi will feed me and Indira Gandhi will give me clothes. I am not going to spend a penny from my pocket." I told him I had drafted a *habeas corpus* petition challenging the detention as also the Emergency. But there was difference of opinion amongst the Opposition parties whether we should approach the court. Some leaders thought that, like during the 1942 Quit India movement, we should not. His immediate reaction was: "This is 1975, not 1942. We are in an independent country. The Courts are ours. If we do not knock at the doors of the judiciary, tomorrow the judges might say we would have given relief. We must make the judiciary face the acid test."

But whatever his personal opinion, he believes in decision by consensus. He said, let me also consult Advaniji, and other party leaders. Shri S.N. Mishra and Madhu Dandavate were also with him in the Bangalore jail. They all decided to approach the Court and their *habeas corpus* petition was filed in Karnataka High Court. A precedent was set. And hundreds of petitions were filed in almost all the High Courts. High Court after High Court held that illegal and *mala fide* detention can always be challenged. But the Supreme Court by a 4:1 decision delivered the blackest judgement, reversing the view taken by nine High Courts. They made the people, the sovereign, the slave, and the servant, the Government, the master.

After the historic election of 1977, his words on the occasion of merger of Jana Sangh with the Janata Party brought a lump in the throat of workers: "During the dark days of emergency our *Deepak* (lamp) was the only ray of hope. But now there is sunrise, and the time has come to snuff our lamp."

During Janata Government, Atalji was the Foreign Minister. This period witnessed an unprecedented improvement in India's relations with her neighbours. It is not difficult to understand the reasons. When he went to Pakistan, his words "Now India will defeat Pakistan only on the hockey field," evoked applause from all Pakistanis. Which Indian or Nepali will not be happy to hear,

"There are no countries on this globe which are closer to each other than India and Nepal. History, geography, civilization, religion and the rivers have tied us together."

He placed before the U.N. the towering ideal *Vasudaiva kutumbakam*, which means the world is one family. After the sudden fall of the Janata Party Government, talking to me about international relations, he said: "If I had a full term, perhaps the disputes with China and Pakistan would have been solved."

The beginning of the eighties saw the return of Smt. Indira Gandhi to power and Atalji again reverted to the Opposition benches. During that time there was a gruesome incident of brutality against the Harijans in Uttar Pradesh and Atalji's programme to undertake *padayatra* of the area was announced. When I asked him how long his *padayatra* would last, he said "It will continue till the goal is achieved."

The *yatra* is on. Almost fifty years have gone by since independence. But now there is a glimmer of hope on the horizon. Due to sheer dedication and hard work of decades by known and unknown workers, the Bharatiya Janata Party has today become a national alternative.

"There are no countries on the globe which are closer to each other than India and Nepal. History, geography, civilization, religion and the rivers have tied us together."

He placed before the U.N. the towering ideal, Vasudhaiva Kutumbakam, which means the world is one family. After the sudden fall of the Janata Party Government, talking to me about international relations, he said "If it had a full term, perhaps the disputes with China and Pakistan would have been solved."

The beginning of the eighties saw the return of Smt. Indira Gandhi to power and Atalji again reverted to the Opposition benches. During that time there was a gruesome incident of brutality against the Harijans in Uttar Pradesh and Atalji's padyatra to understand the plight of the area was announced. When I asked him how long his padyatra would last he said "It will continue till the goal is achieved."

The yatra is on. Almost fifty years have passed by since independence, but now there is a bright ray of hope on the horizon. Due to sheer dedication and hard work of decades by his own and Atalji's own workers, the Bharatiya Janata Party has today become a national alternative.

CHAPTER 2

Atalji: A Profile

V.P. BHATIA*

'Iron fist in a silken glove' is perhaps the aptest description of Atal Bihari Vajpayee's political personality as reflected in some of his public pronouncements on key BJP planks after assumption of office as the first truly non-Congress Prime Minister of India.

This may be elaborated from at least three of his remarks:

(1) There was no conspiracy to demolish the Babri structure; it was precipitated by secularist Centre's shilly-shallying for decades. Ram Mandir will be constructed.

(2) Article 370 may just now be a secondary issue because of the primary problem of curbing terrorism, but we are sure even the Kashmiris will agree to its abrogation if the issue is properly explained to them.

(3) The Muslim problem is there because of aloofness of the community from the mainstream; but this has benefited only the Muslim leaders, not the Muslim masses; they will be well advised to join the mainstream.

Then there was the reiteration that "India never was and never will be a theocratic state", which was in fact the Jana Sangh's declared policy right since Dr. Syama Prasad Mookerjee's pronouncements at the party's first all-India session at Kanpur in January 1953.

---

* The writer is former Editor of the *Organiser* weekly.

Above all, there is his assertion that Hindutva is no longer a matter of controversy after the recent Supreme Court ruling declaring it synonymous with Indianness or *Bharatiyata*. This is, in effect, a constitutional clearance for Cultural Nationalism which is BJP's spinal cord without which it would be an indistinguishable mass of flabby flesh, losing its elan and right to exist. It has now got a popular endorsement for it as a cohesive force, taking it to the peak of popularity. Flexibility in practical politics does not include any compromise on it.

Similarly, he has affirmed again that Rashtriya Swayamsevak Sangh (RSS) is his ideological Mother. In fact, all those who matter in BJP have been committed Swayamsevaks and Pracharaks, forming a collective leadership in a cadre-based party which has no place for personality cult. It is not at all a one-leader party, just as it is not a one-issue party. For example, economic liberalisation and devolution of administrative powers and resources to the States and up to the Panchayat level has been a matter of conviction with it, unlike the Congress for which liberalisation became a matter of compulsion in the wake of the collapse of socialist regimentation.

It may take another election for the BJP agenda to establish itself fully, but there is little doubt that the party has established its dominance in such a way that only the BJP can ensure stability of the political system. The treacherous tribe of V.P. Singh & Co., who enjoyed power with BJP's support not long ago, may now profess to hound it out at any cost, but it is a case of *Bakra ki maan kab tak khair manayegi* (For how long will the she-goat escape the knife?) They are the scared tribe who know their political doom is not far off. Even the worst enemies say that the next round belongs wholly to BJP and that is hardly a year away.

Meanwhile, the installation of Atal Bihari Vajpayee takes my mind back to 1952 when I had the first glimpse of and even a close encounter with him during my brief foray into active politics at the age of 23-24 in 1952-53.

The occasion was the first annual session of the Punjab State Jana Sangh towards the end of 1952 at Jalandhar. I was attending it as a delegate by virtue of being president of the local unit of my adopted town after migration from Pakistan. Among other leaders of the newly formed party, its Founder-President, Dr. Syama Prasad Mookerjee and Pandit Prem Nath Dogra, President of Jammu-Kashmir Praja Parishad, were attending it. It was in this session that Dr. Mookerjee decided to launch a movement in support of Praja Parishad's agitation against Sheikh Abdullah's atrocious communal regime in the State. Pandit Nehru was bent upon sacrificing the Hindus of Jammu by backing the Sheikh to the hilt for what he called 'the prize of Kashmir'.

The first day's evening session continued till late in the night. But the huge gathering kept sitting patiently amidst a barrage of powerful speeches. However, an additional reason why the audience went on swelling as the evening advanced was the announcement that Atalji (an ace RSS Pracharak 'lent' to the Jana Sangh as the P.A. of Dr. Mookerjee at that time) would address the session last of all. This had become the usual way to keep the gathering intact. He was already known as a delectable speaker and a fiery poet specialising in Hindutva poetry. One could see him appearing on the stage off and on till the moment of his spell-binding oratory. And when it did come in fluent Hindi it wafted the listeners on the wings of imagination. A flood tide of emotional stream seemed to flow. One hardly realised when it came to an end. And then followed one of his patriotic poems in a sweet melodious voice. Hardly a soul moved from that pandal till the end.

It was almost midnight when the session ended. Myself and my co-delegate Dr. A.N. Verma, the secretary of my unit, went to a nearby bazar to see if we could get something to eat, preferably with a glass of milk. After much search we spied a shop with light from inside percolating the chinks of a half-closed shutter. As we looked in, we found it was a *halwai's* shop, with a customer sitting inside taking a glass of milk. Encouraged at the prospect, we too went in and sat on a bench near him. And lo and behold, it was none else but Atalji sitting so close to us.

A Model 'Nayak' from Kalidas

Those who have not seen Atalji in his twenties and thirties cannot imagine how handsome he looked. He must have been 27 or 28 at that time. Elegantly dressed in woollen kurta and dhoti with a scarf across his chest, he was the very embodiment of a model *nayak* from Kalidas. With a rose complexion, sensitive face and well-chiselled features he looked a veritable Adonis descended from the heaven. But the most striking feature of his reserved personality was an aura of serenity on his face, of one lost in imagination, with the looks of a poetic seer contemplating far-away things. He was so wrapped in his thoughts that it looked hard to break the ice and make him talk. But we did manage to exchange a few words with him.

In later times one kept hearing of him off and on, particularly about his performance in Lok Sabha to which he was elected from Balrampur constituency of Uttar Pradesh in 1957 for the first time. He had become almost a legendary character in party circles. I had a sample of his reputation when one evening we were meeting Dr. Mangal Sein, then a Jana Sangh MLA from Rohtak (later Deputy Chief Minister in two non-Congress Governments in Haryana) at the local RSS office in Ambala where I was then teaching in a college. Singing paeans of praise for Atalji, Dr. Sein said: "Listening to Atalji in Parliament makes one forget the loss of Dr. Mookerjee." It appeared to me a blasphemous remark because in my view nothing could match Dr. Mookerjee's oratory or compensate the loss of his precious life, and I told Dr. Sein so. He explained that Atalji had to a great extent filled the vacuum as far as humanly possible. I realised the truth of the remark later when I shifted to Delhi and heard him in Lok Sabha a number of times from the Press Gallery. He could overshadow Nehru, or any of his own contemporaries to this day.

Dr. Mookerjee's martyrdom in June 1953, less than two years after the party was founded, had indeed crippled the Jana Sangh for a few years and robbed Parliament of its most glorious orator and the only effective opposition leader, who could challenge Pandit Nehru's steamrolling tactics. It is precisely this greatness that proved Dr. Mookerjee's doom. His precious life was cunningly snuffed out by the Nehru-Abdullah axis, acting in tandem to trap and finish him in far-away Srinagar, beyond the protecting hand of the Supreme Court of India. In those early years, Jana Sangh depended so heavily on Mookerjee's towering personality that there was not even a second rank leader after him. The fact that the orphaned Jana Sangh still came out of the shadows so soon was because of the Herculean labours and dedication of illustrious RSS Pracharaks like Deen Dayal Upadhyaya and Atal Bihari Vajpayee, both brought from Lucknow as all-India Secretaries, apart from Balraj Madhok already in Delhi. Meanwhile, Sunder Singh Bhandari and Nanaji Deshmukh, who built up the party in Rajasthan and U.P., too came to the Centre later on.

In Delhi, the Jana Sangh made its presence felt in a big way when it won nearly one-third of the civic seats in the newly created Corporation in 1957. A year later in 1958, in alliance with dissident Congressmen and Communists (the very people who now profess untouchability to BJP), it was able to have Shri K.N. Sahani installed as Deputy Mayor with the leftist Aruna Asaf Ali as the Mayor. Atalji was the architect of this strategy. A few years later, Prof. Balraj Madhok's victory in a by-election from New Delhi constituency too was a sure signal that Jana Sangh was coming up as a big force.

Nehru's Prediction

Atalji won quite a few compliments from Pandit Nehru as parliamentarian. Nehru is even reported to have prophesied that he would be Prime Minister of India one day. In any case, Nehru had foreseen the takeover of the Government at the Centre by 'Hindu communalists', and openly expressed his nagging fears about it in an official meeting a few months before his death. As a former Foreign Secretary, Y.D. Gundevia, has recorded in his 'From the Archives', Nehru told a meeting of top bureaucrats that 'Hindu communalists' and not the Communists were the serious claimants to power at the Centre. Obviously, he knew in the heart of hearts that not all his authoritarian ways could suppress the soul of India for long. However, the party's successes, prophecies of its ultimate triumph and personal encomiums alerted the enemies of Jana Sangh, particularly the crypto-Communists in the Congress, against Atalji. Though ever since the elections of 1952 Pandit Nehru's ire was mainly concentrated against the Jana Sangh, the 1962 polls were particularly bitter ones, with the charismatic Nehru addressing as many as seven public meetings in Delhi, one in each constituency, so seriously he took the challenge.

The burden of countering Nehru's stormy campaign, made stormier by full play of the official machinery and media against the Jana Sangh, fell mainly on Atalji who was emerging as a counter charismatic personality. He too addressed an equal number of meetings in Delhi, besides a number of others in North India as the party had come to depend mainly on him as a mass speaker. This left him little time for his own election campaign in Balrampur constituency, where the Congress had put up the crypto-Communist Subhadra Joshi. Her campaign was spearheaded by a horde of film stars and writers from Bombay led by Balraj Sahani. They descended on Balrampur with a single-minded mission to defeat Vajpayee. The upshot was that he lost by two thousand votes, and that too by some poll-eve trickery employed by the Communist hordes. Though Jana Sangh lost all seats in Delhi, Nehru's bitter campaign against it had clearly established it as the main challenger of the Congress. This was apparent in the 1967 polls when it won six seats in the capital and lost the seventh, of Outer Delhi, by a few thousand votes. Meanwhile, in 1963, the party was also instrumental in getting Acharya Kripalani and Ram Manohar Lohia elected in bye-elections from Uttar Pradesh. And Atalji was elected to Rajya Sabha. He has in fact been an M.P. almost continuously since 1957.

Another rising star in Jana Sangh by this time was Shri Lal Krishna Advani who was shifted from Jaipur to Delhi in late fifties as journalist who also functioned as Secretary of Delhi State Jana Sangh. I was asked to join *Organiser*, a weekly magazine, as assistant editor in 1968 after Shri Advani left it for wholetime politics a year earlier. The Jana Sangh had made big gains in the 1967 polls. That year was in fact a watershed in the history of Jana Sangh, when it took a quantum jump in national politics. It won 15 seats in Lok Sabha and 96 seats in U.P. Assembly on its own, apart from sizeable blocs in the Assemblies of other North Indian States. The Jana Sangh also won majorities in the Delhi Municipal Corporation and the newly created Metropolitan Council of which Shri Advani was elected the chairman (equivalent of Speaker). Later, in 1970, Advani was elected to the Rajya Sabha.

The Jana Sangh was instrumental in setting up Charan Singh's SVD Government in U.P. besides those in Punjab, Haryana,

Rajasthan, M.P. and Bihar. Apart from dissident Congressmen, almost all other opposition groups including Communists and Socialists were co-partners in these governments. It was a short-lived phenomenon and was followed by Indira Gandhi's massive mandate in 1971, but still it was the beginning of the end of the Congress monolith. It is interesting in this context of SVD governments to recall a reported remark of Pandit Deen Dayal Upadhyaya, that the Jana Sangh should wait till the next elections and then it would come to power on its own in a number of states and later in the Centre also. How true! For, it has taken a twenty years' zig-zag course for the Jana Sangh and its successor the BJP to emerge as a credible alternative. And that too after the BJP has veered to the old Jana Sangh line. This reminds me of an Urdu verse recited by Maulana Anwar Sabri, the then Deputy Mayor of Delhi, in his speech at the founding session of the BJP in April 1980 after the Janata Party's collapse. The ideological thrust of the successor party was being discussed. Pleading that the party should revert to the Jana Sangh line, the Maulana recited the following *shair*:

Jise fizul samajhkar
bujha diya tumne,
Wohi chiragh jalao
to roshni hogi.
(The lamp that you had put out,
thinking it useless,
light the same lamp again
if you want real (ideological) light
to guide your way)

'Lamp' or *Deepak*, it may be recalled, was the election symbol of Jana Sangh. The Maulana, it may be pointed out, was earlier ranked an extremist and had been sharply criticised in *Organiser* by me in the 'Muslim Press' column in 1970, when he was running a weekly paper of his own. Later he joined the Jana Sangh and was made the Deputy Mayor in the Janata days during 1977–79.

However, it is forgotten that the decision to cast the new version of the Jana Sangh in the Janata mould, to cash in on the Janata heritage—as Jana Sangh had been the biggest constituent of the Janata Party with 96 MPs—was a collective decision of the party. Atalji who was the BJP's president for five years was unfairly and ignorantly criticised for adopting Gandhian Socialism as the party's creed. It was even said that he was deliberately casting himself in the image of Jawaharlal Nehru. The hard fact, however, is that as per an amendment incorporated in the Constitution during Smt. Gandhi's infamous Emergency, allegiance to Socialism along with Secularism had become a constitutional obligation for every party. Hence Gandhian Socialism, that is Socialism sans state capitalism and over-centralisation, was thought to be the best *via media*. It was also in keeping with the Jana Sangh heritage.

Moreover, those who never tire of laying the blame for bringing BJP to the plight of a two-seat party in the 1984 polls on Atalji forget how Mrs. Gandhi had relentless tried to project a pro-Hindu image after her restoration to power in 1980. She played the Hindu card with a vengeance to steal the BJP's clothes. To cap it all, her martyrdom in October 1984 led to a terrible Hindu backlash and it cooked the goose of BJP's poll prospects, especially because it had espoused the Sikh cause during the post-assassination riots. "We cannot abandon our Sikh brethren for a few seats", said Atalji at that time.

My first intimate contact with Atalji came in 1974-75 when he rang me up one day, asking me to prepare the draft of a strong statement in my 'usual pithy style' that he wanted to issue against Sheikh Abdullah. Talks were then going on for the Indira-Abdullah Pact to bring the Sheikh back to power. He had demanded restoration of the nomenclature of Prime Minister and withdrawal of all Central laws extended to the State since his dismissal in August 1953. The needful was of course done by me and a blistering statement issued against Abdullah's manoeuvres. Earlier, I had the honour of being chided by Atalji a couple of times when I was holding almost complete charge of *Organiser* when Shri K.R. Malkani became the editor of the newly started daily *Motherland* towards the end of 1970. As the Indo-Soviet agreement was signed in 1971, *Organiser* carried a frontpage headline "People's upsurge against Indo-Soviet Pact." "Where is the upsurge", he asked me angrily, although he added that he too disagreed with some aspects of the Pact. When Smt. Gandhi forced a mid-term poll in March 1971, he advised me not to carry too harsh frontal attacks on her as "once she starts railing against Jana Sangh, she will never stop."

In 1975, a few months before the imposition of the Emergency, when Shri L.K. Advani became the President of the Jana Sangh he included Malkani and myself in the National Executive for the first time. But soon came the Emergency when the offices of the *Motherland* and *Organiser* were sealed after Shri Malkani was arrested in a midnight swoop. I escaped the dragnet by a timely call from a friendly source, but had to remain 'underground' throughout the twenty months' period. The time was, however, spent most fruitfully in editing the English section of the underground literature, published and distributed by an all-India underground network set up by the RSS. I also edited a regular fortnightly bulletin *Satya Samachar*, started at the advice of Jaiprakash Narain after his release on medical grounds. Towards the end of the Emergency, in December 1976 when liberalisation seemed round the corner, I was 'attached' to Atalji for sundry press work when he was under house arrest in his MP's residence at Ferozeshah Road in New Delhi. I had then the occasion of drafting his famous letter to Indira Gandhi containing a severe criticism of her high-handed ways and warning her to retrace her steps. The letter, prepared on the basis of points dictated by him, later underwent several changes. It was really a diplomatic treat to see the words replaced by him, showing his mastery over the nuances of the English language.

1977: Volcanic Outburst of Opposition

Soon after, in January 1977, Indira Gandhi announced fresh elections to the Lok Sabha and relaxed the Emergency. There was almost a volcanic outburst of opposition activity soon, and an era of magazine boom started after a long spell of severe repression. I had then the occasion of writing his interview for *India Today*. Instead of undergoing a regular interview, he asked me to write it myself, complete with questions and answers. Hectic political activity left him little time. As I handed over a typed copy the next day, he sent it to the paper's office without even looking at the contents. I felt inflated by the complete confidence that he had come to repose in me.

During the crucial election campaign in March 1975, besides fighting for his own seat of New Delhi constituency, Atalji had to go out again and again to address public meetings. I again had a chance of drafting some of his statements. One early morning he rang me up to ask why I had not issued a statement rebutting that of his Congress rival, Shashi Bhushan. I replied that he had not given me a blank cheque to issue any statement. He said, "No, you must counter everything. You have my full permission to do so." The rival's statement attributing something false to Atalji regarding his views on the Pay Commission's report had been issued when he was away from Delhi for two days. So I was ordered to prepare the rebuttal within half an hour and dictate it on phone to a person named by him.

Later, when Atalji became External Affairs Minister, I lost regular touch with him, mainly because of my aloof nature, and there were only some chance meetings. Once, during that period, I received a phone call from his secretary who said Atalji wanted to talk to me. "Why are you writing such a long review of my book?", he asked. The book in question was *Kaidi Kavirai ki Kundlian*, a collection of his satirical verses written during the Emergency as a prisoner. I had written a review of it and published it in *Organiser* in two parts. He said it was rather lop-sided and suggested that some more verses in the book might be noticed to restore the balance. However, a third part was never written.

Much has been said about Vajpayee's liberal image among the Muslims. I had a curious experience of it during a visit to Bombay in early 1979 at the house of a near relation who is a noted film-writer and lifelong communist. At an evening drinks session of some leftist veterans, Vajpayee was the subject of discussion when one of the die-hards remarked, "Wonder, what has happened to Khwaja Ahmed Abbas; even he has turned a Vajpayee fan. I told him (Abbas) he is an American agent, but he wouldn't listen."

CHAPTER 3

As Foreign Minister

JAGAT S. MEHTA*

There were undercurrents of deep apprehension amongst officials in the Ministry of External Affairs when they heard that Atal Bihari Vajpayee was to hold the Foreign Affairs portfolio in the Janata Government formed in March 1977. The bulk of officialdom were relieved with the end of the Emergency and were ready to work for the democratically elected new government, but there were also nervous fears, in some ways peculiar to the Ministry of External Affairs. We had basked in the privilege of being the ministry of Jawaharlal Nehru, and were habituated to receive directions from a "cosmopolitan personality" like Indira Gandhi. Nehru and Mrs. Gandhi were at ease in the Western life styles and international diplomatic culture. The new minister was a novice to diplomacy and unfamiliar with representational imperatives abroad, and one feared that India's international credibility might be damaged by cultural parochialism. We were worried that a Jan Sangh Foreign Minister would mean a lurch to the "right" and compromise our "time-tested" non-aligned image and policies.

A nemesis was also feared as some officers even before the Emergency had propagated the idea that the bureaucracy, like party cadres in a socialist state, should be "committed" with unthinking loyalty to the progressive leadership of Mrs. Gandhi.

---

* The writer retired from the Indian Foreign Service after holding several diplomatic appointments and serving as Foreign Secretary, Government of India.

The assumption then was that the Congress Party would or even should remain in power indefinitely (Ironically, this theory was adduced as providing the justification for a wholesale change in the higher ranks of the civil service hierarchy as happens in the United States with a change in the Administration. Officers were not unaware that from time to time, there had been criticism by the opposition in Parliament, and more blatantly outside, that the Foreign Service was full of "brown Sahibs" with no feel for India's own culture. It was known that before and even during the election process some senior officers had privately criticized the Janata coalition, which was perceived as nothing more than a mix of obscuratist and reactionary forces united only in opposing the Congress (I). For all these reasons, one expected there would be a stand-off or even muted crisis in the relations between the new Foreign Minister and the career Foreign Service. It would not have been surprising, therefore, if the new government had decided that there should be new faces in senior posts in the Foreign Office (and not just in important missions abroad) to ensure that the Foreign Service could be depended upon to have full-throated zest to implement the new government's policy.

Supporter of Non-Alignment

The first contact of Shri Atal Bihari Vajpayee with officialdom was when he addressed the senior officers—the secretaries, joint secretaries, directors and heads of divisions, on his first morning in the South Block. He recalled that ever since he came into politics, he had admired and supported the policy of Non-Alignment and had argued that Panditji's approach in Foreign Policy merited all-party support. The historic change of government, he underlined, was proof of the resilient vigour of democracy in India and this must be projected as a national asset abroad. He then went on to assure the officers that because of the change of government, no officers should fear any vindictiveness for having implemented policies which were expressly under the direction of the previous government. He told officers to feel free to offer honest professional advice with integrity and intellectual courage. This address was an unambiguous enunciation of the proper role and ethics for permanent civic servants in a parliamentary system. It was the opposite of the notion of a committed bureaucracy. The many apprehensions in the minds of the officers in the ministry were dramatically eased even if they were not wholly obliterated.

For his part Vajpayee remained true to his pledge. There were, however, extraofficial party pressures to "discipline" the Ministry of External Affairs. From their own sources abroad, the Janata Government leaders had received reports that some officers had shown excessive zest and had harassed people during the Emergency period. Atal Bihari was in a bit of a bind—in some ways he faced a fundamental dilemma of a democracy at having to strike a balance between deference to the party expectations, often coloured by the rhetoric of political campaigning, and the responsibilities and constraints of high office. The dichotomy was sharper both because this was the first time that Jan Sangh had the exhilaration of office in the Centre and because the Emergency was a non-democratic interlude of vicious suppression and arbitrariness in government decisions. In some other ministries the secretaries and senior officers who were zealots of the Emergency were summarily eased out and replaced. Vajpayee seemed to be conscious that morale in the service must not be damaged if policies were to be strenuously implemented. It is to his credit that after careful examinations of outside complaints, some of which were specific in nature, in his first administrative decisions as Minister, he rose above political pressures and thought it fit to demonstrate that the civil service should not be penalized or humiliated with a change of government. No postings were cancelled, no officer was prematurely transferred. One officer who was most vulnerable for being identified with Mrs. Gandhi was nominated to the same post for which Mrs. Gandhi had approved him. It must have been through unmerited magnanimity that I was kept on in my post as Foreign Secretary and head of the Service even though I had been appointed during the Emergency. This was a symbolic affirmation of the fundamentals of the role of the civil service in a Parliamentary Democracy, which has to be predicated on continuity and security of tenure, regardless of political changes.

Atal Bihari Vajpayee proved a model minister from the point of view of professionalism during his tenure as Foreign Minister.

As a rule he did not give his own views without first listening to the official assessment. This was an intangible spur to competence and objectivity in reporting and advice. There was a greater margin to correctly anticipate and describe the international reactions on sensitive problems of concern to India. It was this space for honest advice which facilitated the many important negotiations which took place during his tenure as Foreign Minister. In our far-flung diplomatic network, there were occasional non-authorized departures from the new government's approach and policies but he never publicly criticized or disowned the actions or statements of such envoys in Parliament or outside.

Regardless of calming assurances given by the ministers, individuals with their own calculus for self-preservation and career ambitions could not get over the habit of sychophancy and bending with the prevailing winds, and the fear of being harmed in their prospects and postings. Notwithstanding the non-witch-hunt attitudes of the minister, there were some amusing aberrations to demonstrate loyalty to the new pantheon of power. Vajpayee himself never demanded a show of cultural change of spots, but because he was a known Hindi scholar and poet; some officers started to show that they were not brown Sahibs but true Indians in their command over Hindi and in their sartorial and behavioral style. They started showing off their proficiency in Hindi by reciting their own *kavitas* (poems) on social occasions. For his part, he never put ill at ease senior officers who were from South India for speaking only in, and asking instructions in English. He himself frequently wrote minutes in Hindi, but expressed himself in nuanced English in diplomatic conversations, at home and abroad.

The country was familiar with his powerful oratory but during his tenure in the Foreign Ministry, we learnt that his fluency in Hindi was not just of literary idiom and imagery but reflected deep thought and indeed originality in comprehension of international problems. In Nepal, his public address was one of the best examples of one small phrase becoming a compressed definition and an instrument of persuasion and political impact. Over the previous three decades our relations with Nepal, though fundamentally presuming on each other's friendship, had run into a gamut of problems. The critical factor was a psychological one—

a widely nurtured feeling in Nepal that India's attitude oscillated between a big brotherly domination and callous unconcern for Nepal's progress. In his public address in Kathmandu he expressed honour and respect to Nepal and its national personality by a simple phrase which went somewhat as follows:

> *Jis desh ke har kankar me Shankar hai, uske liye Bharat ko sada shraddha rakhni hi paregi.*
>
> (India will always be obliged to pay deference to the land in which every stone is the abode of Lord Shiva.)

Hindi in the United Nations

Nepal was homeground for our common language and faith but the greater difficulty was when he had to decide whether to use Hindi in the UN. A former deputy ambassador of our permanent mission—and a Muslim at that—had created history by making a short speech in Hindi in one of the Committees with a prearranged availability of the English text. This precedent having been established, Atal Bihari, true to his advocacy of the national language, could not jettison its use in his first formal address to the General Assembly in the year the Janata Government came into office. A draft was prepared by us officials and a Hindi translation prepared by our Hindi Officer, a distinguished academic who was specially deputed to New York. Atalji was not satisfied by the draft. He worked all night revamping the substance and almost retranslating the text. Never before had I come across the power of Hindi, with richness of vocabulary discussing with sophistication and necessary ambiguities, the vast range of international problems. One of our own officers read the English text from the translation booth, so it was carried almost simultaneously in all the UN languages.

The first political decision before the new government was whether to postpone the Non-Aligned Foreign Ministers' Conference which after months of consultations had been fixed for dates barely two weeks after the general elections. The conference schedule had not been altered even after the election dates were fixed, in the implicit confidence that Mrs. Gandhi would remain the Prime Minister and play the ultimate super host to the Non-Aligned. Morarji Desai, in his press conference held within an hour of his swearing in as Prime Minister, affirmed the commitment to "genuine non-alignment" and announced that the proposed meeting would be held as fixed. This was even before the cabinet was formed, but the burden of presiding over the functions and meeting several scores of visiting Foreign Ministers fell on Vajpayee. In some ways it was fortunate as it provided him with an early opportunity to make personal equations with the fraternity of Foreign Ministers whom he was to meet subsequently on diverse occasions.

Multilateral diplomacy in these years had no special problems for India. Kashmir was quiescent and Farakka awaited follow up on the negotiations suspended because of the elections. The real problem was to assuage the anxieties which had arisen because the Janata Government had come to power. As Foreign Minister, Vajpayee decided that the priorities of the diplomatic approaches should be given to the Muslim countries, the Eastern bloc and of course Pakistan. As it happened the Kuwaiti Ambassador was the then Dean of the Diplomatic Corps. In Delhi and so even protocol-wise he had to be the first Ambassador to call on the new Foreign Minister.

Vajpayee met the Soviet Ambassador almost on the second day in office. Sardar Swaran Singh, the previous Foreign Minister, had invited Gromyko to India some years ago but the latter, despite reminders, had not scheduled a visit to Delhi. In the conversation with the Soviet Ambassador, Vajpayee renewed the pending invitation to his counterpart. This was to underline that from India's side there would be no dilution of the importance attached to the Soviet Union. The invitation put Kremlin on test, as to whether to reciprocate with an outward show of continuity or indicate by implication that because the new government was not quite so united in affirming adherence to the Socialist pattern as its preferred socio-economic strategy, the relations between the USSR and India were to be downgraded. As it happened Gromyko promptly accepted the invitation and was indeed the first VIP guest of the new government. The conversations with Gromyko were friendly and the climate of Indo-Soviet relations never suffered any damage during the entire period the Janata Government held office. The Gromyko visit laid the ground for Prime

Minister Desai's formal visit later in the same year when, of course, Atal Bihari Vajpayee accompanied him. A realistic non-ideological frankness strengthened the relations and led to important bilateral agreements between India and the USSR.

Vajpayee knew the trickiest problem was going to be relations with Pakistan. Mrs. Gandhi's government had normalized diplomatic relations and restored road, rail, trade, civil aviation links with the Government of Zulfiqar Ali Bhutto in 1976 which had remained severed since the 1965 Indo-Pakistan War or the conflict in Bangladesh in 1971. The Salal negotiations had taken place and an understanding initialled in October of the same year. The question was whether the Salal Agreement would have to be modified because there was a new government in Delhi. Vajpayee called the Pakistan Ambassador in Delhi with deliberate priority immediately after the conversations with the Soviet Ambassador. Pakistan also responded with alacrity. Agha Shahi who had recently been designated Foreign Affairs Adviser to President Zia-ul-Haque and had been given equivalence to Foreign Minister came with a powerful official delegation. Agha Shahi did indeed seek to review the Salal understanding with Atal Bihari. In fact, with his detailed familiarity with the problem he tried to improve the terms to Pakistan's advantage but in the end the old basis was confirmed. The Salal Treaty was signed by Atal Bihari and Agha Shahi in April 1977 at the end of the visit and was symbolic of bipartisanship in foreign policy. It was, in fact, the first major agreement of neighbourly functional cooperation between India and Pakistan since the Indus Treaty of 1960.

Positive efforts to capitalize on the end of the Emergency and demonstrate the capabilities of new faces in the government was critical to India's international credibility. In the 1977-78 winter, an unbroken relay of foreign dignitaries came to Delhi. Morarji Desai and Vajpayee also paid joint and separate visits to many capitals but they were punctilious not be away too long while Parliament was in session. The Janata Government gave declared priority to repairing relations with the South Asian neighbours. Long-standing problems were successfully negotiated. The interim agreement on Farakka and the separate treaties on Trade and Transit with Nepal broke old gridlocks. But even after the

Salal Agreement, which after all was only a confirmation of the Agreement concluded by Mrs. Gandhi's government, the rooted suspicions between India and Pakistan remained and were at best only muted. The blunt but transparent sincerity of Prime Minister Desai's statement to President Zia on the lines that "We will do no harm to Pakistan but we will retaliate with full vigour against any mischief against India" carried considerable credibility with the Pakistan government but public opinion remained unconvinced, specially with India having Atal Bihari Vajpayee, a former Jan Sanghi, as India's Foreign Minister. Having visited Kathmandu, Thimpu, Kabul and Dacca (with the Prime Minister), it was a challenge whether Atal Bihari would have the political courage to go to Pakistan. He surprised some of his own party colleagues when he told press correspondents that he would not hesitate to go to Islamabad also. The announcement ignited a crescendo of public criticism in Pakistan where many could not stomach the idea of Vajpayee, a person who had opposed the creation of Pakistan, demonstrated against the Simla Agreement and openly disputed the frontiers of the country being allowed to come to Islamabad. It is hard to think of a more diplomatically treacherous journey than when Atal Bihari persisted with a visit to Pakistan in the Spring of 1978.

A Diplomatic 'tour de force'

The mission was not smooth sailing. He had frank but constructively motivated talks with President Zia-ul-Haque and other Pakistan leaders, but public criticism and non-official opinion was not assuaged. Not surprisingly there was mention of Kashmir in the banquet speech but Vajpayee stood politely firm in reaffirming bipartisan adherence to the Simla Agreement. As if to take the bull by the horns, he decided to hold an open press conference—perhaps the first ever held by an Indian minister in Pakistan. The intellectual knives had been sharpened in editorials and comments before, and at the time of his visit, his political past had been recalled in great detail, zeroing on all sensitive differences between the countries and specially on the view in Pakistan that Hindu bigotry was responsible for communal passions against Muslims in India. Vajpayee took the wind out of the sails of the hostile press by himself recalling his own political past; which he acknowledged included opposition to partition, etc., but after volunteering these points with details, he added with disarming credibility that on the basis of mutual respect, he now looked forward to good neighbourly relations with independent Pakistan. Thereafter he answered all questions in fluent Urdu which surprised many Pakistani journalists who thought he was a Hindi chauvinist. The press conference was a triumph of public relations—in turning hostility to respect for his transparent courage and sincerity.

Atal Bihari Vajpayee's visit to Pakistan was a diplomatic *tour de force*, of which there are few comparable parallels in diplomacy in countries with long-standing and deeply entrenched adversarial attitudes. The US/USSR detente was slow to develop; the important preliminary meetings were in neutral capitals and that too after long preparations, and they do not provide an example of a dramatic turnaround because of a high-level political visit. The Vajpayee visit to Pakistan catalyzed a sea-change in the climate of Indo-Pakistan relations which suffered a reverse only after the two countries took divergent paths on the Soviet intervention in Afghanistan in 1980, six months after the Janata Government demitted office. In the Vajpayee conversations nothing was conceded, but deep seated and unwarranted suspicions of permanent hostility were significantly assuaged. Even now most Pakistanis acknowledge that the visit of Atal Bihari Vajpayee heralded a real improvement in the climate of relationship between the two countries. More significantly there was no domestic political backlash in either country against the profession of friendship and confidence in his speeches and statements. The visit to Pakistan was hailed all over the world, including in the Muslim nations and in the Soviet Union as much as in the West.

Vajpayee's diplomatic style carried conviction also in other sensitive capitals like Damascus, Baghdad, Abu Dhabi and Kuwait. President Carter showed keenness to meet him during Vajpayee's visit to Washington when protocol-wise he was not entitled to go higher than the Secretary of State. In every diplomatic contact, Vajpayee showed good anticipation and was always a patient listener and a persuasive respondent. The

Consultative Committee of External Affairs in his time was lively, but he was able to parry questions and criticisms with ease and humour.

Vajpayee was at the Prime Minister's side in conversations with numerous heads of states and governments who came to Delhi. While no discordant notes were ever struck in public between them, one has the impression that, unlike the previous tradition, there were differences in nuances and priorities between the two. Almost for the first time, the Foreign Minister was not simply an implementing instrument of the Head of the Government. Some of these issues/decisions may be of long-term significance. The decision to invite Moshe Dayan on a secret visit was taken by the Prime Minister on his own but one imagines Vajpayee, when told, did not oppose it. Both felt that a rigid anti-Israel policy born out of the fear of Pakistan exploiting it in Muslim countries was unprincipled and needed modification at least in diplomatic contact. But it was made clear that it did not imply endorsing Israeli aggressiveness towards the Arabs and on Palestine. Vajpayee was alone in cautioning against the purchase of the Jaguar strike aircraft as he felt it would revive the competitive arms race in South Asia. It has been argued, subsequently, that had the Janata Government not gone for the Jaguar—which was the first induction of subsonic strike aircraft in the sub-continent—then, even in the wake of the strategic alarm of the USA (wholly unjustified) at the Soviet intervention in Afghanistan, the Reagan administration might not have given the F-16 to Pakistan in 1981. This in turn led India to buy the Mirage 2000 and more sophisticated MIGs 29. The purchase of the Jaguar proved an important step in the vicious militarization of South Asia of the eighties.

As the leader of Jana Sangh and the Parliamentary party, Vajpayee had heavy political responsibilities at home. His house would always be crowded by constituents; political VIPs which had to be accommodated, along with a programme of functions for foreign guests, and requests for calls by resident Ambassadors, etc. With all these constraints many parts of the world remained uncovered by personal visits. (The Janata Government was in office only for two years and three months.) Vajpayee could not, for example, visit any countries in Africa, some of which were of importance to India. The Janata Government had sought to repair the neglect of South East Asia, and in a longer tenure Vajpayee would have wanted to visit Japan, the Far East and South East Asia. In fact, in 1978-79 it had been agreed to have India come as observer to the meeting of the ASEAN in 1980 and so India would have been in an exclusive group of "Observers" which then was limited to USA, EEC and Japan. The exclusion of India from the Asian Pacific Economic Community and the Asia Forum might well have been forestalled. Alas, in January 1980, the newly elected government in Delhi, by taking an indulgent attitude on the Soviet invasion in Afghanistan, and in July by according recognition to the Vietnam dominated Heng Samrin Government in Kampuchea, put India at a disadvantage in the East and South East Asia for the next decade and half.

Outside the circle of South Asian neighbours, the one country of Asia which had special importance for India was of course China. Because of the history of ups and downs of Sino-Indian relations, and with 50,000 square miles still in dispute, and the memory of a humiliating military defeat in 1962 which was followed by a decade and half of diplomatic hostility between the two countries, the Janata coalition government had to be cautious in any initiative towards China. Moreover, after the Indian debacle in 1962 all political parties had united to endorse the Parliamentary resolution pledging to recover the occupied Indian territory. Under the direction of Mrs. Gandhi, in July 1976, a new beginning had been made by reupgrading diplomatic relations to the Ambassadorial level. Some exchanges of delegations had followed but the foreign policies of India and China had remained at cross purposes. China continued to refer to Sikkim as if separate from India. Firm relations between China and Pakistan had got forged into friendship around a parallel hostility to India, and China had publicly argued for self-determination in Kashmir.

With India's somewhat easier relations with Pakistan after the Janata Government came to power, the climate for improvement of relations between India and China did not invite misunderstanding and resistance from Pakistan's side. The real problem—and this was not a question of diplomatic ruffled feathers only—

was because of vicious relations prevailing between the USSR and China. While the Kremlin had welcomed improved India-Pakistan relations, it was seriously alarmed at "beneficial bilateralism" being extended by India in befriending the People's Republic of China. The Communist Party of India, in tune with the USSR, were also very anxious to see that the visit did not take place at all. With these diplomatic potholes Vajpayee reflected cautiously whether he should go ahead to visit China. The last high level visits from the Indian side was Nehru's in 1954 and Vice President Radhakrishnan's in 1957. In 1960, Premier Chou en Lai and Foreign Minister Chen Yi had come to Delhi. Protocol-wise, it was, therefore, India's turn to return the courtesy if a gesture had to be made. Vajpayee decided to pick up the nettle. A visit was nearly fixed for October 1978 but with domestic and international opposition, there was hesitancy and the visit was postponed even after the announcement had been made.

Visit to China

Vajpayee, however, finally did go to China in February 1979. It had been agreed in advance that the border questions would not be taken up but the visit was a great success on every envisaged goal. After the Beijing talks, China ceased to take the initiative to refer to Kashmir or Sikkim and privately pledged not to give arms to the Nagas or Mizos. What has not been noted is that it was only in the Vajpayee visit to the Chinese capital that the Chinese host—in this case the Foreign Minister—in his banquet speech did not carry unfriendly reference to the USSR. It confirmed, at least in objective minds in India and the Kremlin, that India was not going to barter its friendship with the USSR in order to improve relations with China. But much conventional wisdom has come to believe that China's attack on Vietnam while Vajpayee was in Hanchow after the official talks in Beijing were over, was a calculated insult to India. There was an unthinking reply by Deng-Hsia Ping to a question from a correspondent that the operations against Vietnam would be brief "as they were against India in 1962". The fact of the matter is—and this becomes clearer in hindsight—that the timing of the attack on Vietnam had a deterministic logic and chronology which had nothing to do with India and the visit of the Foreign Minister. In my view, the timing of the attack by China on Vietnam was determined, because a treaty with security implication was to be signed between the USSR and Vietnam which would in effect bolster the Heng-Samrin Government in Pnom Penh and put pro-Chinese Khmer Rouge at a further handicap. The Communist Party of India and other anti-government or pro-Soviet sympathizers in India used the ill-conceived Chinese punitive attack on Vietnam to downgrade a successful mission which was an important stage in the rapprochement between India and China.

Vajpayee's last diplomatic mission—and that was after the Beijing visit—was when he accompanied Prime Minister Morarji Desai for a second state visit to the USSR and then on to some Eastern European capitals in June 1979. It was unusual for the Kremlin to arrange a second state visit within twenty months. Three months earlier Premier Kosygin had come to Delhi and sought recognition of the Heng Samrin government in Kampuchea, but the Indian Prime Minister had remained firm that while foreign forces (Vietnamese) remained in the country, India would not establish diplomatic relations with Kampuchea. The Soviets also wanted to have a first-hand impression of Vajpayee's visit to China. After the conversations in Delhi there was no alarm that India had been seduced and entrapped by China. India had its own anxiety, notably about Afghanistan, where the insurgency was challenging the Soviet-supported Democratic Republic of Afghanistan. The Moscow conversations during the visit in June 1979 ranged over the gamut of these problems. Neither side slurred on differences of ideology but there was a clear confirmation of steady warmth and confidence, free of misgivings, on Indo-Soviet bilateral relations.

The second state visit of the Indian Prime Minister and that too as the guest of President Brezhnev and not just of Kosygin, his opposite number, was in some ways the high point in India's foreign policy. India had its own perspectives and did not present different faces to different major powers. It was transparent that India was not playing any one bloc against another. Except for persisting irritation with the United States on the question of the supply of enriched uranium for Tarapur, there was no live major problem in India's political relations with any country. But alas within weeks, the Janata coalition disintegrated and along with the government led by Morarji Desai, Atal Bihari Vajpayee also resigned.

History is likely to applaud Vajpayee's brief tenure. He was the first non-Congress Foreign Minister and came with no previous experience of ministerial responsibility. When he assumed office he aroused serious apprehension amongst career Foreign Service Officers but they came to respect him for a record of fairness and non-subjectivity in personnel administration. He sought to restore the civil service ethics of professional competence, independent judgment and political neutrality. The international prejudice towards his party was also greatly assuaged by his image as Foreign Minister. Most important, the period may go down as the happiest period of relations between India and its immediate neighbours, relieving the world of the dilemma of having to choose on contentious subcontinental issues. This incidentally eased problems of relations with the Islamic countries. In fact, with India/Pakistan and Farakka, etc., off the international headlines and the promise of positive functional cooperation on riparian and economic relations with Nepal, Bangladesh and Sri Lanka, India rose high in international prestige.

What Vajpayee might have achieved if the tenure in office had been longer can only be a matter of speculation. By undertaking treacherous missions, he showed the real potential for Indian diplomacy. His style also showed that with sensitivity, seated fears and hatreds abroad can be mitigated and that domestic opinion on foreign policy can be moulded by political courage and it does not have to yield to populism.

In a democracy, unlike in other systems, political leaders on the opposition benches must oppose with vigour but adjust gracefully when they find themselves on the treasury benches accepting the collar and constraints of responsibility. Vajpayee made this transition with ease and dignity. In the eyes of some observers, Vajpayee's intervention in foreign policy risked his being pushed to the political periphery in his own party. But with the end of the Cold War, in the light of subsequent world developments, Vajpayee's perspective from the Treasury benches holds up well in the stream of time. If this is correct, Atal Bihari as Foreign Minister may have earned in history the accolade of statesmanship.

In the final judgement, Atal Bihari Vajpayee stands out as a consummate parliamentary democrat. He relishes debate and has the capability to dissent with vigour and to carry persuasion with the uncommitted, but he does not allow the decibels of oratory to box him from the vision required for responsibility. In a period of growing cynicism and criminality in politics, while bringing the relish of cut and thrust of verbal rapiers, he also brings glamour, humour and dignity to politics. After four decades in Parliament, Vajpayee comes through in a small group who, like Pandit Nehru and Hiren Mukherji, symbolize India's abiding faith in parliamentary democracy.

—Courtesy:
Parliament Secretariat, 'Eminent Parliamentarians' series.

CHAPTER 4

Retrospect and Prospect

ATAL BIHARI VAJPAYEE*

Time passes off quickly. Almost forty long years have elapsed. Still it looks as if all this happened only the other day.

It was the year 1957. The second general elections for Lok Sabha were in the offing. My party—Bharatiya Jana Sangh—was engaged in the gigantic task of establishing itself. The benign presence of Dr. Syama Prasad Mookerjee was no longer there. Neither was there a distinguished leadership nor was there a wide mass base. Candidates were hard to find to fight the elections. There was none who was willing to spend his own money to face forfeiture of security deposit. Even so, elections had to be fought: what better chance could there be to spread the message of the Party to the vast masses, to the maximum possible extent?

It was decided to field me from three constituencies: Lucknow, Mathura and Balrampur. I had earlier fought the bye-election for Lok Sabha from Lucknow. Victory was out of question. Yet I had polled a good number of votes. I helped to boost the morale of the Party. Accordingly, it was decided to field me again from Lucknow. There was hardly any candidate of stature ready to stand from Mathura. The few, who after great persuasion and difficulty were prevailed upon to fight the election, wanted to stand for the

* From *Four Decades in Parliament: Atal Bihari Vajpayee*, ed. N.M. Ghatate, Shipra Publications, Delhi, 1996.

Legislative Assembly. Firstly, it involved less expenditure. Secondly, there was hope of saving one's security deposit. Thirdly, if luck favoured, one could even get elected. But for Lok Sabha no suitable candidate was forthcoming. I had made some name. People had started to flock around to hear my speeches. In my name funds could also be easily raised to fight the election.

To Lok Sabha from Balrampur

So far as contesting the election from Balrampur was concerned, the position of the Party was relatively better there. Late Shri Pratap Narain Tiwari, first as whole-time Pracharak of Rashtriya Swayamsewak Sangh (RSS) and later as full-time worker of Bharatiya Jana Sangh, had succeeded in raising a strong organisational structure of the Party in Balrampur. The youth, farmers, employees, teachers and shopkeepers were drawn to the Party in sizeable number. From the Party's angle there were good chances of winning the election from Balrampur. After filing my nomination papers from Lucknow and Mathura I went to Balrampur.

Prior to this I had never been to Balrampur. Neither did I know its geography nor was I familiar with its history. The Balrampur station was located on the metre gauge, which ran from Gonda to Gorakhpur. The train used to leave Gonda at midnight reaching Balrampur in early hours. I was familiar with the metre gauge. Between Gwalior and Bhind there used to be a narrow gauge which was even smaller. The train used to run leisurely and took lot of time to reach the destination. On the same ticket and at the same fare one could experience the joys of a long journey! I boarded the train from Gonda. After spreading my bed on the narrow berth, I went to sleep. When I woke up I found the train standing at a station. When I raised the shutter to have a view, I found that hundreds of crows, perched on nearby trees, were crowing aloud. Their crowing virtually rented the whole sky. I enquired about the name of the station. The answer was, "It is Kauwapur."

The Balrampur station situated between Kauwapur and Intiathok was a place of halt for passengers bound for Nepal. The town stood on the banks of river Ghagra. Balrampur was a princely state which was merged with Uttar Pradesh in 1947. People had found in Bharatiya Jana Sangh an alternative to Congress. They were attracted to it. The nationalistic ideology of Jana Sangh made an impact on them. Though monarchy was abolished, the Zamindari still continued. Several landlords were Muslims by faith. Besides indulging in economic exploitation, they discriminated on religious grounds. During my election campaign I toured many places in my constituency where striking of gongs and blowing of conch shells was prohibited. Although things had considerably changed after independence yet the winds of change had not reached the remote areas. Small and medium level farmers, who lived under the perpetual terror of landlords, gathered around Bharatiya Jana Sangh. As a result thereof I got elected to Lok Sabha from Balrampur. There were in all 4,82,800 voters. Out of them 2,26,948 electors exercised their franchise. I got 1,18,380 votes, while Shri Haidar Hussain lost by nearly 10,000 votes. Had the Congress fielded a Hindu candidate, perhaps I would not have won the election. Shri Haidar Hussain was a reputed lawyer of Lucknow. For him to maintain contacts with people in Balrampur was not easy. He used to win elections on the support of Congress. Resentment against Congress was on the increase. As a result I was successful in the battle of the ballot.

As against this success I lost in the other two constituencies with heavy margins. In Mathura, I even lost my security deposit. At the eleventh hour even the staunch supporters of Bharatiya Jana Sangh deserted it and went with the independent candidate Raja Mahendra Pratap. People had great respect for Raja Saheb. He had participated in the freedom struggle and had been the first President of the Government of Free India formed abroad. The Prem Ashram founded by him was doing commendable work in the field of education. He succeeded in fully exploiting the anti-Congress sentiment. His being a Jat also helped him. The local unit of the Party should not have, in the first place, persuaded me to fight the election from there; or if it had fielded me it should have remained firm in its resolve to get majority of votes cast in my favour.

In Lucknow, the Party got good public support. The winning candidate Shri Pulin Behari Bannerji of the Congress polled 68,579 votes, whereas 57,034 votes were polled in my favour. Had the Communist candidate cornered, some more votes the Congress could have been defeated. It appeared that in a bid to defeat Jana Sangh, voters with pronounced leftist leanings too had cast their votes in favour of the Congress.

In 1957, only four candidates of the Party, including me, got elected to Lok Sabha. The Party had scored victory in the Hardoi (Reserved) Constituency. Two other members Shri Uttam Rao Patil and Shri Premji Bhai Aasar were elected from Maharashtra. In Maharashtra the Opposition parties had waged a collective struggle for the formation of united Maharashtra. Jana Sangh was a co-participant in this struggle. It was decided to fight the elections there jointly. Shri Uttam Rao Patil got elected from Dhulia, whereas Shri Premji Bhai Aasar was elected from Ratnagiri. Shri Patil was an advocate by profession and Shri Premji Bhai Aasar was a businessman. Thus all the four members of Jana Sangh in a way represented the entire society.

In the beginning of 1957 there were doubts whether the elections would be held or not. It was only a year ago that the states were reorganised and linguistic states had come into existence. Although the general atmosphere was disturbed in many areas, yet the elections were held on time. An estimated 20 crore voters took part in the elections. Elections to Legislative Assemblies were also held alongwith elections to Parliament. Congress polled 42.8 per cent votes and as compared to the last elections it increased the strength of its members in the House by seven. The Communist Party of India got 8.9 per cent votes and the number of its members rose from 16 to 27. The Praja Socialist Party polled more votes as compared to the votes cast for the Communist Party, but it was successful only at 19 places. Bharatiya Jana Sangh succeeded in retaining its all India recognition, while several other parties, namely, the Hindu Maha Sabha, the Scheduled Caste Federation and the Ram Rajya Parishad failed to retain their recognition for not being able to secure the minimum 3 per cent votes. The Bharatiya Jana Sangh, on the other hand, succeeded in securing 6 per cent votes.

The President of the Hindu Maha Sabha, Shri Nirmal Chandra Chatterji, and the General Secretary, Shri Vishnu Ghanshyam

Deshpande, lost the election. In Orissa, the Gana Tantra Parishad made its appearance on the political scene. The advent of Dravida Munnetra Kazhagam (D.M.K.) in Tamil Nadu (Madras) was a significant development. The Sanyukta Maharashtra Samiti, which fought for the creation of a separate Maharashtra State by reorganising the Bombay State, and the Maha Gujarat Parishad which spearheaded the movement for the formation of a separate Gujarat State, achieved notable successes in the elections to Lok Sabha.

After the elections the Council of Ministers formed under the leadership of Shri Jawaharlal Nehru included top leaders like Maulana Abul Kalam Azad, Shri Gobinda Ballabha Pant, Shri Morarji Bhai Desai and Shri Jagjivan Ram. Shri Krishna Menon also became Minister without Portfolio. The Opposition benches were graced by the presence of veteran parliamentarians and political leaders like Acharya J.B. Kripalani, Shripad Amrit Dange, Shri Narain Ganesh Gore, Professor Hiren Mukherji and Shri Minoo Masani. Smt. Vijaya Raje Scindia, who today sits in the front row of the Opposition in Lok Sabha, was in those days in the Congress. Besides her Smt. Sucheta Kripalani, Smt. Parvathi Krishnan and Smt. Tarakeshwari Sinha were very active in the House and used to make significant contribution to the debates.

We, all the four members of Bharatiya Jana Sangh, had entered Parliament for the first time. None of us had ever been a member of any legislature. We were quite new to legislative work. We neither had any previous experience nor was any experienced member there, to whom we could turn for help. Being only a few in number we had been allotted seats in the House on the back benches. From there it was difficult to catch the Speaker's eye. During discussions on various issues time was allotted according to the strength of the Party in the House. Members of smaller parties hardly got any time. Even now they rarely get any.

Interest in Foreign Policy

Foreign policy has been my favourite subject. In those days discussion on the international situation used to be an important event. Prime Minister Shri Nehru was also the Minister of Foreign Affairs. When demands for grants to the Ministry of Foreign

Affairs were discussed in the House it used to be packed to its capacity. The visitors gallery tended to be overcrowded. There was virtually no space left unoccupied in the Diplomatic gallery. The Communist Party being the major Opposition party, its leaders used to initiate discussion on the international situation and India's policy towards it. The Praja Socialist Party too used to project its viewpoint. But there was great difficulty for the Bharatiya Jana Sangh in getting time to speak. The Party hardly got three to four minutes as its share. A definite time was fixed for the Prime Minister to reply to the debate.

On one occasion I had to stage a walkout to register my protest against non-allotment of time. Whatever time was allotted to the Party, the Jana Sangh members tried to make full use of it.

My very first speech on Foreign Policy attracted the attention of the House. English used to dominate the proceedings. Most of the speeches on Foreign Policy were usually delivered in English. Of course Shri Brajraj Singh of the Socialist Party, as a rule, did speak in Hindi. My Hindi was chaste. The members liked my fluent style. On 20th August, 1958, Prime Minister Shri Nehru after concluding his speech in English in reply to the full debate sought the permission of the Speaker to speak something in Hindi. The members welcomed this gesture by clapping their hands. When Shri Nehru after referring to me by name started speaking in Hindi the members once again expressed their happiness over it. Shri Nehru said in the course of his speech:

> "One of the many speeches delivered yesterday was that of Shri Vajpayee. During his speech Shri Vajpayee had said that in his opinion our foreign policy was correct. I am thankful to him for having said so. But he had also said one thing more. He had said that in order to speak, speech is needed but to keep silent both speech and discretion are required, I am in complete agreement with him on this point. You may well be aware that this could work in other councils, but in the councils of world this may not work. At least so far as our foreign policy is concerned, sometimes we may be caught up in our enthusiasm and at times we may suffer an illusion. But I have always wanted that we should speak the least and interfere the minimum. I had once said perhaps

here in this House or somewhere else that if all the foreign diplomats of the world observe silence for at least six months then it would do immense good to the world, will better its lot and will not harm anyone. But our dilemma is that when we do not speak, many others say that you have developed cold feet and that you are afraid.

Shri Vajpayee said, and Acharya Kripalani too had referred to something similar, that in respect of the summit conference in question we reacted in haste. To some our prompt response gave an impression that we were eager to attend it and to participate in it. I would like to narrate what actually happened.

It is just possible that we may not derive any benefit out of it, but outright refusal is also incorrect. In the case of Korea as well as of Indo-China we got involved because it became very difficult for us to decline the invitation, especially so because all the people requested us with one voice to participate in it. We are surely among those few countries which are in a way trusted by both the blocs. For this very reason we went to Korea and precisely for the same reason we went to Indo-China.

The fact is that for this summit conference I received a telegram from Shri Khrushchev. This telegram came at a time when the situation had taken a critical turn. When the British and the American forces were sent there, then it was obvious that such a step may lead to grave consequences and may escalate into a large scale war. It was just possible that in retaliation the other side launch a bigger offensive.

Had even a single provocative action been taken you could have surely witnessed within the next 24 hours the total destruction of scores of cities. Once a decision was reached and a button was pressed the hell would have been let loose. All the strategic plans were already there and the armies knew it well that they had to move from here to there to destroy a particular city and drop atom bombs at such and such place. During these agonising moments I got Shri Khrushchev's telegram. This was the same telegram, which he had sent to other countries, the bigger ones. I don't mean to say that our reply would have either added to or lessened the grimness of the situation but the fact is that we had very little time. After considering all these aspects I decided to send the reply at once. The reply was that if at this juncture all concerned so desire and deem it right and we too think that by going there we can be of any service, then we are ready to go.

I was sad at my failure to get elected to the Third Lok Sabha. The span of time from 1962 to 1967 was the most significant period in the life of independent India. During this short period the nation went to war twice. The cruel hands of death snuffed out the lives of our two Prime Ministers. The Chinese invasion left Shri Nehru a shattered man. Their betrayal had shaken him to the core of his heart. Thereafter he never again looked his old lively self. On seeing him one felt as if he had lost his zest. Shri Lal Bahadur Shastri died of a massive heart attack. He had been a heart patient but the circumstances in which he died naturally led to the suspicion that he was subjected to great pressure to sign the Tashkent agreement and that his heart could not endure it.

In the Third Lok Sabha the majority of Congress was slightly reduced. The strength of its members fell from 371 to 361. The Communist Party improved its tally by 2 seats. The fortunes of Bharatiya Jana Sangh registered a long jump. The strength of its members in the House rose from 4 to 14. By winning as many as 28 seats the Swatantra Party ranked second in the Opposition. The Praja Socialist Party lost 7 seats. The strength of its members fell to 12.

The notable feature of the Third Lok Sabha was that Opposition stalwarts like Acharya Kripalani, Lohia and Masani got elected to it through bye-elections. There was a wave of anti-Congressism in the country. The Opposition parties fought the elections jointly. Unfortunately the leader of Bharatiya Jana Sangh Shri Deen Dayal Upadhyaya, who contested the election from Jaunpur, failed to get elected. The void created by his death continues to be still felt by the Party.

My failure in the elections for the Third Lok Sabha was unanticipated. I had looked after my constituency well during my five-year term. In and outside the Parliament I had forcefully represented the Balrampur constituency. Being an Opposition member I had made Government the target of my scathing criticism, and as spokesman of the Bharatiya Jana Sangh had nurtured it and had succeeded in establishing its separate identity. Its detractors were dismayed by its growing influence. They conspired to defeat me at the hustings. It was decided to shift the President of the Sampradayikata-Virodhi Samiti from Haryana to contest against me from Balrampur. Subhadra Joshi enjoyed the support of all the leftist forces. She also claimed to have the blessings of Shri Jawaharlal Nehru. On reaching the constituency, she launched a vituperative attack on Bharatiya Jana Sangh in general and the RSS in particular. To her, the Sangh was a fascist organisation and its founder Dr. Hedgewar had gone to Germany and the RSS was being organised on the lines and pattern of the Nazi Party. Although such baseless talk did not make the desired impact on the public, yet it provided an issue to the Congress to fight the elections. They were adopting aggressive attitude. They had no shortage of resources. They intimidated the district and local authorities into submission by claiming to have access to Delhi. To influence the election all types of unfair means were used. So much so that on behalf of the Brahmins an appeal was addressed to Brahmin voters in support of the Congress. Planned efforts were made to generate communal tension in the area. On the day of election a conspiracy was hatched to engineer a stabbing incident in the Balrampur city to intimidate the voters, especially the women voters, who had gathered since early morning at the polling booths to cast their votes for Jana Sangh and force them to return to their homes without casting their votes. In some areas polling had to be suspended. Majority of those voters who had gone to their houses did not turn up again for voting.

Still I had a hope of victory, because I enjoyed wide public support. In spite of having brought Shri Nehru to canvass support for the Congress candidate, her chances had not shown any marked improvement. In fact the sentence in Shri Nehru's speech that there are some good people in Jana Sangh had actually helped me. Possibly what Shri Nehru had said was not said keeping me in view, but most of the voters interpreted it as pointing towards me.

Almost all people admitted that had I not stood from Balrampur Shri Nehru would never have taken the trouble to visit it. Good polling was reported to have taken place in favour of Jana Sangh at all other places except the Balrampur city.

But a common complaint received from several places made me apprehensive. The complaint was that the Congress supporters in a bid to cause confusion among the voters had started the propaganda that if they wanted to support me in the Lok Sabha elections then they should put stamp on the election symbol of Deepak (the earthen lamp) on the pink coloured ballot. In those days, elections for Lok Sabha and State Assemblies were held simultaneously. Every voter was given two ballot papers of separate colours. Seeing the growing popular support for me the Congressmen asked the voters to cast their votes for me on the ballot paper of a different colour. Some officials posted at polling booths also helped to spread this confusion. When counting took place the result of the well-planned and deep-rooted conspiracy came out in the open.

I lost the election by a margin of 2,000 votes. I polled 100,208 votes, whereas the Congress candidate secured 102,266 votes. What intrigued us most was the fact that out of the five candidates put up by my Party for Legislative Assembly, four romped home with handsome margins. Sardar Baldev Singh won from Tulsipur by more than 6000 votes. From Balrampur (S.C.) constituency Jana Sangh's winning candidate Shri Sukhdev Prasad secured 2000 votes more than what the Congress polled. From Atraula also Shri Suraj Lal Gupta was ahead of his Congress rival by 4500 votes. Shri Avadh Ṇarain Singh won the Sadulla Nagar seat. The Jana Sangh lost only one Assembly seat, that too by a paper thin margin of 55 votes. Perhaps Balrampur was the only Lok Sabha constituency of its kind where a Party had won four of the five seats in the Assembly segment but its Lok Sabha candidate lost the election. This could happen only under two conditions. Firstly, if the candidates for the Legislative Assembly had solicited votes only for themselves and bypassed the Lok Sabha candidate. Secondly, if confusion had been created in the minds of the voters about the colour of the ballot paper and the voters thought that they were casting their votes in favour of the Lok Sabha candidate whereas actually they were the candidates for the Legislative Assembly who got their votes. There was hardly any possibility of candidates contesting the elections for the Legislative Assembly seeking votes only for themselves. In reality they hoped to win the elections on the wave of popular support for me. But what happened was that they were able to cross the river, but I was drowned midstream. After the election results were declared many voters met me and expressed shock over my defeat in spite of their having voted for me *en masse*. Obviously the Congress had succeeded in creating confusion in the minds of the voters.

Members of Parliament and Legislatures are expected to look after their constituencies well, to visit them frequently and share the joys and sorrows of their electorates. This expectation is not unjust. I was elected member of the Lok Sabha for the first time from Balrampur. I had always taken good care of my constituency. Ever since my election to the Lok Sabha I had maintained close contacts with my electorate and brought Balrampur into prominence in Parliament. After I lost the election I resolved not to lose contact. I was firmly determined to seek re-election from Balrampur. I had to avenge my defeat. Before the 1967 general election some senior leaders of Congress suggested to me that I should leave the Balrampur seat and seek election from elsewhere. Their logic was that I could win election from any constituency, but for the successful Congress candidate to leave the Balrampur seat would be a disgrace. I turned down their suggestion. I again contested from Balrampur and won the seat. This time I won by a margin of more than 30,000 votes. I secured 1,42,446 votes, while the Congress candidate polled 1,10,704 votes. Along with me four other candidates contesting the elections for the Legislative Assembly also won on Jana Sangh ticket.

First Joint Session of Parliament

In the history of our Parliament, 6th May 1961 will always be remembered. On that day a joint meeting of both the Houses of Parliament took place for the first time. There is a provision in the Constitution for convening such a meeting. Barring the matters relating to finance and money, both the Houses enjoy equal rights. I had the privilege to be a member of both the Houses. Rajya

Sabha is the Council of States whereas members of Lok Sabha are directly elected by the voters and represent the whole country. Members of Rajya Sabha too represent the country, but they are at the same time the representatives of their respective States. In certain matters Rajya Sabha has some special privileges, which the Lok Sabha does not have. It is a continuous body not subject to dissolution.

It is not surprising that the difference between the two Houses arose on a relatively small issue like dowry. But as a matter of fact, dowry is not a small issue. It concerns with the social structure, old conventions, past traditions and religious beliefs. In a tradition-bound society whenever a social reform is brought about, it creates great controversy. The heat and dust generated by the Hindu Code Bill all over the country is quite well known. In fact the convening of a joint session of Parliament on the question of dowry was more surprising because as against Lok Sabha, the Rajya Sabha had taken a more progressive stance. Rajya Sabha is considered to be more mature and is a House of elders. The utility of a second House lies in applying the brake but in the matter of dowry the Rajya Sabha was in favour of taking a rapid stride.

The majority of members in both the Houses were of the view that dowry was a social evil, which must be eradicated. They also did not differ on the necessity of enacting a law to curb this social evil. The main issue on which members differed was how stringent the law should be made. The Rajya Sabha was in favour of enacting a rigorous law.

Many members were of the view that if at the time of marriage of the daughter, her father and other relatives wished to gift cash and jewellery to her of their own accord, in that case such cash and jewellery should be excluded from the meaning of dowry. But majority was against *thehrauni* (agreement money). *Thehrauni* means such part of dowry as is agreed upon as a pre-condition of marriage. Before a marriage is solemnised the father of the girl is made to agree what items and how much cash he will give along with his daughter to the boy's father in lieu of the boy's marriage with her: in short, how much the bridegroom will cost. The law aimed at stopping such type of dowry. Many members expressed the apprehension that if in the law exemption was granted in respect of gifts or presents then the very purpose of enacting a law would get defeated. Their fears were further confirmed by an amendment proposed by the Government. The whole discussion centred round an explanation appended to the main clause. The explanation read: "To remove the apprehensions, if any, it is hereby stated that at the time of marriage any gifts given to a party to a marriage in the form of cash, jewellery, clothes or other items of use will be excluded from the meaning of dowry under this clause except in case they are given as consideration for the marriage of the contracting parties."

The Government did not concede the demand for dropping the explanation. It was of the view that if at the marriage of a daughter cash, jewellery, etc., are given voluntarily, then how it can be stopped. I suggested that a middle path be found out. By way of an amendment I suggested that the total cost of the items to be given at the time of marriage be limited to 2000 rupees. In 1960, rupees 2000 was considered a big amount. Now this amount looks like a peanut. Some members suggested a limit of 51 rupees. My amendment failed. The amendment to drop the explanation was also rejected by 192 to 230 votes.

This Bill proposed to make both giving and taking of dowry a penal offence. It also provided for imprisonment upto 6 months. Besides, demanding of dowry was also categorised as a criminal offence punishable with imprisonment upto one month. The strangest thing was that to the expression 'demanding of dowry' the words 'directly or indirectly' were added. The evidence for demanding dowry directly can be produced but how indirect demanding of dowry will be proved? Will this not be misused? I proposed the amendment that the words "directly or indirectly" be dropped. The House did not approve it. Some members desired that in the matter of dowry the police should have the right to intervene. But the Government took the rigid stand that the court will not take cognizance of offence relating to dowry as long as prior approval of the State or an officer appointed by it is not obtained.

There was no doubt that the anti-dowry law was made quite innocuous. But it was a matter of satisfaction that both the Houses had, by reconciling their differences over the legislation, taken a concrete step in the direction of social reform. Nowadays the evil of dowry has assumed demoniac proportions. Every year hundreds of newly wed daughters-in-law are sacrificed on the altar of dowry. The dowry seekers do not hesitate to burn their daughters-in-law alive by dousing them with kerosene. The law has been made quite severe. Still dowry-related crimes are on the increase. What is required is that the law should be enforced strictly and honestly. There is also need to awaken the conscience of the people. In my speech I said: "What is needed is that the country should make economic progress, education should spread, caste barriers should be broken and boys and girls allowed to marry each other without any inhibition. Marriages should no longer be arranged in heaven but should be fixed by mutual consent. This alone can end the system of dowry."

Nearly forty years have passed. There is neither adequate economic progress nor the objective of total literacy has been achieved. The caste affiliations instead of weakening have been strengthened. The number of inter-caste marriages is very low. To give away a daughter in marriage is still regarded as a humiliating act. Even educated people, on joining the bridegroom's procession are seen indulging in unrestrained behaviour. As we get more and more modern, we are more and more forgetting the human qualities and values. Perhaps nobody knows where these trends will lead.

What Role for Rajya Sabha?

I was elected to the Rajya Sabha twice—first time in 1962 and second time in 1986. In 1962, our Party had only two members in the House. In spite of this the then Chairman of Rajya Sabha, Dr. Radhakrishnan, allotted me a seat in the first row. There was hardly any occasion when we were not given a chance to put forward our Party's viewpoint during the course of discussion. Dr. Radhakrishnan used to conduct and control the proceedings of the House with great modesty and dignity. Later, Dr. Zakir Hussain assumed the office of Chairman. He used to get distressed by the unruly noise witnessed immediately after the Question Hour.

The members of the Rajya Sabha, being limited in number, get more time to speak. In accordance with convention, members could speak on a non-official motion or Bill for as long as they liked. On such a motion, the Communist member Shri Bhupesh Gupta set a new record by his marathon speech which lasted six hours.

In 1986 when I got elected to Rajya Sabha for the second time, the constitution and the complexion of the House had changed perceptibly. The young members outnumbered the seniors. Because of the youthful Prime Minister Shri Rajiv Gandhi, many young persons connected with the Youth Congress got elected as members of Rajya Sabha. The Opposition was less in number but was more effective quality-wise.

The question arises: when the founders of our Constitution took the decision to constitute a Rajya Sabha, what was their objective? Has that objective been realised? During a discussion in the Constituent Assembly Shri Loknath Misra, a member from Orissa had said that the Rajya Sabha in its present form would be unnecessary. But his plea was not accepted. Shri Anantasayanam Ayyangar advanced three arguments in favour of the retention of the Rajya Sabha. First, there is great enthusiasm among the people for participation in politics, for which they must be provided a chance and they should be given opportunities to make use of their talent. Secondly, the Rajya Sabha can apply the brake of 'go slow' on any legislation passed by Lok Sabha in a haste. Thirdly, the Rajya Sabha will be a standing House, whereas the Lok Sabha will not. Shri Ayyangar concluded that for the progress of the country the second House was a must.

In the matter of providing opportunity to more people for participation in politics the Rajya Sabha has succeeded in its objective. But it has miserably failed in its aim to apply brakes on the haste of the Lok Sabha. The biggest reason for this is that even though the members of Rajya Sabha come as representatives of the States, yet they function as the representatives of their Party. They are tied to the discipline of their Party and project only the policies decided by it. In a situation like this there is hardly any scope for exercising any control. In the beginning the usual practice was that various political parties used to honour their senior members, who besides being older in age were also more experienced, by nominating them to Rajya Sabha. Nowadays, even this practice is not being observed. The Rajya Sabha is a House of elders only in name. There is no visible difference with regard to the constitution of the two Houses and the categorisation of their members according to their age-group. Only this much difference is there, that for contesting the election to Lok Sabha one should be of 25 years of age, whereas a minimum age of 30 years has been prescribed for election to Rajya Sabha.

To me it appears that the political parties should exercise greater caution in choosing members for Rajya Sabha. The senior leaders of parties can be honoured with the membership of Rajya Sabha, but at the same time, it is equally necessary that they should be quite experienced and knowledgeable. If the political parties, while making selection of their nominees, endeavour to give primacy to competent persons of various sections of the society then this will not only give strength to them but also enrich the complexion of the Rajya Sabha in a meaningful way. Retired personnel of armed forces, educationists, scientists, industrialists and constructive workers can contribute a lot to make the discussions in Rajya Sabha more useful.

In the general elections of 1984, which were held soon after the diabolical murder of Smt. Indira Gandhi, the Opposition suffered a humiliating defeat. The wave of sympathy towards Congress uprooted the Opposition. The Bharatiya Janata Party in terms of the percentage of votes polled in its favour got the same public support as it had received in 1971. But while in 1971, the Party had secured 22 seats in Lok Sabha, in 1984 the number was reduced to a mere two. I also lost the election. In the north other political parties too suffered heavy losses. The Lok Dal could get elected to Lok Sabha only three members. The numerical strength of Janata Party too did not reach a dozen. The reason for its securing larger number of seats vis-a-vis Bharatiya Janata Party and the Lok Dal was that the sympathy wave was not as effective in the south as it was in the north.

The impression that if I had, instead of shifting to Gwalior, fought from my old constituency of New Delhi which had elected me in 1977 and 1980, I would have surely won is not correct. The sympathy wave had its impact in Delhi also. The Bharatiya Janata Party could not get a single seat from Delhi. The position in New

Delhi was relatively better in 1980 when the Bharatiya Janata Party lost all other seats for Lok Sabha in Delhi but got the New Delhi seat. Perhaps on this ground it was surmised that I could have retained the New Delhi seat even in the face of the sympathy wave.

It is also not correct to say that I had gone to Gwalior in search of a safe seat. The truth is that being burdened with Party responsibilities, I could not give as much attention to the New Delhi constituency as I should have given. From an organisational angle some areas of New Delhi have always been weak. While discharging the responsibilities of an all-India campaign it was not possible for me to give the requisite time for work in New Delhi. It was in this context that the suggestion to shift to Gwalior was made, since I had earlier (in 1971) got elected from there. In those days Gwalior was represented in Lok Sabha by Shri Shejwalkar. He was not willing to fight election again. The former Maharaja had been elected from Guna. Before taking the final decision I had one day enquired of him in the lobby whether he intended to contest the election from Gwalior. He replied in the negative. But at the eleventh hour he filed his nomination papers from Gwalior. I did not have enough time to file my nomination papers from elsewhere. The secrecy and cleverness with which the whole strategy to tie me down to Gwalior was planned came to light only after the Janata Dal was formed.

In fact there was a dual policy behind the whole plan. Firstly, to confine me to Gwalior so that I would not be available to tour the whole country to campaign against Congress. Secondly, whatever be the outcome of the election it suited the political objectives of a faction in the Congress. If I lost, the Opposition would be weakened. If by any chance Shri Madhav Rao Scindia lost, chances for which were least, even then it would have served their limited purpose.

But there was no possibility of the defeat of Shri Scindia. He was contesting the election from Gwalior for the first time. Even now people have great regard for the royal House of Gwalior. Being the only son of his father he has always reaped the benefit of his influence. Rajmata Vijaya Raje Scindia too wields immense influence. The dignified personality of Rajmata and her commitment to principles has attracted the people towards the Party. Whatever success the old Jana Sangh and the new Bharatiya Janata Party have achieved in the Gwalior region is all due to Rajmata Scindia. It is needless to say that her influence has evidently helped the party to a great extent. I do not know what would have been the outcome if in 1984 instead of me Rajmata Vijaya Raje Scindia had taken the decision to seek election from Gwalior and if her election rival had been none other than her own son Shri Madhav Rao Scindia. But I wanted to avoid any such confrontation at all costs. The rift that has somehow developed between the mother and the son has never been liked, least of all by me. Political differences are one thing but generation because of it of bitterness in the inborn, natural and tender relationship between the mother and the son is absolutely another thing.

Rajmata Scindia had asked me not to go to Gwalior unescorted to file any nomination paper and had expressed a wish to accompany me for this purpose. But I did not think it proper to trouble her. I was also apprehensive that if she herself filed the nomination papers along with me, it may be difficult to withdraw later on. Afterwards when some friends asked Shri Madhav Rao Scindia why he stood against me to contest the elections, he is said to have replied that after filing my nomination papers I had thrown a challenge to him to contest the election and find out for himself what his real worth was in the eyes of the public. This is absolutely a concocted story. It is not in my nature to behave rudely with my political opponents. I always had a natural affection and respect for Shri Scindia. It was I, who had in the first place, enrolled him as a member of Jana Sangh.

Shri Scindia should have acknowledged that he was pressurised to stand from Gwalior and that, as a conscientious Congressman, he had no option except to fight from there. Though I would not term the treatment he meted out to me by filing his nomination papers at the last minute as breach of faith, yet after weighing his action in the criteria of mutual relationship I would not be able either to describe it as proper. Today he may even deny that he had said to me anything about his not contesting the election from Gwalior but it is an incontrovertible fact that he was fielded from Gwalior at the last moment only in order to defeat me.

Because of the sympathy wave as well as the personal influence of Shri Scindia my defeat was a foregone conclusion. If the former ruler knocks at the door and solicits votes for himself, then it becomes very difficult to say 'no' to him. But had there been no sympathy wave, in that case, in spite of a sense of respect and loyalty towards the ruler, the Bharatiya Janata Party would have received far wider public support. In Jammu Dr. Karan Singh, who contested election against the Congress, could not score election victory in spite of his being former ruler of the state.

Why did I contest the elections to Lok Sabha in 1991 from two constituencies? This had a background of its own. In those days I was a member of Rajya Sabha. I had announced that I would not contest the election for Lok Sabha. My term in Rajya Sabha had not as yet expired. But the Party decided to field me from Lucknow. The Party wanted to form its Government in Uttar Pradesh. To boost the election campaign it was very necessary to field from there a person who could muster more public support for the Party. Dr. Murli Manohar Joshi, being the national President of the Party, had already taken the decision not to stand for election. There was also no question of shifting Rajmata Vijaya Raje Scindia or Shri Lal Krishna Advani from the seats they had won. The Party needed a good candidate to contest the Lucknow seat. I had my old contacts with Lucknow and had contested the elections thrice from there. It was because of this that a decision was taken to field me from the Lucknow constituency.

But when it was decided that Shri Advani should contest elections from New Delhi as well as from Gandhi Nagar, I was also called upon to stand for election from two seats. It was already known that the New Delhi seat was not a sure seat. But the victory from Lucknow was a foregone conclusion. Even if the Congress Party had fielded a top film star from Lucknow it would not have been easy for him to win the seat. Uttar Pradesh was flooded with Ram wave. The Opposition was not only divided but had earned a bad name in the bargain. The excesses committed in Ayodhya on the *Karsewaks* had roused the ire of the people. To defeat Bharatiya Janata Party the Opposition had held several rallies. The presence of the members of the minority community in these rallies in large numbers, and the delivering of inflammatory speeches by them, helped the BJP all the more. Had the *Karsewaks* in Ayodhya not been fired upon, and had such speeches not been delivered as to hurt the sentiments of the majority community, the Bharatiya Janata Party would not have achieved so much success in the elections. The division of anti-BJP votes also helped to carve out this victory.

In the final picture that emerged after the conclusion of the 10th General Elections to Lok Sabha, the Bharatiya Janata Party by securing 119 seats became the main Opposition Party in the House. The Congress by winning 227 seats emerged as the largest single party. When the President Shri Venkataraman invited Shri P.V. Narasimha Rao, the leader of the Congress Parliamentary Party, to form the Government, the Congress Party did not have a majority in the House. In a situation like this, before inviting the Congress to form the Government, the Bharatiya Janata Party too should have been consulted. Perhaps the President was so much disgusted by the political instability of the last one and a half years that he did not even think it necessary to have consultations with any other party.

As a matter of fact, in the history of Indian politics the period of 1990-91 will always be remembered as the period of political instability. The Congress got defeated in the general elections, but the National Front, which included the Janata Dal, failed to get a clear majority in the House. The Bharatiya Janata Party and the Communists decided to extend support to it from outside without joining the Government. On this basis, the President invited Shri Vishwanath Pratap Singh to form the Government. If in 1984, the Indira wave had given Congress a massive majority in the House, the anti-corruption wave, of which Bofors was a symbol, forced the Congress to lick the dust.

In the elections the non-Congress parties had promised the people that they would not repeat the history of 1979 and this time they will work together. The people had voted on this trust. But the National Front, especially the Janata Dal, failed to maintain its unity. The mutual distrust, which developed on the very first day, eventually led to the collapse of the Government itself. The disgraceful history of 1979 was repeated in spite of the assurances given to the contrary. The Congress by extending its support to the group which separated from Janata Dal, under the leadership of Shri Chandrashekhar, ruined the second historical experiment of a non-Congress Government at the Centre. But for this the non-Congress leaders were more responsible than the Congress.

V.P. Singh's Folly in Pursuit of Power

Like 1979, this time too the rift in the Janata Dal did not occur on any question of principle or matter of policy. The infinite lust for power was alone responsible for the rift in the party. The recommendations of the Mandal Commission were used by V.P. Singh as a weapon to give an ideological twist to this rift. Even this was done in hasty and in a clumsy way. The parties supporting the Government were neither taken into confidence nor any effort was made to create within the country a favourable opinion, especially among the younger generation. Had it been announced on day one that along with social and educational backwardness, economic backwardness will also form one of the criteria, and some posts will be reserved for younger people of the so-called forward classes keeping in view their economic conditions, the anti-reservation movement would not have taken such a violent turn. The younger generation suspected that the announcement to give 27 per cent reservation to the backward classes was not motivated by any sense of social justice but was guided by the sole desire to remain in power.

The issue of reservation is very sensitive. It needs to be tackled with great caution. The maintaining of a balance between the declining number of employment opportunities and the rising aspirations of the younger people demands wisdom of a very high order. The problem cannot be satisfactorily solved either by fanning caste prejudices or by linking this question to the politics of vote. While on one side among the younger generation of the backward classes a feeling of resentment is gradually growing against the social injustices, on the other the younger people of forward classes are fast losing patience. A solution can be found only on the basis of a national consensus on this question. But the Janata Dal, torn by its internal dissentions, had become so much entangled on this issue that not only its Government fell, but also the question of reservation is still not satisfactorily solved.

Because of the internal strife of Janata Dal and its policy to give more weightage to the leftist parties than what their strength warranted, the question of Ayodhya instead of getting solved became more complicated. The objective of Shri Advani's *Rath Yatra* was not to bring down the then Government. It was undertaken with the sole aim to mobilise wider national support in favour of the reconstruction of the Shri Ram Temple. It did succeed in this aim. As the *Rath* rolled on, it became increasingly clear that the question of building a Ram Temple deeply touches the emotional chords of the majority community. During the past 40 years role of the Congress, the policies and programmes adopted by it in the name of secularism have, rightly or wrongly, left an impression on the minds of the Hindus that they are not being treated well.

In the Shahbano Case the judgement of the Supreme Court was first welcomed but later on the Constitution was amended to reverse the judgement. This wounded the psyche of the Hindus. The challenge to the integrity and solidarity of the country in Kashmir and Punjab has also agitated the Hindu mind. The politics of vote pursued by the Congress and the Leftist parties has also made adverse impact on them. The *Rath Yatra* became the symbol of their disenchantment. A solution would have been possible if instead of postponing the Ayodhya issue Shri Vishwanath Pratap Singh had made sincere efforts to solve it. But he allowed himself to be caught by mutually contradictory pressures and refused to appreciate the acute feelings of the majority community. The Muslim voters had given the Janata Dal wide support. Muslim religious leaders too were, in large number, associated with it. Had the leadership of the Janata Dal tried to convince them about the wisdom of adopting a conciliatory attitude on this issue they would have surely succeeded in finding a solution. But it did not attempt any such thing. It kept itself busy with the equation of votes. It calculated that the minorities and the backward classes together constitute a large vote bank on the strength of which elections can be won. But it did not cross its mind that the question of building a Ram Temple can also affect the backward classes and they could also vote differently.

Due to the rift in the Janata Dal the National Front Government fell on 7th November 1991. The Rashtrapati Bhawan turned into a centre of political activities. Shri Venkataraman started consultations with leaders of various political parties. The President was implored not to encourage switching of partly allegiance. But what was the alternative left to the President? If Janata Dal breaks and the Congress gives assurance of support to the breakaway group and on the strength of this support it stakes its claim to form the Government, then what can the President do? He had the apparent option to order fresh general elections but there was also another question before him: whether it would be advisable to order general elections so soon. Would elections help to establish political stability? Would any party get absolute majority?

Now it is a well-known fact that during the first week of November, 1990 when the fall of Janata Government was imminent and a faction of the Janata Dal was trying hard to form its Government with Congress support, the President Shri Venkataraman felt convinced of the necessity to install a National Government and even held informal discussions with the leaders of different political parties in this regard. He was deeply worried about the future of the country. How will the nation tide over the present crisis in the absence of an eluding political stability?

I had publicly welcomed the idea of the formation of a National Government. Later on the Bharatiya Janata Party also expressed its agreement with this idea. But things did not go further, because other parties were not willing to opt for it. This time the main difficulty was not how to make the Communists and the BJP sit together. That chapter had closed in November 1990 itself. Even the logic of Shri Madhu Limaye did not work i.e., if in Poland an organisation called 'Solidarity', which was considered to be an extension of the Roman Catholic Church, could form a coalition government with the Communists, then why can't the BJP and the Communists function together on a minimum based programme? But this time there were other difficulties.

Need for Consensus on National Issues

The relations between the Janata Dal and the BJP had become embittered. The anti-Congress attitude of Janata Dal had also hardened. Would the formation of a National Government be possible under these circumstances? In the event of war the necessity to form a National Government can be understood, but in times of peace how far will its formation be justified? What will happen in the next elections? Will the parties in the Government fight the elections on a common platform? If not, will not the preparation to fight the elections on separate identities start while still working together in the Government? The experiment of coalition did not succeed in 1977–79 nor did it succeed in 1990. In what way would a National Government be different from a coalition government?

One question which was discussed in those days in whispers, and about which there is a lot of misunderstanding even today, is that the President Shri Venkataraman himself wanted to be the Prime Minister and the whole exercise of the formation of National Government was in fact directed towards this end. In my capacity as the leader of the parliamentary group of BJP I took part in almost all the discussions held in this connection. On the basis of my talks with the President Shri Venkataraman I can confidently say that when he made the suggestion for the formation of a National Government the idea of becoming Prime Minister had not even once crossed his mind. The truth is that during the discussions if it was ever suggested that none other than him was better qualified to head such a Government, he summarily dismissed it. He was of the view that a person who was occupying the high chair of the President should not even allow such a thought to enter into his mind. If the question of leadership ever arose, though the truth is that the suggestion for the formation of a National Government never reached this concrete stage, Shri Venkataraman mentioned the name of Shri Shankar Dayal Sharma. In this connection, whosoever has accused Shri Venkataraman of being ambitious, has done a great injustice to the former President. They are either ignorant of facts or they are suffering from their own prejudices. Had Shri Venkataraman wished, he could have easily got himself elected President for another term. But the way he relinquished his high office willingly and smilingly, leaving behind all the paraphernalia of Rashtrapati Bhawan, is an example for others to follow.

I am, as in 1990 and 1991, even today of the view that to strengthen and to bring prosperity of this large country with many diversities it is essential to evolve consensus on all national problems. Solely on the strength of Government and administration no single party or group of parties can keep the nation either united or fulfil the demands of its development. We may not have a united Government but we must not be divided in our resolve. This is the message of *Sam vo manaansi jaantaam* (Let there be a union of minds).

Nehru and his Successors

I have had the opportunity of coming into close contact with all of India's Prime Ministers, from Pandit Nehru to Shri Narasimha Rao. Among them Pandit Nehru was the only one to leave an indelible stamp on Parliament.

With his complete commitment to democracy Nehru considered the institution of Parliament a sacred temple and was ever alert about preserving its prestige. He not only attended Parliament regularly himself but encouraged all ministers to take parliamentary business with due seriousness. Be it Question Hour or a discussion on any subject, Pandit Nehru made it a point to be present if his presence was required and listened to the debate attentively. As Leader of the House he discharged his duty diligently and also cooperated with the Speaker in the discharge of his duties. His very presence changed the atmosphere in the House, lending it greater prestige, greater seriousness.

Pandit Nehru was by nature a democrat, but he was also somewhat headstrong. If he thought something was right he would stick by it. His capacity to take the House with him was unparalleled. If and when necessary he did not hesitate to act in accordance with the sentiment of the House.

I recall the time when there was great resentment in the House over certain adverse remarks that Shri M.O. Mathai, Pandit Nehru's Special Assistant, had made about members' behaviour. Members of almost all parties had objected to Shri Mathai's statement. A notice of breach of privilege was given against him and the matter of contempt of House was also raised. My resolution was accepted by the Speaker. When it came up for discussion

Pandit Nehru sought to save his Special Assistant by arguing that it was not a matter of breach of privilege but of impropriety. But Members did not accept the contention. Even Congress MPs were not happy with Shri Mathai's general behaviour. The unanimous demand was made that the matter be handed over to the Privileges Committee. Pandit Nehru immediately assessed the situation. Sensing the mood of the House he realised that it would be futile to say anything in Shri Mathai's favour. He agreed to hand over the matter to the Privileges Committee. What he said in the House on that occasion is guidance for future Prime Ministers. He said when a substantial section of the House is of the view that something needs to be done in a certain matter it is not proper for the majority to disregard the feelings of that section. He also said nothing should be done here that would lead the people to feel that something is sought to be covered up or hidden from the public eye. This small incident throws ample light on Pandit Nehru's personality.

LAL BAHADUR SHASTRI

Shri Lal Bahadur Shastri's election as Prime Minister after Pandit Nehru highlights both the maturity and the apparent contradiction of Indian democracy. Nehru had regal upbringing on the one hand, and on the other hand Lal Bahadur Shastri fought his way through abject poverty. A barrister who had acquired Western education and imbibed Western culture at Cambridge University on the one hand, and Lal Bahadur who had obtained the 'Shastri' degree at the Kashi Vidyapeeth on the other. Despite this dissimilarity Shri Shastri proved a worthy successor to Pandit Nehru, which shows the inner strength and elasticity of the Indian society. Before becoming Prime Minister Shri Shastri had impressed everybody with his capacity by working ably in many positions. I still recall the time he presented his budget as Minister for Railways in Hindi.

Shri Shastri rose to dizy heights during the Indo-Pak War. Had he lived he would have changed the direction of Indian polity. The mystery that covered the circumstances of Shri Shastri's tragic death in Tashkent has now been more or less removed. No basis has been found for the suspicion that his death was not natural. I was greatly relieved to read in the book by Shri Shastri's special assistant Shri C.P. Shrivastav that I was not the cause for worry for Shri Shastri that fateful night in Tashkent. What happened was that when the news of the Tashkent agreement reached Delhi, the press asked for my reaction. I criticised the agreement severely and called it a surrender. This news was conveyed to Shri Shastri in Tashkent. When the news of his death due to heart-failure arrived, I got the guilty feeling that my harsh criticism may have deeply affected him. But Shri Shrivastav's narration of that fateful night in Tashkent has lifted a big burden off my mind.

During the Indo-Pak War Shri Shastri made arrangements to keep Opposition leaders posted with news from the front every evening. When necessary he would personally contact them and brief them.

Shri Shastri's sudden death posed before the country the question of choosing a new Prime Minister. There were many claimants for the post. Once again Congress President Shri Kamaraj played a decisive role. He had already decided in favour of Smt. Indira Gandhi. Other senior Congress leaders too did not wish to see a formidable person like Shri Morarji become Prime Minister. In the belief that Indiraji would be pliable in their hands they disregarded abler and more experienced leaders and put the reins of the country into Indiraji's hands.

In the innermost recesses of his heart Pandit Nehru might have certainly wished his daughter to succeed him, but it does not appear that he made any special effort in that direction. He must have certainly liked Indiraji being made Congress President and indirectly he may have even helped in it, but it seems other Congress leaders were more responsible for making her Congress President, as they sought to influence Nehruji through her. The participation of Congress in the "liberation struggle" against the first Communist Government of Kerala and later the Centre's decision to topple it exposes senior Congress leaders' strategy in making Indiraji Congress President.

INDIRA GANDHI

In contrast to her father, Indiraji generally stayed away from Parliament. In the beginning she was so silent that she was called a dumb doll. But that was unfair to her. She believed in talking little. After listening to all, she formed her opinion and expressed it at the end if at all.

Morarji Desai's personality was just the opposite. He expressed himself even before listening to others. He had some firm beliefs, some definite opinions, and he never hesitated to express them. Indiraji was cleverer in this respect. Instead of attending the House she used to turn the levers of power sitting in her office. She kept a sharp eye on what was happening at home and abroad, what was going on in Parliament, what was happening within Opposition Parties. She impressed the world by ruling for 14 years and she bested the Opposition many a time.

Whenever I met Smt. Indira Gandhi, I felt she was in the grip of some unknown fear. There was a deep sense of insecurity in some corner of her mind. Watching everybody, not saying anything openly, thinking that the whole world was conspiring against her—all this indicates a mindset that needs to be analysed in depth if we are to fully understand Indiraji's personality and actions.

It was this mentality of hers that made her ensure Shri Neelam Sanjiva Reddy's defeat even after filing his nomination for the President's post. She thought if Shri Reddy became President he would not let her continue as Prime Minister for long. Later events proved that this was a baseless fear and President Reddy did not pose any danger for her.

Had Indiraji resigned from the Prime Ministership after her election was nullified in 1975 and taken up leadership of the Congress, there was no one to challenge her within the party. But she had no confidence in herself, and this led her to declaring an Emergency. She preferred throttling democracy for the sake of saving her position of power. History will never forgive her for this. Later she did succeed in regaining power, but the blot on her name can never be washed away.

Indiraji's role in the creation of Bangladesh will always be appreciated. The firmness and statesmanship with which she formulated the strategy to defeat Pakistan, as a result of which Pakistani forces were forced to lay down arms, has become a legend full of pride and glory. The then Defence Minister Shri

Jagjivan Ram made a substantial contribution to this success, but it is Indiraji who is given the credit of creating an independent Bangladesh. However, when India was humiliated by China the entire blame had been laid at the door of the then Defence Minister, Shri Krishna Menon. No one can say how and to whom the cycle of events would do justice or injustice in apportioning praise and blame.

I was also one of those who praised Indiraji highly for her successful leadership in the Bangladesh crisis, but the impression is wrong that I once called her Durga. I had certainly praised her but had not called her Durga. I have clarified this fact a number of times, but this impression is so deep-seated that people still praise me by saying that in that hour of crisis I rose above party politics, extended full cooperation to the Government, and described Indiraji as Durga. Smt. Pupul Jayakar wanted to mention this when she was writing Indiraji's biography, but though she refrained from doing so on my objecting to it, she did make a detailed investigation about it. After going through Parliament's proceedings and newspapers of the time she was convinced that I had not hailed Indiraji as Durga. The question arises—how did the impression spread? I think some leader described her like that at that time, and some newspapers attributed it to me.

I often clashed with Indiraji in Parliament, but she never let political differences affect personal relationships. Her tragic assassination removed suddenly from our midst a personality that will not only be remembered as the worthy daughter of a worthy father but also for her own ability, dexterity, decisiveness and firmness.

RAJIV GANDHI

Shri Rajiv Gandhi became Prime Minister at a tragic juncture. He had no administrative experience. He did not even have any interest in politics. He was happy to be a pilot. Once when I alighted from a plane I saw a young man wearing his cap standing below and greeting me with a smiling *Namaskar*. I could not recognise that he was Shri Rajiv Gandhi, son of the Prime Minister. On another occasion, when he was going out of Delhi with his family, there was unexpected delay in the plane's departure. Had he so wished he could have returned home with Smt. Sonia Gandhi and the children, but he decided to spend time in the airport's resting lounge. He kept playing and chatting with his children. But Prime Ministership greatly changed his informal and simple nature.

Shri Rajiv Gandhi was always particular about etiquette. Whenever he met anyone he did so heartily. He would try to understand the other's point of view and make him understand his own. But his lack of experience and absence of proper advice made him commit many grave mistakes. I saw him at close quarters as a pilot, as General Secretary of the Congress, and as Prime Minister. He showed great fortitude in the wake of his defeat in the elections. As Leader of the Opposition he never missed an opportunity to put the Government in a difficult position. But because of lack of adequate experience his decisions at times bordered on impropriety. The way he behaved in Srinagar as a member of the All Party Parliamentary Committee set up for studying the situation in Kashmir was not liked even by his well-wishers. Similarly by being present at the independence celebrations of Namibia he greatly embarrassed not only Prime Minister Vishwanath Pratap Singh but himself as well. He took a long time to realise the fact that he was no longer in power and as the Leader of the Opposition he had to play a constructive role.

Indian Democracy — Strength and Weakness

India is the largest democracy of the world. Leaving aside the short span of 1975 and 1976 the reign of democracy has remained uninterrupted. Adult franchise, impartial elections, independent judiciary, multi-party system and free press are the cornerstones of our democratic set-up. People change Governments through the ballot. In 1977, the people defeated even a formidable Prime Minister like Smt. Indira Gandhi at the hustings. In 1980, the Janata Party Government, which had ascended the throne of power on the tide of people's wrath against the excesses committed in the Emergency, and had the blessings of Lok Nayak Jaiprakash Narain, was similarly swept out of power by the same people. In 1989, even the Government of Rajiv Gandhi, to which just five years earlier the people had given a massive mandate to rule, was in a similar way swept off by the same electorates. In the States also people have changed Governments in this way and demonstrated the decisive power of the ballot.

Does it mean that Indian democracy is inwardly as strong and mighty as it looks alive and vibrant outwardly? Are all democratic institutions discharging their responsibilities properly? Are the democratic values of life being defended in the country? Has democracy taken deep roots in our land? While searching for answers to these questions one is sorely disappointed.

In Parliament there is less discussion but more noise. Elections have been reduced to a farce because of the use of money power on an extensive scale. The party system is getting eroded due to the unethical trend of horse-trading. Accusing fingers are beginning to be raised at the impartiality of the judiciary. The Election Commission has become a target for charges and countercharges. Politics is becoming increasingly criminalised. The outer shell of democracy is, no doubt, intact but it appears to be motheaten from inside.

Democracy is not a game of simple majority of numbers, a majority of 51 versus a minority of 49. Our election system is such in which it is not necessary for the winning candidate of the victorious party to secure even 51 per cent votes. The Westminster system already suffers from the defect of feigned majority on the strength of minority of votes. The multiplicity of parties, and more than it the division of vote on account of the presence of a large number of candidates in the elections, is giving rise to a strange phenomenon. Parties are forming Governments on the strength of 30-35 per cent of votes, and by securing even a lesser percentage of votes candidates are getting elected to Lok Sabha and State Legislatures. This system is basically defective.

In accordance with the Westminster system the Leader of the Opposition is accorded a special status and he gets salary, allowances and perquisites equal to what members of the Council of Ministers receive. Following the British convention in India too the office of the Chairman of the Public Accounts Committee goes to the Opposition. So much so the tradition of giving the post of Deputy Speaker to the Opposition is also somehow or other being honoured. At the root of these Westminster conventions and traditions lies a genuine respect for the Opposition. It is needless to say that this sentiment is conspicuous by its absence in our country. Far from basic respect for the Opposition, even an attitude of tolerance towards it is lacking. The Opposition is treated as enemy. Not only are they treated as such, but declarations to this effect are publicly made. In fact the growing intolerance is posing a serious danger to the democratic fabric. As a result of imitating the Westminster electoral model, many divisive factors which were already present in the Indian polity became more acute. Society, divided by considerations of caste, subcaste, modes of worship, languages and different life styles, is getting gradually disintegrated. Communalism is at its worst. The poison of casteism is playing havoc with public life. The factors which once united the people have now assumed a divisive role. Politics has now been reduced to a game of power. To capture power by questionable methods and, after usurping it, to remain in power by whatever means has become the sole objective of politics. In their lust for power the political parties do not refrain from giving encouragement to secessionist forces; they do not desist from hobnobbing with anti-national elements.

For the success of democracy it is very essential that the party system should be strong. In a large country like India with diverse traits the two-party system, unlike in Britain, does not seem to be practicable. Nonetheless, it is imperative that whatever be the number of parties, they should be based on policies and programmes, should observe democratic norms, have regular membership, hold regular organisational elections and on the basis of their clear-cut manifestos should go before the voters to solicit their support.

Due to historical reasons the Congress has acted more as a political platform and less as a political party. From communists to communalists, all have played politics under its umbrella. The Congress has changed with times as much as it hasn't. It may have taken 60 years to journey from the goal of creating a socialistic society to its new haven of free economy but it has from the angle of ideology traversed that distance with great ease. Its flexibility may have been an asset to it, but it has been a source of great embarrassment to other parties. There is a very thin line of demarcation between pragmatism and opportunism. The proverbial saying *Jaise bahe bayar, peeth tab taisi dijiye* (As the wind blows, so set your sails) may be a sure formula for leading a comfortable life, but it cannot induce a newly independent nation to strive hard for building it anew. For this, a deep commitment to certain values of life is essential.

CHAPTER 5

Building India Anew

(Presented here are extracts from speeches made by Atal Bihari Vajpayee on various cultural, social and economic issues in Parliament during the last four decades.)

Hindutva is Indian Ethos

It is said, in English, that ours is a secular country; and it should remain secular. There is no objection to it. But the difficulty arises when the word is translated as *Dharamnirapeksh* in Hindi. Not only in my opinion but in the common man's opinion, ours is a religious country. To be religious or having good qualities mean much the same thing these days. I would like to submit to the so-called custodians of secularism that *Dharamnirapeksh* is not the equivalent of the word 'secularism'. It is creating confusion among the people. Is the Government anti-religious? Does the Government want to make the country non-religious?. . .

What is the identity of this country which we call Bharat, Hindustan or India? Where are the life roots of this country? No new nation was born in the year 1947. The nations which emerged in Europe after the Second World War are in a process of disintegration at present. But this country has remained united for centuries.

Nehru said: "Since thousands of years, a chain of life continued and I am proud that I am also a link of that chain. I do not want to separate myself from that chain." Which is this chain? Is it not Hindu? But an objection has been raised to the word Hindu after independence or after the division of the country.... If this is not a Hindu country or if it is not integrated by the Hindu culture, then what other factors are responsible for the integrity of this country? Who were those great men who inspired the people for making sacrifices at the time of foreign invasions? Why do Shivaji and Maharana Pratap Singh inspire the people of this country even today?

The hon'ble Home Minister said the other day that the RSS members consider Hinduism as nationalism. He should understand that the term Hinduism is not used as Hindu religion.*

(Lok Sabha, 2nd March 1993)

Two Aspects of Ayodhya

We as well as the Government of Uttar Pradesh had requested the Central Government to get the matter expedited in the Court either way. How long would the case be kept pending?... The assembled *Karsevaks* were of the view that they would get some opportunity for construction work. But they could not get the same. However, efforts were made to control the situation. The General Secretary of the RSS had been requesting the people, in southern languages, that no *Karsevak* should go towards the structure. He should not take part in demolition activity.

The press reporters who went there told me that Shri Advani was very sad when the structure was demolished. He was in tears. That is why he sent in his resignation, expressing his regret over the incident. Owning the responsibility, Shri Kalyan Singh (BJP Chief Minister of Uttar Pradesh) also resigned...

We would like to know who was that group, from where it came and who organised it. I repeat it again that the *Karsevaks* who took part in demolishing the structure should come forward and reveal their participation in the demolition. If punishment is given, they should accept it...

But there is another aspect also of this issue. There was a temple as well. Namaz was not offered in the mosque. Even entry to the mosque was prohibited. But prayer was offered in the

* This affirmation by Vajpayee anticipated by nearly three years the unanimous judgment of a three-member bench of the Supreme Court, on 11th December 1995, that there is no inherent or necessary contradiction between Hindutva and secularism. Extracts from the judgment are given in the Appendix II.

temple by the orders of the court....

The reaction to the happening in Ayodhya throughout the country and abroad is more or less over-reaction. I think that primarily the outlook and the approach of Government to the problem is no less a factor to be blamed for it. We did not point out to the world that it was a disputed structure. It was repeatedly stated that there was a mosque. We never clarified that, along with the structure of the mosque, there is a temple also, in which prayer and worship is being done, and this dispute has been going on for the last 500 years. There are umpteen examples like this throughout the world. When Russia occupied Warsaw, a (Russian Orthodox) church was built there. When Poland became independent, the first thing it did was demolition of the church. History bears testimony to this. When Toynbee visited India he taunted us that it is possible in India alone that a mosque has been erected after demolishing a temple. We have allowed wrong propaganda in the world... Had they known the fact that an ancient temple was razed to the ground in order to build this mosque, then they would have asked the Muslims to settle the issue amicably.

(Lok Sabha, 17th December 1992)

Why Muslim League in Free India?

Why is the communal atmosphere in the country deteriorating? Why does a section of the Muslim society say in Bombay we are not prepared to say Vande Mataram? Vande Mataram is not anti-Islamic. When believers in Islam recite the Namaz do they not bow their heads to the 'pak' (pure) soil of this country?

Shri S. A. Shamim: That is for Khuda.

Shri A. B. Vajpayee: But the head is touched to the ground. We eat the food this soil produces. It is the soil that gives us shelter in our final moments.

When the same Muslim member interrupted to say that the National Anthem is Jana Gana Mana and not Vande Mataram, Vajpayee clarified the position by quoting the statement made on the subject by the Chairman of the Constituent Assembly on 24th January, 1950: "The composition consisting of the words-music known as Jana Gana Mana is the National Anthem of India subject to such alteration in one word as the Government may authorise as the occasion arises, and the song Vande Mataram which has played a historic part in the struggle for Indian freedom shall be honoured equally with the Jana Gana Mana and shall have equal status with it". Atal Bihari Vajpayee went on to say:

The trouble in Bombay started when students of Urdu madrasas refused to stand up to sing Vande Mataram on January 26 (Republic Day).... Tomorrow they may say we will not bow before the tricolour because we bow before Allah. Every man living in India will have to bow before the tricolour. . .

Let us close this unfortunate controversy over Vande Mataram. The Muslim League raised it. And it did not remain confined to the League. Shri Khandvani, leader of the Congress party in the Bombay Corporation, also sided with them.

The Prime Minister says the victory of communal forces in the Bombay Corporation is causing riots there. But who gave life to communalism by forming a government in Kerala in alliance with the Muslim League? What is the need of the Muslim League in independent India? Parties should have their doors open for all. But instead of condemning the Muslim League, a government is formed in league with it. The Prime Minister feels unhappy when that same Muslim League opposes Vande Mataram and wins in Bombay. You will have to eat the bitter fruits of the seeds you sowed. I would say communalism is like a double-edged sword. You cannot fight the communalism of other classes by encouraging Muslim communalism.

(Lok Sabha, 29th March 1973)

Politics from Places of Worship

In view of the circumstances in which the country was partitioned, and of the evil effects of that partition which we have not yet been able to forget, we have to prevent the repetition of events that strike at the secular form of the Indian republic and incite communal passions again. We have established a secular state. A natural corollary of this is that politics and religion should be kept apart.

In the past, all freedom struggles were linked with religion, but now there is no propriety in linking a mode of worship with politics. Of course if there is any difficulty in worshipping in a temple or a gurudwara, or if the Government is adopting any discriminatory policy in purely religious matters, it can be considered. But if *fatwas* regarding elections are issued from mosques, a political and communal agitation for a separate State is conducted from gurudwaras, churches are made the centre of separatist activities, and if then, as a result, people start going to temples for political activities, it cannot be supported.

Let us not tolerate the communalism of any community, whether it is a minority or a majority. All rules apply equally to all. But we see that in Punjab the police cannot enter a gurudwara, whereas in Chandigarh the police can enter an Arya Samaj mandir. I do not support conducting political activities in Arya Samaj mandirs. I say no one should have the right to conduct such activities, whether it is a gurudwara or a temple or a mosque or any other religious place.

(Lok Sabha, 17th February 1961)

If politics in this country is played from masjid, from the church, from the gurudwara, then it cannot be stopped from reaching the door of the temple. There are people who go to the mosque during elections to take orders from the Imam. We do not go.

I have never been to any Shankaracharya till today to seek blessings during elections. During the elections, I had gone to a certain area. I got the opportunity to meet one Shankaracharya. The newsmen asked me as to what sort of talk I had with him, whether I sought blessings for the Party. I said, no, I asked for blessings for the country. Parties may exist, they may not exist, but the country must exist.

Mr. Speaker, Sir, the Congress Party in Mizoram seeks votes in the name of installing a Christian Government and writes so in its election manifesto. If they seek vote in the election in the name of installing a Christian Government in Mizoram, it will not do. The matter is pending in the Supreme Court since long. I can present this manifesto. One-sided action will not do, there can be no one-sided battle against fundamentalism. Encouraging communalism on the one hand and fighting it on the other cannot go together.

The Congress Party talked about minority communalism for the first time in the Tirupati conference. This has been said for the first time. Was the country not partitioned because of minority communalism?

My submission is that if communalism is to be fought, if the feeling of nationalism is to be created in its true sense, if communalism is to be rooted out, then there cannot be different yardsticks to measure communalism. If we want to curb narrow-mindedness then we must fight it out wherever it is seen. If you compromise with communalism for the sake of securing votes, then the tendency to compromise with other types of communalism will grow.

Shri Ram Vilas Paswan: We will fight out evil with evil means....

Shri Vajpayee: I do not want to start a verbal dual with him but throughout the country he is saying that the President is Brahmin, Vice-President is Brahmin and the Prime Minister is also a Brahmin.

Shri Ram Vilas Paswan: That is what I am saying even today.

Shri Vajpayee: He has stated that the leader of the Opposition is also a Brahmin. I did not know the caste of Shri Advani. We never go into the caste. Mr. Speaker, Sir, is it not another way to spread venom?

People who themselves enacted a new legislation keeping aside the verdict of the Supreme Court in the Shahbano case, and amended the Constitution, should not give sermons to us.

(Lok Sabha, 17th July 1992)

Social Regeneration

This Bill is proof of the fact that during the past 22 years our efforts to end untouchability have failed, and now it has become necessary to stiffen relevant laws still further. When our Constitution was framed in 1950 we had made a declaration in Article 17 of it. The declaration was: "Untouchability has been ended and its practice in any form is prohibited. Practice of any uneligibility due to untouchability will be an offence punishable by law".

The framers of the Constitution declared that untouchability was at an end, but the mere declaration did not end untouchability. A law was also passed to end it. But now even that law seems insufficient. Will the Hon. Minister tell us how many people were prosecuted all over the country for practicing untouchability in contravention of the existing law, and how many of them were punished? Is it not true that it is very difficult to prove such cases in court?

Untouchability is a cognizable. The police need not wait for a complaint to be lodged. It can intervene on its own. But even the police include people who believe in untouchability; even those who do justice in such cases in the court have untouchability ingrained in their cultural influences. This is why law cannot eradicate this evil.

No one can be against your stiffening of the penalty under law. If you are going to stiffen it, stiffen it still further. But we would be making a mistake if we think we have put an end to untouchability by merely passing a law.

THE SHAME OF UNTOUCHABILITY

Untouchability is a sin. We are atoning for this sin for hundreds of years. But this sin is not yet at an end. To some extent untouchability is practiced even in the United States. Untouchability in India is worse than racial discrimination based on pigmentation. In it discrimination is practised on the basis of how fair or dark your skin is. But here everyone has the same skin colour, the same features, the same blood flows through their veins, and yet there is discrimination on the basis of birth. This is against humanity. This is against Indian philosophy, even against our religion.

I do not agree with those who equate untouchability with the Varna system. In Vedic times, the Varna system was not based on birth. The same father had sons belonging to different Varnas, but they all lived together, ate together. There were also inter-marriages. But later this system got vitiated and we have to remove the evil that crept into it. Today we do not need the Varna system on the basis of birth or on any other basis. Now we all belong to the same Varna. So along with the passage of a law we need a social revolution.

The current of revolution that flowed till 1947 got blocked after the advent of freedom. Swami Dayanand, Mahatma Gandhi, Dr. Babasaheb Ambedkar brought about an awakening. They roused the people and filled their hearts with the spark of rebellion. They made them feel the present order must change, no one must be considered high and no one low. But once independence came, we thought it would be enough to pass a law. This decelerated our pace towards social awakening.

The House may pass this law but a countrywide campaign for the eradication of untouchability needs to be launched on a social level. You know that even today Harijan students are not allowed to sit on the matting, Harijan villagers cannot wear chappals, they cannot sit on horseback at weddings, their women cannot wear ornaments. Even in the Central Secretariat there is a separate *surahi* for Harijan employees and no attempt has been made to end this system. Everyday news comes of Harijan women being stripped naked and paraded through the market place. There is a boycott of Harijans near Poona. The Scheduled Castes Commissioner's report is full of such instances. All these events should stir the mind of the society. Along with law we need a nationwide campaign on the non-political level.

I will conclude with a suggestion. The National Integration Council that has been set up is so far involved only in the problem of communalism. It may tackle it, but I suggest that the National Integration Council should hold a special meeting to consider the problems of Scheduled Castes and Tribes and a campaign should be launched all over the country with the cooperation of all parties. Let us fix the target to fashion an India free of untouchability at the end of five years. It is necessary to draw a line in this matter. Let us change the circumstances and let us also change the mindset. We cannot do this with law alone. Along with it social awakening is called for. But the Hon. Minister does not even mention a need for social awakening in his speech. The presence of members in the House too does not provide evidence of realisation of the seriousness of the subject. The subject merited the Prime Minister's presence in the House.

(Lok Sabha, 23rd May 1972)

We are discussing an important national issue. It cannot be denied that during recent years atrocities on Harijans have increased. The figures collected by the Home Ministry support the fact that there has been a substantial increase in the incidents of burning Harijans alive, torching their houses, unauthorized occupation of their lands, and otherwise humiliating and harassing them.

The social aspect of this problem is familiar to all. For centuries a system has prevailed in this country in which one man has been considered inferior to another, considered untouchable on the basis of birth.

An Hon. Member: This system was made by the Brahmins.

Shri Vajpayee: Who made it is not the question. Whoever made it, it is wrong. That it still continues is shameful for the country. In the rural areas these barriers of discrimination still stand. The Constitution has declared untouchability as a punishable offence, attempts are being made to stiffen anti-untouchability laws, and yet determination is being practiced between man and man. We need a national campaign to solve this problem.

In the days of the freedom struggle non-official efforts were going on in this direction. The Arya Samaj did significant work for removal of untouchability. The constructive programme under the leadership of Mahatma Gandhi tried to bridge this gap. But once power came into our hands, non-official efforts came to a halt. Now no non-official efforts are made to rouse the soul of the society and motivate the high castes to atone for this. These efforts are necessary. The Home Minister is reviving the National Integration Council and its initial meeting is to be held tomorrow. We could decide in it to launch a national campaign with the cooperation of all classes and all parties which could prove an effective instrument for ending social aspects of discrimination and untouchability.

But it is not only a social problem, it is also an economic problem. It is true that even after earning money a person considered low by birth cannot get a respectable place in the society. This is a social curse. But if they are landless—a majority of such persons are Harijans—if they have no means of livelihood, if their handicrafts have fallen backward because of progress in science and technology, and are even dying down because they cannot stand competition, these people are also faced with an economic crisis. This crisis cannot be resolved by giving them representation in jobs—which we have not been able to give so far. Their industries should be safeguarded and changed in conformity with modern conditions so that they can stand competition in the market. This economic aspects needs also to be attended.

The principle behind reservation is that only equal opportunity is not enough. The backward will have to be brought up to a higher level by giving them special concessions. Then alone can they last in the race. Otherwise an opportunity means nothing for a Dalit or the oppressed. If we cannot stand everybody taking part in the race in line, the race will not be run according to rules. This is why reservation has been advocated. But reservation should lead to immediate progress. We must not get the feeling that these crutches are for ever.

HARIJANS AND DOMINANT CASTES

This is not just a clash between Brahmins and Harijans. It is also assuming other forms. In various regions and various fields the class in power, the group or sub-caste in power is stepping up its atrocities because it does not want to give up the power that has remained in its hands for centuries. On the other hand Harijans have woken up, are recognising their rights, and have started sharing power. I would like to give an example. In Haryána the struggle is not between Brahmins and Harijans, it is between Jats and Harijans. My Jat friends should not get annoyed. I am not saying this to annoy them. I could give the example of Maharashtra. In Maharashtra the struggle is not between Brahmins and Harijans. Those who are Marathas, those who are Kshatriyas, those who are in a majority, those who are influential in the villages, those who dominate the Government.... Now Harijans want to contest Panchayat elections, they want to become the Pradhan. They want to share power. This is a natural desire and also necessary. They should get a share in it. But those who had the monopoly of power do not want to share it either on the social level or even the political level, whether it is in Maharashtra or in Uttar Pradesh. This is the political aspect that is coming into focus, and it needs to be considered. This problem cannot be solved by only differentiating between high caste and Harijan. In whatever fields a particular group dominates it will have to be persuaded to share power, otherwise democracy will lose all meaning.

There is also a fourth aspect to this, and it is administrative. Incidents of excesses are on the increase. It is a symbol of social awakening, it is also proof of social change. While such incidents cause a sense of anxiety, they also rouse the hope that Harijans are no longer prepared to take it lying down. Now they will raise their voice, they will speak out, and they will fight for their rights. Perhaps they may have to face being burnt alive, but even if it comes to that their burning bodies would create a light in which those who burn them will see their face and hang their head in shame. This is a good sign, but our administrative apparatus has failed this test. It is true that the Home Minister has sent directives, the Prime Minister has held a conference of Chief Ministers, and attempts have been made to fix local officials' responsibility. But incidents take place, they are not immediately reported, and, as Shri Nawal Kishore has rightly said, many more incidents remain in the dark than coming to light, as there are no reports. Those who report are threatened. If there is a report, the matter is settled in the name of a compromise. The offenders are saved, those who should be punished go scot free. The police do not discharge their responsibility. The officials are also not vigilant. In the ultimate analysis their conduct betrays the class to which they belong. Hence the stress on recruitment in the services in large numbers. They should be placed in important positions where they may not practice partiality but where they could resent injustice. At present we have not been able to create such resentment, such anger, so we should try for it. Incidents must be immediately reported. Look at Bihar. The Bihar Government woke up when the matter was raised in the Assembly. In the Bawra incident even those in power were involved. A social boycott was imposed on those Harijans who had embraced Buddhism. They cannot drink water, they cannot work in the fields. This atrocity is being perpetrated in an organised manner. But the Government machinery did not budge, because this machinery was influenced by those who had a direct hand in the incident.

So on the one hand a decision has to be taken on the political level and on the other the administrative apparatus needs to be strengthened. It will have to be activated. The most stringent action will have to be taken, and those officials who do not do their duty, who delay action, whose conduct shows that they have been deliberately negligent, deliberately careless, will have to be meted severe punishment. Everyone must come to know that the Government at the Centre or those in power in the States will not tolerate any laxity in this matter. We can do this job only by making the administration efficient.

In the Constitution we have provided for a Commissioner for Scheduled Castes and Scheduled Tribes. He submits his report. But the report is delayed. If and when it does come, we do not get a chance to discuss it. If we do get a chance we cannot extract from it what we want. Now the Commissioner's difficulty is: How can he get information? How can he receive information when an incident takes place? In the past he had separate offices in the regions. He could visit them, call for information and get an immediate report. The Home Ministry should think about this. It is necessary to strengthen his position. The Scheduled Castes and Tribes Commissioner should be given a machinery that would activate sources from New Delhi, that would bring the truth to light if the State Government is lax or if the local official fails to do his duty. Then the House could consider it. We should work for this as well.

As I said in the beginning, this is a national problem. The time, the energy and the resources we spent for national unity were spent for unity that was limited to Hindu-Muslim; we neglected Harijans and *Vanvasis*. This was not good. We have no time to lose. Sometimes I feel it would be easier to close the gap between the rich and the poor than between the high caste and the Harijan, and so long as this equation does not change, the country will not move. This relationship must basically change. This must be considered a national issue.

The politics of votes will go on, the clashes between parties will go on for ever, even charges and countercharges can be accepted as a part of democracy. But there are certain problems on which the whole nation must come together, make up its mind and launch its efforts; otherwise we will never be able to fulfil our dream of making a new India where there is no discrimination on the basis of birth, on the basis of caste, on the basis of race. This is the test. The test is whether we do what we say. I hope this discussion will inspire us to forge ahead in this direction.

(Lok Sabha, 23rd August 1973)

Do not Politicise Reservations

How many Scheduled Castes and Scheduled Tribes students are there in medical colleges? Our young people do not understand that injustice has been done to them for centuries. They say, all right, injustice has been done for centuries, but we did not do it, so why should we suffer?

They do not have fellow-feeling, they do not have a pain in the heart, and if we have lost anything in these thirty-three years it is this pain, it is this camaraderie. It is a misfortune that all problems have been politicised. The country is divided into parties, and parties are getting divided into castes. Not only the country, not only the parties, even hearts have been divided.

This matter has so far been limited to educational institutions. Now, the employees of Gujarat are making demands. When they are asked, they say we can put up with reservation in recruitment but we cannot understand this business of reservation in promotion—our junior becomes our senior. I too could not satisfy them.

Reservation is understandable in recruitment. In respect of even promotion, the Supreme Court has ruled that it is right and we are implementing it. But the employee in the office says this is not proper. You may bring them up to the level by giving them concessions, but once they are equal to others, leave it at that. He who is capable of going ahead will go ahead. They show me the roster and ask, who will be the deputy secretary five years hence? I say, do not worry about who becomes the deputy secretary, let him become, after all he is our brother. But this is an economic question, a question of bread and butter. Man has become such an economic being that nationalism, social unity, brotherhood, camaraderie, love, affection—these values do not appeal to anybody. In this we have failed.

Now organisations are breaking down one by one, conventions are dying down one by one, traditions are getting trampled upon one by one. Those who are in power want to remain in power, and those who are in the Opposition want to exploit all opportunities for what they are worth. But our Congress friends should not complain about this. Uttar Pradesh had a Lok Dal Government. There was a disturbance in Narainpur, atrocities were committed on Harijans, and women were involved. Prime Minister Smt. Indira Gandhi went to Narainpur. When she was coming out after meeting the women, a press reporter asked, can it be said you have come to exploit the mistake of the Lok Dal Government that is in power here? The Prime Minister replied, if the Opposition makes a mistake why should we not exploit it? This was her reply. Now our workers show us that reply, and say: you will not understand politics, Smt. Gandhi knows how to play politics. When during the Janata regime reservation was applied to backward classes, the Congress Party did not openly support it. They kept silent. Even now the statements that are being made are quite clever—a little on this side, a little on that. I tell you, this won't do. This country will not run on cleverness, it will run on character, it will run on values. You do not have to fear, you are in a majority, you have the power, but you will have to take courage in your hands to take a decision. And for that you will have to be willing to take everyone with you. The way the reservation policy is being implemented may create some problems, and I have referred to them.

The other day the Communist Party member Shri Bhogendra Jha had introduced a Bill, a non-official Bill—he is not of the BJP, and there is no question of his being of the RSS—and in that Bill he said along with education and the socially backward, pay a little attention also to the economically backward. Does poverty depend only upon caste? Is not poverty just poverty? You may not have any reservation for it, but at least give some concessions for it. We do not think of those who are poor, those who are beggars.

Then, should we have reservation in promotion too? This should also be considered. No one can say the reservation that has gone on for 33 years has not benefited anybody, but we have also to look to whether those who ought to get the benefit get it. Are only some people get the benefit, while the rest are being deprived of it?

All these points are such that all should come together, discuss them and arrive at a political consensus. But this has to do with the Prime Minister, and the Prime Minister is not present in the House; so this discussion has no meaning.

(Lok Sabha, 18th March 1981)

Reform not by Laws Alone

I welcome the spirit in which this Bill has been presented before the Lok Sabha. No thinking person can support the dowry system. It has become a curse for us. It is an indication of the pitiable plight of women in Indian society. It is an index of man's selfishness. It is a sign of our social backwardness. Everyone will agree that this custom of sale and purchase of brides and grooms must be removed from the roots.

But the question is, what is the right way to eradicate this vicious custom, which has distorted our culture down the ages? The Law Minister has agreed in his speech that social evils cannot be eradicated by law alone, and if we consider the experience with laws that have so far been passed for removing social evils we would reach the conclusion that if the people are not enlightened, if there is no expression of an enlightened public opinion, if there is no social awakening such laws merely decorate the shelves. They are unable to fulfil our objective of basic social transformation.

In this connection the Law Minister has referred to the child marriage ordinance. It may be possible to book those engaged in a child's marriage at the time of the marriage, but how practicable would it be to arrest them at the time of giving or receiving dowry if there is no complaint from either side? And he would not complain if he himself wants to give or take it. If a third party complains, it would be a big problem for him to marshal witnesses. So we must admit there would be practical difficulties in implementing this law.

This law with all its clauses may well stop this business at the time of marriage, but giving gifts by the back door would begin. But what I say should not be taken to mean that I am a supporter of the dowry system. I have already said that this custom should be eradicated, but for that it is not a law that is required first, it is social awakening. I charge that those who criticise the dowry system remain silent in this respect when it comes to bringing about a change in their own social and family life. All their activities are limited to politics, they are oriented towards attainment of power, and those who attain it only care for keeping it. But when the problem of social reforms comes up in the Lok Sabha we assume the mantle of sentinels of social reform and its alert advocates.

In respect of laws regarding untouchability I find that before making a law efforts were made to enlighten the society on the matter. Now, this does not happen. Now, social workers feel there is a law and it is a cognizable offence, now it is for the police to look into it, why should we care? If social reform laws are made without social awareness they slow down the efforts for social reform. Social reform organisations think our job is over, a law has been passed, now what is left for us to do? This is not a good situation for the country. Even if a law is passed it cannot be implemented so long as the society and every individual is not alert.

Actually I wanted the Law Minister to throw light on how the anti-dowry laws passed by two States were implemented there and what their experience has been. Laws were made in Bihar and Andhra. What is the experience of these two States? Has the dowry system been really checked by law? If the law is in force and reforms continue to be talked about and the dowry custom also continues, this would not be a healthy situation. The test of social reform is not the growing number of laws. We should not just pass laws and think that the society is making progress. The Government as well as non-official organisations motivated by the Government will have to work for it.

So I propose that this Bill be publicised for popular awakening. We should take this Bill to the people—not for finding out if the people are in its favour or not, but for ensuring that once it becomes law the people would cooperate in its implementation. This law cannot become effective so long as the people do not themselves come forward to implement it. What steps is the Government taking to bring about this social awakening?

Regarding expenditure on marriage, a lady member said that

the sum of Rs. 2000 that has been fixed is too big, it should be decreased. But if it is big for someone it may be small for someone else. My objection is not what is given to the bride. We can understand it if the bride's parents want to give something as *Kanyadan* for the future happiness of their daughter. But if there is no cut in the overhead expenses in marriages these days, it would mean continuing the dowry system in another form. How many people should be in the *Barat*? If, on the one hand, you disallow accepting more than two thousand rupees but allow that 500 people may come in the *Barat*, their railway fare should be paid for, and everyone of them should be given 10 rupees by way of *Dakshina* as well as a shawl as a parting gift, the bride's side would be squeezed dry and the law would not be able to intervene.

So this matter is not as simple as it is made out to be. After all this is a question of reforming the society. There are complexities in the social structure and the law cannot meet these complexities. It only gives cosmetic treatment. Perhaps by passing this law against dowry the Government wants a pat on the back for taking a step ahead in social reform. Doing so would be to ignore this serious problem. Its seriousness has not been fully assessed. If this law prevents only the dowry given and taken at the time of marriage but giving and receiving go on after marriage this law would not be useful.

It was just now said that the police should step in, it should be made a cognizable offence. This sounds fine but I can fully appreciate the Government's difficulty in this. What will happen if the Government takes cognizance but it does not get a witness and the case falls through? So I want to know the experience of those two States in this matter. Our Law Minister has made an emotional speech. We agree with the feeling that the evil custom of dowry is a blot on the fair face of our nation, but the question is, how can we wash it off?

(Lok Sabha, 5th August 1959)

Economics and Ethics

Atal Bihari Vajpayee has been urging over the decades that economics should not be divorced from, but should on the contrary be governed by, ethical values. Supporting the tax on expenditure introduced by T. T. Krishnamachari as Union Finance Minister, Vajpayee said in the Lok Sabha on 17th July 1957: "Unrestrained expenditure is against our tradition and culture. Indian culture believes in restraints, and these restraints should apply to individual expenditure also. Unrestrained expenditure by an individual produces social tendencies that shake the very basis of society."

During a general discussion on the Third Five-Year Plan, Vajpayee agreed that planning is necessary in an underdeveloped country, but urged that "along with material prosperity we should preserve our life values."

He wanted planning to be village oriented, and deplored the neglect of cottage and small industries. India being a democracy, he said the five-year plans should have been prepared in consultation also with political parties other than the party in power.

Nationalisation no Panacea

Cautioning against the belief in nationalisation as a cure for all ills, Vajpayee said in the Rajya Sabha on 6th December 1963 on a resolution on the nationalisation of banks: "Nationalisation is not a panacea for all ills. It has come to mean governmentalisation. I am not opposed to socialism but I do not consider it a complete philosophy of life. Man is not merely a slave of lucre, nor is a creature of carnality. We cannot violate moral and spiritual values of life."

Warning against over-government and the notion that the Government is to do everything, he said: "In that case we have to take one more decision—that there will be no democracy in the country."

Condemning the nationalisation of the major commercial banks through an ordinance issued forty hours before Parliament was to meet, Vajpayee said in the Lok Sabha on 21st July 1969: "An ordinance can be issued if there is a crisis. The Prime Minister will have to explain what that crisis was. So far as we can see, there was a political crisis, a party crisis; it was a crisis not of the banks but of the party."

On the unwisdom of inscribing socialism, retrospectively, into the preamble of the Constitution, Vajpayee recalled on 2nd March

1993, in the Lok Sabha, how Dr. B. R. Ambedkar had opposed any reference to socialism in the Constitution. When K. T. Shah tried to get the word included somehow in the Constitution, "Dr. Ambedkar did not accept it. The argument given by Ambedkar shows his farsightedness. He said that socialism is a hypothesis of an economic set-up. The economic system keeps on changing. A time may come when a better economic system than socialism may come into being and the same is accepted by the people. I do not want to put limitations for the future generations."

Maruti: Elitism and Corruption

On the subject of corruption in Government, Vajpayee's comments were unsparing. Speaking on the Maruti car project, promoted by Prime Minister Indira Gandhi's second son Sanjay Gandhi, he said in the Lok Sabha on 22nd December, 1972 that it showed the priority wrongly being given to the production of luxury goods. Recalling that a small car project in the public sector had been originally thought of but transferred now to the private sector, Vajpayee asked: "Do we need such a car at all?" Cars, he said, did not call for priority in the allocation of investible resources.

The other aspect of the Maruti car project which he found deeply disturbing was that favour shown to it in the allocation of steel, coal, etc: "This is not Maruti Limited. This is Corruption Unlimited." It was not good for the Prime Minister's prestige, he said, that governmental favours were being shown to her son.

1997, in the Lok Sabha that Dr. B. R. Ambedkar had opposed any reference to socialism in the Constitution. When K. T. Shah tried to get the word inserted somewhere in the Constitution, Dr. Ambedkar did not accept it. The argument [illegible] Ambedkar gave for [illegible] was that socialism [illegible] system of economics set up [illegible] changing [illegible] time may come when better [illegible] evolved [illegible] may come into being and the same is [illegible]. He did not want to put limitations for the future generations.

[illegible] and Corruption

In the subject [illegible] was [illegible] important [illegible] by [illegible] the Lok Sabha [illegible] showed the [illegible] to any [illegible] originally [illegible] said [illegible] not call [illegible] [illegible]

The [illegible] aspect of [illegible] was [illegible] that [illegible] was not good for the [illegible] said that governmental [illegible]

Part II

FRACTURED FREEDOM AND AFTER

CHAPTER 6

Factors that Led to Partition

From the time of the Sindhu (Indus) Valley Civilisation which flourished for a thousand years from 2700 B.C., there was in the Indian sub-continent a mingling of races and faiths remarkable for the synthesis that followed each initial conflict. Up to about 1000 A.D., Indian history offered a study in the assimilation of people who differed in their skin colour and appearance and who followed different forms of worship. The amalgam of numerous creeds that prevailed in the sub-continent was referred to by outsiders as Hinduism, or the religion of the Hindus. The people themselves were so named as they were inhabitants of the land of the river Sindhu, pronounced with an aspirate as 'Hindu' by the ancient Persians. This was subsequently rendered by the Greeks as 'Indos'—from which are derived the English names Indus, for the river, and India, for the country.

High tribute has been paid by scholars and historians like Monier Williams and Arnold Toynbee to the tolerance and catholicity of the religion of India. Some of their remarks are quoted in the Supreme Court's judgement of 11th December 1995 in the Hindutva case, excerpts from which are given in Appendix II.

A notable example of the integration of Aryan and non-Aryan elements in Indian culture is the deification of Krishna, a dark-hued chief of the Vrishni clan, who came to be ranked with the Aryan king Rama in the Hindu pantheon. Another instance, designed to bridge differences between worshippers of the deities

Vishnu and Siva, is the charming legend that Parvati, consort of Siva, is Vishnu's sister. A polytheistic religion in which mother goddesses abound, Hinduism has been more tolerant and kinder to women, compared to the monotheistic Semitic faiths with their fanaticism, proselytism and male chauvinism. The difference is brought out vividly by Aruna Asaf Ali in *The Resurgence of Indian Women* (Radiant, 1991.)

India's liberal and syncretist ethos received rude shocks from the eleventh century onwards. Northern India was invaded by marauders who sought to sanctify their loot, rape and rapine by invoking the Quran. The first of the marauders was Mahmud of Ghazni, who burnt the temple of Mathura and sacked the shrine at Somnath.

Humanists and Fanatics among Muslims

The later Muslim conquerors made India their home. Some among them had a humanist outlook that was in contrast to the barbarism of the early invaders who destroyed temples, violated the human rights of the native Hindu, i.e. Indian population and imposed a punitive tax known as *Jazia* on those who did not convert to Islam.

The human face of Islam was presented by the mystics among Sufis. When conversion to Islam in India was not at the point of the sword or from hope of material advancement by adopting the faith of the new rulers, it was because of the appeal of the saintliness of Sufi mystics. Another factor in unforced conversions was the hope of the lowest of the so-called low castes among Hindus, of securing freedom from the social indignity and insult which they had to suffer at the hands of every caste above them in the brahminical hierarchy. (It is a different matter that this hope was most often belied, whether it was Islam which victims of the caste system embraced during Muslim rule or, subsequently, Christianity during British rule.)

The mingling of Islamic Sufism and Hindu Bhakti, in which good men of the two faiths reached out to each other, gave rise to a new religion, Sikhism, based on the teachings of Guru Nanak (1469-1538). Though Sikhism was a proselytising religion, and was gaining adherents from the ranks both of Hindus and of

Muslims, the broadminded Mughal emperor Akbar did not regard the new religion as a threat to Islam or to the State. He admired the saintly lives of the Sikh Gurus of his time. Akbar also arranged for translation into Persian of the *Atharva Veda*, the *Ramayana* and the *Mahabharata*. According to the historian Abdul Qadir Badauni, a contemporary who was an orthodox Sunni and disapproved of Akbar's eclecticism which he ragarded as un-Islamic, Akbar prohibited the killing of cows since it offended Hindu sentiment, refrained from eating meat on certain days, and celebrated non-Islamic festivals.

A great difference might have been made to the history of India had Akbar's grandson Shah Jahan been succeeded by the liberal-minded Dara Shikoh rather than Aurangzeb. When Shah Jahan fell ill in September 1657, a war of succession broke out among his four sons: Dara, Shuja, Aurangzeb and Murad. Aurangzeb, who combined religious fanaticism with ruthlessness in the pursuit of power, emerged the victor. Crowning himself emperor in Delhi in 1658, he had Dara executed the following year after getting him condemned by the Mullahs for deviation from the Islamic faith and parading the prince in disgrace through the streets of Delhi. Murad's turn for execution came in 1661. The dethroned Shah Jahan—kept imprisoned in Agra fort under harsh conditions—breathed his last in 1666. Forced to drink brackish water from the wells within the fort though the river Jamuna was nearby, the unhappy emperor wrote to Aurangzeb:

> Praised be the Hindus in all cases,
> As they ever offer water to their dead.
> And thou, my son, art a marvellous Mussalman
> As thou causest me in life to lament for water.

In 1675, angered by Guru Teg Bahadur's support to the Hindus of Kashmir in their resistance to oppressive measures, Aurangzeb caused the Sikh divine to be brought to Delhi where he was asked to choose between death and conversion. Preferring to die rather than recant his faith, the Guru was beheaded. The martyrdom of Teg Bahadur, which enranged the Sikhs, was followed in 1679 by the reimposition of the Jazia tax on the entire non-Muslim majority of the population. The Mughal empire was riven by conflicts with Rajput, Sikh and Maratha rulers. A disunited India became vulnerable to penetration and eventual conquest by European powers.

Dara Shikoh: Inter-Religious Ecumenism

Dara Shikoh spent much time in the company of Sufis—one of the reasons for Aurangzeb's dislike of him. A Sufi mystic who was a friend and mentor of Dara Shikoh was Sarmad. He was put to death in 1657 on the orders of Aurangzeb. Sarmad came to India from Iran initially as a merchant. According to Bankey Behari, he was "a companion of Emperor Shah Jahan and tutor of Prince Dara whom he taught the Upanishads and the Bhagwad Gita." An echo of Vedic pantheism can be heard in Sarmad's invocation:

> You manifest Your glory in innumerable forms,
> Sometimes in the hyacinth, sometimes in the cypress,
> and oftener in jasmine are You seen;
> In the mountains, in the desert and in the garden
> You lie hid.
> And at other times You turn into the light
> of the lamp and scatter effulgence.

Sarmad asked those who came to hear him:

> Why do you seek His abode only in the temple
> and the mosque?
> See you not His creation above and below? Wherein
> does he not abide?

Sarmad accepted and respected the gods and heroes of the land of his adoption. A saying attributed to him is that he had passed from Jewish faith into Islam and had wandered from Islam "into the garden of Sri Rama and Laxman."

Dara Shikoh also held in high esteem Mullah Shah Badakshani (d. 1661) of the Qadiri order. Dara says in the preface to his translation into Persian of a selection of Upanishadic verses (referring to himself in the third person) that, in 1640, "he went to Kashmir, the resemblance of paradise, and by the grace of God and the favour of the Infinite, he obtained the auspicious opportunity of meeting the most perfect of perfects, the flower of the gnostics, the unitarian accomplished in the Truth, Mullah Shah." Dara found that Advaita or non-duality among Hindus was manifest from "their heavenly books which are the Rig Veda, the Yajur

Veda, the Sama Veda and the Atharva Veda... And it can also be ascertained from the Holy Quran that there is no nation without a prophet and without a revealed scripture... The summum bonum of these four books are called the Upanishads. . . . He (Dara) obtained from these the essence of the most ancient of all heavenly books in point of time. Happy is he who. . . . shall study and comprehend this translation entitled *Sirr-i-Akbar* (The Great Secret), knowing it to be a translation of the words of God." It was from a Latin and subsequently French translation of Dara Shikoh's Persian rendering that the West came to know the Upanishads for the first time. M. Mujeeb in his book *The Indian Muslims* says of Dara: "What he represents socially is the culmination of that understanding between Muslims and non-Muslims of which Akbar laid the foundation... The translation of the Upanishads was not due to literary curiosity, like the translations of the Mahabharata and the Ramayana and other works of Sanskrit literature made in Akbar's time and earlier; it was the result of a passionate search for truth."

In his *Majma-ul-Bahrain*, (The Mingling of the Two Oceans), Dara Shikoh expounded the fundamental unity of the teachings of Hinduism and Islam, observing that the difference was only in terminology. This work has been preserved in the Persian as well as in a Sanskrit version known as *Samudra-sangama-grantha*. No wonder that K.R. Qanungo, biographer of this worthy great-grandson of Akbar, has said: "Anyone who intends to take up the solution of the problem of religious peace in India must begin the work where Dara had left it, and proceed on the path chalked out by that prince."

For the leaders of India's freedom movement spearheaded by the Congress, there could have been no better strategy for countering the British imperial policy of divide-and-rule, and the alien feeling fomented by Muslim separatist leaders, than to revive the Bhakti-Sufi ethos of unity among Hindus and Muslims. But this was not attempted by the three most prominent leaders of the national movement in its final phase—Mahatma Gandhi (1869-1948), Jawaharlal Nehru (1889-1964) and Maulana Azad (1888-1958). The reasons were different in each case.

Mahatma Gandhi, a devout Hindu, in his campaign against

untouchability and for other reforms addressed the Hindu masses directly, over the heads of orthodox religious leaders, offering his own humanist interpretation of the Hindu scriptures. But Gandhiji did not address the Muslim masses directly, over the heads of the *Imams* and *Mullahs* who upheld Muslim orthodoxy, to exhort them in the name of Sufi saints to reject separatism. He thought that the work of reforming the outlook of Muslims should be left to Muslim leaders.

Turning to Maulana Azad, he was in his youth a revolutionary in his religious as well as political thought. He wrote in 1910 an essay on *Sarmad Shaheed* in the course of which he praises Dara Shikoh highly. Following is an extract from that essay, published in English translation by the Indian Council for Cultural Relations in 1991 under the title *The Rubaiyat of Sarmad*:

"During the last days of Emperor Shah Jahan, Dara Shikoh was heir-apparent. A man of Sufi temperament, he was unique among Mughal princes. It is a blot on historical veracity that the pen which recorded the history of the Mughal period was always held by Prince Dara Shikoh's enemies. Dara's writings indicate that the author was a man of excellent taste. The overwhelming proof of his taste is that in pursuing his goal he lost the distinction between the temple and the mosque. The humility with which he met the Muslim divines was matched by the devotion with which he bowed his head before the Hindu saints and sadhus. Who can deny the purity of this principle? Because, in this exalted state of mind, if one can still distinguish between Kufr and Islam, then what is the difference between blindness and vision? The moth should seek the flame. If it is desirous of the lamp which is lit only in the mosque, its desire for self-immolation is not complete. In Alamgir's eyes, Sarmad's greatest crime was his closeness to Dara Shikoh."

However, Maulana Azad was overtaken in later years by a spiritual counterpart of the hardening of arteries. Like the English poet Wordsworth who was in his youth a mystic and a worshipper of nature but became, over the years, an orthodox Christian, Maulana Azad became a conventional Muslim though he remained a nationalist. The essay on Sarmard remained a literary masterpiece; its theme did not permeate his later speeches and writings.

In any case Azad, aloof by temperament, was not a man of the masses. Jawaharlal Nehru would often confer with Azad but, as will be seen in the next chapter, ignored his colleague's advice that the Indian State should ensure the instruction of students, at every stage of education, in the humane values of all the major religions at their best.

Jawaharlal Nehru exemplified in some respects the effect which Thomas Babington Macaulay expected English education, introduced in the 1830s, to have on Indians. ("A single shelf of a good European library", Macaulay wrote insolently in his ignorance, "is worth the whole native literature of India and Arabia.") Macaulay's aim was "to form a class who may be interpreters between us and the millions whom we govern; a class of persons Indian in blood and colour, but English in taste, in opinions, in morals and in intellect." Macaulay also looked forward with relish to the subversion of the religious faith of English-educated Indians: "No Hindu who has received an English education ever remains sincerely attached to his religion. It is my firm belief that if our plans of education are followed up, there will not be a single idolator among the respectable classes in Bengal thirty years hence. And this will be effected without any effort to proselytise; without the smallest interference in their religious liberty; merely by the natural operation of knowledge and reflection."

In the case of Jawaharlal Nehru, the Macaulay effect was reinforced by that of Karl Marx with his poor opinion of India which had 'no history'. Nehru writes to Gandhiji on 11th January 1928: "I neither think that the so-called Rama Raj was very good in the past, nor do I want it back... You have criticised strongly the many obvious defects of industrialism and hardly paid any attention to its merits. It is the opinion of most thinkers in the West that these defects are not due to industrialism as such but to the capitalist system which is based on exploitation of others."

A reference to the problem of untouchability, in the course of a letter to Asaf Ali on 12th October 1933, shows Nehru's censorious attitude towards his Hindu heritage: "The aspect of the Harijan movement which appeals to me most is that it will weaken the Hindus in the sense that it will create a split amongst them." Nehru had no interest in Bhakti-Sufism and, though he was a keen student of history, was simply unaware of the significance of Dara Shikoh. Sufism does not figure in his *Glimpses of World History*; and in the later work, *The Discovery of India*, there is only a glancing reference to Sufism and no mention of Dara Shikoh. Since Nehru discusses various Mughal personalities at length, the reason could be (Dara Shikoh lost the war of succession) "a certain contempt for the weak" which Nehru notes as part of his own make-up in the candid self-portrait that he wrote in the *Modern Review* in 1937. His friend Edward Thompson, referring to the discussion of the French Revolution in the 'Glimpses', twitted Nehru about his 'Napoleon worship'. This tendency finds expression in Nehru's discussion of Indian history, too, as in his remarks about Mahmud of Ghazni. Nehru quotes, in the 'Glimpses', from an account given by Firdausi, the following description of the city of Mathura by Mahmud: "There are here a thousand edifices as firm as the faith of the faithful; nor is it likely that this city has attained its present condition but at the expense of many millions of dinars, nor could such another be constructed under a period of 200 years." Nehru omits to mention that Mahmud proceeded to loot and to torch the city which he so greatly admired.

It speaks volumes for Nehru's lack of interest in popularising the best insights of the various religions, so as to promote their cooperative co-existence, that there is no road in New Delhi named for Dara Shikoh. Many roads formerly named after British monarchs and their colonial agents in India were renamed during Jawaharlal Nehru's prime ministership. Among the Mughals commemorated by road names in free India's capital are the invader Babar and the fanatic Aurangzeb, and mercifully also Akbar—but not Dara Shikoh.

British Patronage of Muslim Separatists

Unlike the Muslim invasions of India, the establishment of British rule over India was the result of a creeping conquest. It was in the guise of trade, and through the practice of intrigue and taking of sides in quarrels between Indian princes. The success of the East India Company's forces at Buxar in 1764 reduced the Mughal 'emperor' in Delhi to a nullity. The Company secured from him the *dewani* of Bengal, with the right to collect land revenue and to maintain law and order in that vast province which at that time included present Bihar and Orissa.

Since the anti-British uprising of 1857 was ostensibly in support of the last Mughal emperor Bahadur Shah Zafar, the British initially perceived Muslims as their main enemy, though many Hindu sepoys and chieftains had also taken part in the uprising. On the other hand the Sikhs fought against the Muslims, in the service of the British, at the siege of Delhi in 1857-58. This was because of bitter memories of the torture to death of the fifth Sikh guru in Jehangir's time, the execution of the ninth guru by Aurangzeb in 1675, and the killing of two sons of the tenth and last guru by the Muslim governor of Sirhind.

Sikhs were shown special favour under the new dispensation following the assumption of direct responsibility for the governance of India by the British Crown. Michael O' Dyer, Lt. Governor of Punjab in the early part of this century, pointed out that the province occupied only a thirteenth part of India but furnished sixty per cent of the army. The high preference shown to Sikhs in recruitment to the army continued to be in evidence for decades after India's independence. Sikhs (for whom separate electorates were established in Punjab under the Government of India Act of 1919) were also shown preference in recruitment to the civil services. When the Constituent Assembly was debating a draft clause that sought to authorise the State to make provision for reservations in favour of classes not adequately represented in the public services, a fear was expressed by Sardar Ujjal Singh that the words might be interpreted to mean that no minority community would be given representation in the services on a scale higher than what it would get on a population basis. He said that this would be 'unfair' to Sikhs for whom 20 per cent of public appointments were at the time reserved in the Punjab though they formed only 13 per cent of the population of the province.

Very soon, the British overcame their hostility towards the Muslims and began to favour them along side of the Sikhs. The foreign rulers saw that Hindus were to the fore in utilising the system of modern education through English introduced in the first half of the 19th century, and were beginning to ask for steps towards self-government. Muslims were therefore to be encouraged as a counter to the nascent Indian nationalism. Unlike the Sikhs, Muslims had a substantial all-India presence and accounted for about 20 per cent of India's population as against less than 2 per cent in the case of Sikhs.

The Secretary of State for India, Sir Charles Wood, gave detailed advice on the art of divide-and-rule to Lord Elgin, then Governor-General, in a series of communications starting from 3rd March 1862. The Secretary of State said: "We have maintained our power by playing off one part against the other, and we must continue to do so. Do what you can, therefore, to prevent all having a common feeling... The natural antagonism of the races is no inconsiderable element of our strength. If all India was to unite against us, how long could we maintain ourselves?"

Lord Dufferin, the next Governor-General, was assured by an English official, Sir W.H. Gregory, in a letter of 24th February 1886, that the policy of encouraging Muslims in education and in employment was sound, and would pay off: "I am confident that it will bear good fruits; indeed it seems to have done so already, by the complete abstention of the Mohammedans from Brahmin and Baboo agitation. It will be a great matter to sweeten our relations with this portion of the Indian population, the bravest and at one time the most dangerous. They all with one voice declare they got their whipping in 1857, and they take it like men. They now look to us alone, not to be subjected to Hindu domination."

This letter was written within two months of the first session of the Indian National Congress at Bombay. The outstanding Muslim personality in public life of that time, Badruddin Tyabji (1844-1906), had been invited and was to attend, but was detained outside Bombay on urgent business and could not come. He had to miss the second session too. His absence led some loyalist Muslims to claim that he was, like themselves, keeping away from the newly formed Congress.

Badruddin Tyabji not only attended the third session of the Congress, at Madras in 1887, but presided over it. And in his address he said that he failed to understand why Muslims should not work shoulder to shoulder with their fellow-countrymen for the common benefit of all.

Tyabji, who was the first Indian to become Chief Justice of the Bombay High Court, pulled up a British barrister who had made disparaging remarks about the Indian National Congress: "I have always regarded it (Congress presidentship) as the highest honour, higher than being on this Bench. Let me tell the counsel that in my Court no contemptuous references to that body will be permitted."

When Syed Ameer Ali invited Tyabji to attend a Muslim political conference that was proposed to be held at Calcutta, he replied: "You are no doubt aware that I have always been of opinion that in regard to political questions at large, the Mohammedans should make a common cause with their fellow countrymen of other creeds and persuasions, and I cannot help deprecating any disunion on such questions between ourselves and the Hindus and Parsees. If, therefore, the proposed Mohammedan Conference is started simply as a rival to the National Congress, I should entirely oppose it, as it seems to me that the proper course is to join the Congress and take part in its deliberations."

A section of the Muslim intelligentsia shared Tyabji's robust nationalism. Others shared the fear voiced by an older Muslim leader, Syed Ahmad Khan, that in India democracy based on representative government would result in Hindu domination and would be harmful to Muslim interests. Ahmad Khan wanted the Muslim community to offer its loyal co-operation to the British Government. This attitude was welcome to the British authorities, who did everything to encourage it.

At the root of this separatist trend was the delayed start of Indian Muslims on the path of modernisation through English education as compared to the Hindus, not to speak of Indian Christians and Parsees who had taken to western education with alacrity. This gap, which was to have profound consequences for the development of the sub-continent's polity, is marked by the life-spans of Rammohun Roy, namely 1772-1833, and of his counterpart as the initiator of social reform and modern education among the Indian Muslims, Syed Ahmad Khan (1817-1898).

The Muslim elite withdrew into sullen isolation after the 1857 revolt was crushed. Muslim parents who could afford at all to educate their children sent them to traditional schools for religious instruction, rather than to schools run by missionaries or by the government, where English was taught. It was only after two or three decades that the Muslims started coming out of the protective shell of orthodoxy into the sunlight of the contemporary world and modern knowledge. Virtually a whole generation thus missed the process of modernisation. It was Ahmad Khan who founded in 1875 the Muhammadan Anglo-Oriental College, which was raised in 1921 to the status of a university as the Muslim University of Aligarh. In the sphere of social reform, Ahmad Khan attacked the Purdah system which symbolised the seclusion of women. He also deprecated the tendency to attribute supernatural powers and miracles to the Prophet and saints.

Partition of Bengal: Curzon's Design

Though the Congress was established in 1885 with official blessing, its resolutions and the speeches thereon soon dismayed the British rulers. By 1900 the Viceroy, Lord Curzon, had decided to destroy the Congress. He said in a letter of 18th November, 1900 to Lord Hamilton: "My own belief is that the Congress is tottering to its fall, and one of my greatest ambitions while in India is to assist it to a peaceful demise." The partition of Bengal, mooted in 1903, was Curzon's brain-child. Of the 18 annual sessions of the Congress between 1885 and 1902, four had been hosted by Calcutta. Bengali nationalist leaders had presided over as many as six of the 14 annual sessions held outside Calcutta. The Bengali presence was thus conspicuous on the stage of Indian nationalism. And the Bengali nationalist intelligentsia was largely Hindu. Curzon decided to strike where, as he thought, it would hurt the cause of Indian nationalism most. Ironically, the partition of Bengal was, instead, to mark the beginning of the Indian struggle for freedom.

It was ostensibly for improvement of the administration that the division of Bengal, a Presidency of unwieldy size, was undertaken. It included, besides Bengal proper, Bihar, Orissa and Chota Nagpur. If administrative considerations had been primary, there were rational ways of reorganisation: for example, a reduction of the Bengal Presidency's size by constituting a new Chief Commissioner's province comprising the non-Bengali areas of

Bihar and Chota Nagpur. The aim was different. Northern and Eastern Bengal, with Assam, was to form a new Province of Eastern Bengal and Assam; and Western Bengal with Bihar and Orissa was to constitute the Province of Bengal. Bengalis in Western Bengal would be separated from their kith and kin; and Bengali Hindus would be a minority in both the provinces. Commending the scheme to London, the Viceroy said in a despatch: "Calcutta is the centre from which the Congress Party is manipulated throughout the whole of Bengal and indeed the whole of India. Its best wire-pullers and its most frothy orators all reside here... If we are weak enough to yield to their clamour now, we shall not be able to dismember or reduce Bengal again, and you will be cementing and solidifying in the eastern flank of India a force already formidable and certain to be a source of increasing trouble in the future."

To the Muslims of Eastern Bengal, Curzon's appeal was frankly communal. Addressing a gathering at Dacca, he said: "When a proposal is put forward which would make Dacca the centre and possibly the capital of a new and self-sufficing administration, which must give to the people of these districts by reason of their numerical strength and their superior culture, the preponderating voice in the province so created, which would invest the Mohammedans in Eastern Bengal with a unity which they have not enjoyed since the days of old Musalman viceroys and kings, which must develop local interests and trade to a degree that is impossible so long as you remain the appendage of another administration—can it be that the people of these districts are to be advised by their leaders to sacrifice all these great advantages from fear? Do you mean to be so blind to your future as to repudiate the offer?" The first Lt. Governor of the province of Eastern Bengal and Assam, Joseph Bamfylde Fuller, said with reference to the two main communities—Muslims and Hindus—that they would be like two queens of his, the first being the favoured one.

The decision to partition Bengal was announced by the Government on 20th July 1905. It set off a mass movement of protest in Bengal, with sympathetic reaction in other parts of the country, the like of which had not been witnessed before. The repressive measures adopted by the British authorities were also unprecedented. Economic boycott of Britain was forged during this movement as the weapon of a weak nation against a strong power. Starting with cloth made in Manchester, the boycott movement soon widened to cover Liverpool salt and foreign sugar, and social boycott of those using British goods.

The Swadeshi movement spread to other parts of India. Confidential reports received by the Government from the intelligence bureau showed that, by the end of 1905, the Boycott-Swadeshi movement had affected 23 districts in the United Provinces, 15 towns in the Central Provinces, 24 towns in the Bombay Presidency, 20 districts in the Punjab and 13 districts in the Madras Presidency. In rural Delhi the people of Larsoli village took an oath to discard the use of imported sugar. When a trader was caught selling it, he was fined ten rupees. The Panchayat announced that any person who informed it of such a breach would be given a reward of ten rupees and the culprit would suffer eviction from the village. There were similar instances of social boycott elsewhere, including Bengal itself, during the anti-partition movement. These examples appear to have inspired Asaf Ali to propose social ostracism as the 'sanction' for the parallel system of people's self-government proposed by him in 1920 (discussed later in this chapter).

Creative writers contributed significantly to the national awakening. One of the earliest among patriotic writers was Bankim Chandra Chatterji (1838-94). While he valued English as a unifying link among educated Indians (Bankim Chandra was in the first batch of Calcutta university graduates), he cautioned against alienation of the English-educated intelligentsia from the common people. He stressed the importance of Indian languages for communicating with the masses. Bankim Chandra's song 'Vande Mataram', which he incorporated in the novel *Ananda Math*, became the battle-song of the movement against the partition of the province in 1905. The British banned its singing, and at the Bengal provincial conference held at Barisal in 1906, the delegates were severely beaten for singing the song in defiance of the ban.

The repressive measures bore heavily on students. On 10th October 1905 a government circular was issued over the signature of R.W. Carlyle, saying that students were being used for political purposes and "it is impossible to tolerate this in connection with institutions which Government either assists or countenances." The circular warned that unless heads of educational institutions prevented students' participation in the Swadeshi movement, their grant-in-aid would be withdrawn and the University would be asked to disaffiliate the institutions. If the head of an institution was himself loyal to the government but unable to prevent student participation, he should prove his loyalty by furnishing to the educational authorities a list of the offending students.

This produced a strong reaction in the two Bengals. The outcome of the 'anti-Circular' movement was the establishment of the Jatiya Siksha Parishad, or Council of National Education. The Council wanted to impart education—literary as well as scientific and technical—on national lines, not in opposition to but standing apart from the existing systems of primary, secondary and university education. It stood for education ordinarily through the medium of the vernaculars, but with English as a compulsory subject. The Bengal National College was inaugurated on 14th August 1906, with Aurobindo Ghose as principal. The example inspired the formation of similar institutions under the auspices of national education councils in various parts of the country. The anti-partition movement thus anticipated two important features of the Non-Cooperation Movement launched by Gandhiji in the early 1920's: boycott of foreign goods, and the establishment of institutions of national education.

A natural sequel to the creation of a Muslim-majority province by dividing Bengal was the encouragement by the British of the formation of an all-India Muslim political organisation. Lord Minto, Curzon's successor, received on 1st October 1906 a Muslim delegation headed by the Aga Khan. That the delegation was sponsored by the British authorities is clear from an entry of the same date in the diary of Lady Minto: "This evening I have received the following letter from an official: 'I must send Your Excellency a line to say that a very, very big thing has happened today. A work of statesmanship that will affect India and Indian history for many a long year. It is nothing less than the pulling back of sixty-two millions of people from joining the ranks of the seditious opposition'."

What was this momentous event? It was the Viceroy's acceptance of the principle, urged by the delegation led by Aga Khan, of a separate Muslim electorate. This was the beginning of a process which was to break up the sub-continent four decades hence. The delegation told Lord Minto that representative institutions of the European type should be "adapted to the social, religious and political conditions obtaining in India". Pointing out that the Muslims formed between one-fifth and one-fourth of the total population of India, the delegation wanted that they should be given a more than proportionate share both in the legislatures and in public employment: "The position accorded to the Mahomedan community in any kind of representation, direct or indirect, and in all other ways affecting their status and influence, should be commensurate not merely with their numerical strength but also with their political importance and the position which they occupied in India a little more than a hundred years ago, and of which the traditions have naturally not faded from their minds." In other words, Muslims wanted to be treated as more important than, and not as equals of, other Indians.

Lord Minto responded most sympathetically. He agreed that "any electoral representation in India would be doomed to mischievous failure which aimed at granting a personal enfranchisement regardless of the beliefs and traditions of the communities composing the population of this continent."

Shortly after this, Nawab Salimullah proposed the formation of a Central Muslim Organisation to the leaders of the community who had gathered at Dacca for the Mahomedan Educational Conference. Accordingly, on 30th December 1906 a political association called the All India Muslim League was formed. Its objects were "to promote feelings of loyalty towards the British government and to protect and advance the political and other rights of the Muslims of India."

In this atmosphere of separatism, a series of Hindu-Muslim riots broke out in Eastern Bengal, particularly in the districts of Mymensigh and Comilla. These were followed by a chain of communal disturbances in the ensuing years in Peshawar, United Provinces and Bihar.

Separate Muslim Electorate

Separate electorate for Muslims—or the election of Muslim members of legislatures by Muslims only—were provided for in the Indian Councils Act of 1909. The Act treated Muslims as more equal than other citizens, giving them disproportionately large representation in the Imperial and Provincial councils. Even Lord Minto, the then British Viceroy who was the author of the scheme, felt qualms. "I shall not be at all surprised if we have serious trouble over the excess of representation granted to Mohamadans", he wrote in November 1909. *Empire*, an Anglo-Indian newspaper of Calcutta, said: "When the Councils meet there seems every probability of the Government finding themselves in a position analogous to that of the Light Brigade in the famous verse, slightly adapted:

'Moslems to right of them
Moslems to left of them
Moslems behind them
Volleyed and thundered.'

Probably the Government never imagined that they would have so many Mohammedans to deal with, but there the fact remains."

According to Minto, Gopal Krishna Gokhale's advocacy of democratic representation was a fine idea only from the Congress point of view: "It is misleading to talk of the many populations composing the people of the Indian Empire as if they were one nationality." Separate electorates were the means he devised for keeping Hindus and Muslims divided. Over the years, the British rulers carried their flattery of Indian Muslims so far that they treated the basic Indian identity as Muslim and described the rest of the Indian population as 'non-Mohammadan'. Thus we find in the officially published proceedings of the Central Legislative Assembly of the 1920's that not only is Lala Lajpat Rai of Muslim-majority undivided Punjab described as member from 'Jullundur Division: Non-Mohammadan' but members from the south too, where the Muslims are a small minority, are similarly described. Thus A. Rangaswami Iyengar is member from 'Tanjore-cum-Trichinopoly: Non-Mohammadan Rural', and C. Duraiswamy Aiyangar is member from 'Madras ceded districts and Chittoor:

Non-Mohammadan Rural'!

Lord Hardinge, who replaced Minto as Viceroy towards the close of 1910, realised that there could be no peace till the partition of Bengal was ended. The annulment was announced on the occasion of the visit of the British King and Queen, George V and Mary, for the Delhi Durbar in December 1911. Bihar, Chota Nagpur and Orissa were formed into a Lt. Governor's province; Assam reverted to Chief Commissionership; and the rest of the area constituted the province of Bengal. Simultaneously, it was announced that the capital would be shifted from Calcutta to Delhi.

The annulment of Bengal's partition had already become a major Muslim grievance within India when the blows struck at the Ottoman empire by European powers in 1912, in the course of the Balkan wars, evoked sympathy for Turkey. Its ruler was regarded by many Muslims the world over as their Khalifa or guardian. Syed Ahmad Khan, writing nearly four decades earlier, had questioned the propriety of regarding the Sultan of Turkey as having any jurisdiction over Muslims outside Turkey: "Khilafat literally means succession, and the person who succeeds is called the Khalifa.... Their Khilafat or government is confined to the Muslim inhabitants of that country alone over which they rule.... He (Sultan of Turkey) can in no sense be the Khalifa for those over whom he has no such authority." But in the popular estimation Turkey continued to be the symbol of Muslim power. Anti-British feeling ran high when the First World War broke out in 1914 with Britain and Turkey ranged on opposite sides. The attack on Turkey by Greek troops in 1919 created bitter resentment.

Gandhiji's Support to Khilafat

It was at this juncture that Mohandas Karamchand Gandhi finally returned to India from South Africa. He earned the title of Mahatma (Great Soul) for his successful struggle through non-violent means for securing elementary civic rights for Indians who had settled in South Africa.

Gandhiji saw in the anti-British mood of Indian Muslims on the Khilafat issue an opportunity to draw them into the freedom movement from which most of them had kept aloof till then. He threw himself heart and soul into mobilising Hindu support for the Muslim cause. He even subordinated to this political objective his moral scruple about boycott of British goods, which seemed to him to denote hatred in contrast to his own advocacy of loving the enemy.

M. Asaf Ali, who had served the British administration but broke away from it on the issue of Khilafat, recalls in the course of his autobiography (*M. Asaf Ali : Memoirs*, Ajanta Books, 1995) the proceedings of the Khilafat Conference in Delhi in November 1919:

> Among the draft resolutions, we of the younger group had set our hearts on the one which called for boycott of British goods. When I showed the draft resolution to Gandhiji, he at once expressed his disapproval of boycott on the ground that it savoured of hate. The elders among the convenors of the Khilafat Conference including Hakim Ajmal Khan, Dr. M.A. Ansari and Syed Riza Ali were also strongly opposed to it, and we had carried it in the drafting sub-committee despite their opposition. They thought it was premature, being a drastic sanction which should be considered only if representations to the British Government failed. But Gandhiji's point was different. Boycott to him was an expression of hate, and therefore 'violent'. Who among Muslims could appreciate this?

Leaders of the Indian Muslim community persisted in the demand for boycott; Gandhiji thereupon reversed his attitude. In January 1921 he drew up an eleven-point programme of non-cooperation which included boycott of foreign goods. Bonfires of foreign cloth were made in Bombay city and elsewhere.

The poet Rabindranath Tagore was shocked. He wrote in the *Modern Review*: "Consider the burning of cloth, heaped up before the very eyes of our motherland shivering and ashamed in her nakedness. The command to burn our foreign clothes has been laid on us. I, for one, am unable to obey it. Firstly, because I conceive it to be my very first duty to put up a valiant fight against this terrible habit of blindly obeying orders. Secondly, I feel that the clothes to be burnt are not mine, but belong to those who most sorely need them."

The method of boycott apart, there were nationalists and

foreign-born friends of Indian freedom who were opposed to the very cause of Khilafat and Gandhiji's advocacy of it. Among them was Bipin Chandra Pal (1858-1932), veteran of the movement against the partition of Bengal. In 1918 he could not attend the annual session of the Congress, the first to be held in Delhi, because the British authorities forbade him and Tilak to enter Delhi and Punjab. Bipin Chandra Pal warned against the danger of political pan-Islam, and kept aloof from the non-cooperation movement because of its association with Khilafat. He deprecated the tendency to venerate Gandhiji blindly.

Another notable non-participant in the Khilafat movement was M. A. Jinnah. He was at that time a staunch nationalist. At the Nagpur session of the Congress in 1920, he said to Gandhiji: "For God's sake, do not mix up religion with politics. You do not know what you are doing." It is a different matter that Jinnah himself, after he became a Muslim fanatic and separatist, mixed religion and politics with a vengeance.

Khilafat would prove an *afat* (calamity), said Vinayak Damodar Savarkar (1883-1966), the revolutionary who was sentenced to two transportations for life and was confined under savagely harsh conditions in the cellular jail at Port Blair in the Andamans. He was brought back to the mainland in May 1921 and kept in prison at Ratnagari.

In contrast, C. Rajagopalachari, Gandhiji's southern lieutenant, remarked naively at the time: "Is it not a beautiful thing that India could present the spectacle of one religion not merely tolerating but actually fighting for a sister religion?" Rajaji lived to witness the culmination of the Khilafat mentality in the adoption by the Muslim League, in March 1940, of the resolution demanding partition of the sub-continent to create a new Islamic State of Pakistan.

Gandhiji's support to Khilafat was roundly criticised by C. F. Andrews, a friend and co-worker who, after the initials of his name, was hailed by many Indians as "Christ's Faithful Apostle". He wrote to Gandhiji on 23rd September 1920: "I hate the Khilafat doctrine of a Turkish empire which was too sacred to be touched, and which involved the refusal of independence to another race. My objection to that still holds, and until you can get Mohammed and Shaukat Ali to be absolutely frank on that question, and not to equivocate, you cannot expect to have my wholehearted support. You have not made your meaning clear. Will you or will you not accept Arab and Armenian and Syrian independence in lands which are obviously theirs and not the Turks'?" Gandhiji said in reply, in the columns of *Young India*, that the British government's encouragement of Arab nationalism in the territories of West Asia ruled by Turkey was motivated by Britain's anti-Turkish policy and not by genuine attachment to the principle of self-government. This was an accurate statement, but did not answer the essence of C. F. Andrews' objection.

Saintly Self-Abnegation

Gandhiji's tendency to self-abnegation was evident in his total and uncritical identification with Maulana Mohammed Ali, his chosen comrade-in-arms in the Khilafat-cum-non-cooperation movement. Gandhiji's saintly self-abnegation translated in political terms as appeasement.

So strong was Mohammed Ali's attachment to his religion that he was "impelled by the love I bear towards Mahatmaji to pray to God that he might illumine his soul with the true light of Islam." Whereas Mohammed Ali could see the truth only in his own religion, Gandhiji respected his colleague's faith to the point that he took no exception to, indeed approved of, the following fanatical statement by Mohammed Ali: "As a follower of Islam, I am bound to regard the creed of Islam as superior to that professed by the followers of any non-Islamic religion. And in this sense the creed of even a fallen and degraded Mussalman is entitled to a higher place than that of any other non-Muslim irrespective of his high character, even though the person in question be Mahatma Gandhi himself."

Gandhiji's toleration of Mohammed Ali's Islamic zeal was in curious contrast to his earlier deprecation of Christian proselytisation. Addressing a conference of Christian missionaries in Madras on 14th February 1916, Gandhiji had stressed the importance of each person remaining true to and acting in accordance with the best teaching of his own religion: a Hindu should be a good Hindu, a Muslim a good Muslim, and a Christian a good

Christian. Explaining his concept of Swadeshi in relation to religion, Gandhiji said Swadeshi is "that spirit in us which restricts us to the use and service of our own immediate surroundings to the exclusion of the more remote. Thus, as for religion, in order to satisfy the requirements of the definition I must restrict myself to my ancestral religion, that is, the use of my immediate religious surroundings. If I find it defective, I should serve it by purging it of its defects."

Gandhiji knew that the great majority of Indian Muslims and Indian Christians are descendants of Hindus who were converted at various points of time to the foreign religions. Many of these conversions were brought about through coercion or inducement. Raja Rammohun Roy (1772-1833), father of the Indian renaissance in the modern period, has described both these aspects of conversion to Christianity. On the activities of the foreign missionaries who received aid and encouragement from the British authorities, Rammohun Roy said: "It is true that the apostles of Jesus Christ used to preach the superiority of the Christian religion to the natives of different countries. But we must recollect that they were not the rulers of those countries where they preached. Were the missionaries likewise to preach the Gospel and distribute books in countries not conquered by the English, such as Turkey, Persia, etc., which are much nearer England, they would be esteemed a body of men truly zealous in propagating religion and in following the example of the founders of Christianity. In Bengal, where the English are the sole rulers, and where the mere name of Englishman is sufficient to frighten people, as encroachment upon the rights of her poor, timid and humble inhabitants and upon their religion cannot be viewed in the eyes of God or the public as a justifiable act."

And on inducement, and the possibility as well as desirability of reconversion of proselytes to the Hindu fold, Rammohun Roy said in the course of a letter to the Rev. Henry Ware of Harvard College, U.S.A.: "Several years ago there was a pretty prevalent report in this part of India that a native embracing Christianity should be remunerated for his loss of caste by the gift of five hundred rupees, with a country-born Christian woman as his wife; and while this report had any pretension to credit, several natives offered from time to time to become Christians. The hope of any such recompense being taken away, the old converts find now very few inclined to follow their example. This disappointment not only discourages further conversion, but has also induced several Moosulman converts to return to their former faith; and had Hindoos with equal facility admitted the return of outcasts to their society, a great number of them also would, I suspect, have imitated the conduct of their brother Moosulman converts."

Shuddhi Movement

In promoting Shuddhi, or reacceptance into the Hindu fold, Swami Dayanand (1824-83) gave practical shape to Rammohun Roy's suggestion. A Gujarati by birth who settled in Punjab, Dayanand anticipated Gandhiji's crusade for the reform of Hindu society. He campaigned against untouchability and the relegation of women to inferior status. Taking his stand on the very Vedas which were invoked by the orthodox among Hindus, Dayanand denounced short cuts to salvation through fasts and pilgrimages, or through listening to the Puranas and other medieval texts. He founded in 1875 the Arya Samaj which did much good work in and around Punjab in the spread of education, specially among girls, and in improving the condition of the so-called lower castes.

Subsequent leaders of the Arya Samaj, like Lala Lajpat Rai, followed the lead given by Swami Dayanand when they organised the Shuddhi movement for reacceptance into the Hindu fold, and thereby the psychic rehabilitation, of those who felt uncomfortable in the way of life into which their forefathers had been inducted through coercion or inducement. The opening chapters of Prof. M. Mujeeb's work on *The Indian Muslims* are replete with instances of how the descendants of those forced or inveigled into Islam cling to the old Hindu beliefs and practices.

Shuddhi became a live issue when the Islamic zeal worked up during the Khilafat movement resulted in some forced conversions, as during the days of the Muslim invasions of India. As a tragic consequence of Khilafat, the Muslims of Malabar known as Moplahs turned against their Hindu neighbours. A series of communal riots broke out in various parts of the country, and in

September 1924 there was violence against, and forcible conversion of, Hindus in the north-west frontier region. Annie Besant, friend of Indian freedom who had served as President of the Indian National Congress, wrote in *New India*: "It has been one of the many injuries inflicted by the Khilafat crusade that the inner Muslim feeling of hatred against 'unbelievers' has sprung up naked and unashamed. We have been forced to see that the primary allegiance of Mussalmans is to Islamic countries, not to our motherland. How much sympathy with the Moplahs is felt by the Muslims outside has been proved by the defence raised for them by their fellow-believers, and by Mr. Gandhi himself who stated that they had acted as they believed that their religion taught them to act. I fear that this is true; but there is no place in a civilised land for people who believe that their religion teaches them to murder, rob, rape, burn... People in the 20th century must either educate persons who hold these Middle Age views, or else exile them. Their place is in countries sharing their opinions."

While the Khilafat movement ended in Hindu-Muslim riots in India, in Turkey itself the people discarded their Sultan and established a republic. But Gandhiji did not regret his espousal of the pan-Islamic cause. His saintly self-abnegation led him to take certain further positions which strengthened Muslim intransigence. When some Muslims objected to the singing of Vande Mataram, the patriotic song which inspired the movement against the partition of Bengal and became popular all over India on the ground that it celebrated Mother India as a goddess, Gandhiji advised that it should not be sung even if a single member of a mixed audience (i.e., one which included Muslims) objected. In a remarkable exercise of casuistry, he said that the song was so great that it would not suffer from non-use.

When there was a movement early in 1939 for responsible government in Rajkot, a principality in the Kathiawar region of what is now Gujarat, the Hindu ruler found it convenient to cite the fears of the Muslim minority while turning down the demand for popular government. Gandhiji said on that occasion that the special interests of the Muslims would be safeguarded, and that "if they wanted separate electorates in Rajkot with reservation of seats, I would see to it that they got them."

In 1939 Gandhiji advised the State Congress in Hyderabad, then under the fanatical Nizam's autocratic rule, to suspend its agitation for freedom of worship and for responsible government since the Arya Samaj, which he regarded as 'communal', had launched an agitation on similar lines. He did not want the distinctness of identity of the Congress from that of the Arya Samaj to get blurred. A second reason was, as he wrote in *Harijan* of 19th August 1939: "I was anxious not to embarrass His Exalted Highness the Nizam's Government as long as I could help it." In contrast, at the time of the accession of Jammu and Kashmir to India, Gandhiji said at his prayer meeting on 25th December 1947 in New Delhi: "The Maharaja should clearly say that he is no longer the ruler; it is the Muslims of Kashmir who are the real rulers and they may do what they like." Here was a clear case of applying double standards.

Confusion of Roles: A Sanyasi in Politics

As a sanyasi (renunciant) who doubled as a political leader, Gandhiji frequently commended saintly behaviour to ordinary mortals. In an article he wrote on 'Hindu-Muslim tension: its cause and cure' in *Young India* of 29th May 1924 (following the communal riots which broke out after the euphoria of the Khilafat movement evaporated). Gandhiji said: "There is no doubt in my mind that in the majority of quarrels the Hindus come out second best. My own experience but confirms the opinion that the Mussalman as a rule is a bully, and the Hindu as a rule is a coward.... Between violence and cowardly flight, I can only prefer violence to cowardice... Those Hindus who ran away to save their lives would have been truly non-violent and would have covered themselves with glory and added lustre to their faith and won the friendship of their Mussalman assailants if they had stood bare breast with smiles on their lips, and died at their post."

Gandhiji returned to the theme of converting the adversary through self-immolation in the course of a speech at Surat on 5th September 1924. Referring to an injury suffered by Jamnalal Bajaj when he intervened to pacify two angry groups of Hindus and Muslims, Gandhiji said: "Jamnalalji's hand was injured. It made me happy. If he had been killed while stopping the conflict, even then I would have been happy... If Jamnalalji had died, both the feuding groups would have felt ashamed and would have wept for him. You should win the hearts of Muslims by such display of courage."

The monumental example of the Mahatma falling between the two stools of the saint and of the political leader was during 1947, on the crucial question of the partition of India demanded by Mohammad Ali Jinnah and the Muslim League.

On 1st June 1947 Gandhiji reiterated his opposition to partition, and said: "Let not the coming generations curse Gandhi for being a party to India's vivisection." The Congress Working Committee met in Delhi for considering the Mountbatten scheme for partition that was formally announced on 3rd June 1947. Under this scheme, in view of the increasing scale of communal violence which was having a bad effect on the administration, the date for transfer of power was advanced from June 1948 to 15th August 1947. At the meeting of the Congress Working Committee the only members who voted against partition was Khan Abdul Ghaffar Khan, according to Acharya Kripalani in *Gandhi—His Life and Thought* (Publications Division, 1970).

Mahatma Gandhi soon reconciled himself to what seemed inevitable. He said at his prayer meeting on 9th June 1947: "Lately I have been receiving a large number of letters attacking me. A friend points out how ineffective were my words when I said that vivisection of the country would be the vivisection of my own body, and calls upon me strongly to oppose the partition of the country... When I said that the country should not be divided, I was confident that I had the support of the masses. But when the popular view is contrary to mine, should I force my own view on the people?" This inclination to follow, rather than to shape, public opinion was in curious contrast to Gandhiji's affirmation less than a year earlier: "I must continue to bear testimony to Truth even if I am forsaken by all." (*Harijan*, 25th August 1946). Gandhiji the political leader could not always act up to the standard of Gandhiji the saint.

The final instance of Gandhiji's mixing of roles was on the eve of his assassination. When Pakistan launched an invasion of Jammu and Kashmir by proxy, through tribal raiders armed and financed by it, the Nehru Cabinet decided to postpone (not repudiate) the payment to Pakistan of a sum of Rs. 50 crores as the remaining instalment of its share of the cash balances of undivided British India. As Jawaharlal Nehru put it, "Our difficulty was that if we made any payments now, when a kind of undeclared war was going on between us, that money would be used in carrying out the war against us. It would be foolish for us to make those payments until the Kashmir business had been settled."

Gandhiji felt otherwise. His unhappiness at the Nehru Government's decision to withhold payment to Pakistan, as well as at the state of Hindu-Muslim relations in Delhi and elsewhere, prompted him to begin an indefinite fast on 13th January 1948. The Nehru Government reversed its decision. Then followed, on 30th January, the tragedy of Gandhiji's assassination by Nathuram Godse, indignant at what he regarded as the Mahatma's appeasement of Muslims and of Pakistan.

Gandhiji's imposition of his own morality of the sanyasi or renunciant on his non-sanyasi followers has been brilliantly analysed by Prof. K. Swaminathan who was Chief Editor of the Collected Works of Mahatma Gandhi for a quarter century from 1960. He wrote in the Deepavali annual number of *Swatantra*, English weekly of Madras, in 1952: "Dr. A.D. Lindsay in his 'Two Moralities' brings out the important distinction between the Morality of My Station and its Duties, and the Morality of Grace or the Challenge to Perfection. The argument of the book is for observing ourselves and enforcing on others 'the rules of the game' so long as we play it. The Rules of the Game should be real and actual and observed in practice by all the parties to the game, and not by one party only. The Lower Morality is strictly reciprocal and consists of rights claimed as well as duties owed; and we should be prepared to use organised force for establishing the rule of law impartially on all groups and individuals. The best of us should be ready and willing to do the morally 'dirty' but socially necessary work of policemen, jailors and soldiers. This doctrine is very close to the teaching that Arjuna receives in the Gita, and it cannot be too often or too emphatically repeated.

"The higher morality springs from the inner life and is not owed to any other person, and should not be demanded of any one. The morality of grace, which consists in loving your enemies, is essentially anarchic, for he who loves his enemies has often to let down his friends. It can only be practised by the idealist who cares less for the social structure than for his own soul, by the seeker whose pursuit of perfection has taken him beyond the *grahastha* and well towards the sanyasa stage...

"The extraordinary power of Gandhiji arose from his being a true and typical *vanaprastha* evolving into a sanyasi. If like Ramakrishna, Ramana or Aurobindo he had taken the promotion due to him, if some time between 1942 and 1947 he had withdrawn from the world, all would have been well with him. But he underrated his own achievement and over-rated the capacity of others; he ignored the yawning gulf between his *adhikara* and that of his fellow-countrymen. The success of soul force vis-a-vis Cripps and Pethick-Lawrence, and its failure vis-a-vis Jinnah, ought to have opened Gandhiji's eyes to the difference between a people who have accepted the lower morality and can conceive the higher morality, and a people who have not accepted the lower morality and cannot conceive the higher morality. But Gandhiji was too far committed to the higher morality to question its universal validity; and he made the fatal mistake of attempting to impose it on a society which was not yet ready for it... When, in the great Calcutta killing of August 1946, the Muslims called upon all Hindus to behave like so many Gandhis, events inevitably followed which culminated in the first (and let us hope the last) martyrdom in Indian history."

Nationalist Muslims Let Down

Nationalist Muslims felt let down from time to time by the ambivalence of Gandhiji, and of the Congress, towards Muslim separatists. Among such nationalist Muslims were A. M. Khwaja, Dr. M.A. Ansari and Khan Abdul Ghaffar Khan.

A. M. Khwaja, a prominent Congressman of the United Provinces, wrote on 12th March 1931 to Gandhiji, when the latter expressed his readiness to compromise on separate electorates: "It means that you are prepared to surrender the Congress Muslims who have fought the battles of the country side by side with you, to those Mussalmans who have done nothing except for themselves, their seats, their posts, their salaries and their lunches and dinners at the Government Houses.. .So far they (Congress Muslims) have fought against the Government and against the self-seekers of their own community.... If now they are thrown overboard by the Congress or by you, they must either clear out of the field altogether or must henceforth fight against the Congress." (Quoted by Mushirul Hasan in his biography, *A Nationalist Conscience: M. A. Ansari, Congress and the Raj*, Manohar, 1987).

Ansari's biographer writes: "The Congress preferred to negotiate with their (Congress Muslims') rivals and was willing to compromise.... Congress Muslims at best were bargaining counters; when not so, they could easily be stored in the deep freeze. This placed Ansari and his friends in a quandary and damaged their credibility in the eyes of their followers."

The British Government's Communal Award of 1932 extended the pernicious principle of separate electorates (first introduced in the Indian Councils Act of 1909) beyond Muslims and Sikhs to the Depressed Classes. The Award gave Muslims in provinces in which they were a minority a much higher proportion of seats in the legislatures than was warranted by their numbers. Mushirul Hasan writes: "The Act of 1909 was the beginning and the Communal Award the culmination of the Government's strategy of leaning heavily on the Muslims and giving them a distinct political identity which they did not actually possess.... Muslims alone had reasons to feel satisfied. It is true that their main demand—statutory majorities in the Punjab and Bengal legislatures—was not conceded, but in both the provinces they retained not only their separate electorates but they were also given more seats than any other community in the provincial assemblies." The Award gave Muslims of Bengal and Punjab "considerable opportunities to win a clear majority for themselves" if they were able to capture some of the seats reserved for special interest groups or secure their support.

On the position taken by the Congress that it neither accepted nor rejected the Award, Mushirul Hasan comments: "It was an extraordinary decision, yet it could hardly be very different. It was the inevitable outcome of the past neutral and feeble policy of the Congress. A strong line adopted at an earlier stage and followed regardless of short-term consequences would have enabled it to resist all forms of communal demands. But it had been unwilling to do so... Ansari's own views on the Communal Award were unmistakably clear... He characterized the Award as a vicious document based on the principle of divide and rule. Reaffirming, along with Azad and Sherwani, the position that joint electorates with adult suffrage constituted the only acceptable basis for India's constitution, he asserted that the Award would create fresh communal groups and interests and impede future prospects of Hindu-Muslim cooperation... Given the choice, Ansari would have campaigned against the Award and rallied his band of followers. But Congress strategy to play it safe clipped his wings. In the end, he performed the role expected of him: to explain and defend Congress policy."

British imperialism had driven Indian nationalists into a corner by conferring on Muslims and other religious minorities, beginning from the first decade of the 20th century, not only separate electorates but weightage in representation in the legislatures or government services or both. The Congress could have chosen to set its face firmly against separatism and taken the stand that V.D. Savarkar, the patriot and revolutionary, took vis-a-vis the Muslims. He told them in effect: 'We shall fight for freedom along with you if you will join us, without you if you do not, and despite you if you stand in the way.' The other course was to win the favour of Muslims by outbidding the British—which was clearly impracticable. The Congress oscillated between rejection of and, more often, acquiescence in separate electorates. This resulted in acute embarrassment for nationalist Muslims. If they stood out for uncompromising opposition to the imperialist-Muslim separatist combine, they could be taunted with inability to influence the Muslim masses. If nationalist Muslims, even at the cost of their own claims, advocated a compromise with the Muslim League in order to forge a joint front for advance towards self-government, they were liable to be suspected as disguised Muslim Leaguers. If, going against the current of opinion, they advocated a settlement with the British authorities in the larger national interest as Maulana Azad and Asaf Ali did (when the entire Congress Working Committee was held in detention at Ahmadnagar Fort during World

War II) in view of the imminent Japanese invasion of India and the famine and epidemics that raged in Bengal, colleagues would raise their eyebrows.

The final act of letting down nationalist Muslims was the acceptance of India's partition on the basis of religion by the Congress leaders, and the Mahatma's acquiescence in it. Acceptance of the partition scheme worked out by the last British Viceroy, Lord Mountbatten, was a cruel blow to nationalist Muslims, notably Khan Abdul Ghaffar Khan—popularly known as the 'Frontier Gandhi'. Under the partition scheme, a referendum was to be held in the North-West Frontier Province, overwhelmingly Muslim, where the Khudai Khidmatgars led by Ghaffar Khan and his brother Dr. Khan Saheb had won the elections held for the provincial assembly the previous year.

Aruna Asaf Ali was staying at that time along with her sister Purnima Banerji at Constitution House (where the UNCTAD flats now stand) on Curzon Road (now Kasturba Gandhi Marg). The wartime tenements were utilised for accommodating members of the Constituent Assembly. Their next door neighbour was Ghaffar Khan. Aruna Asaf Ali recalls how he remarked bitterly to her: "We have been betrayed."

The story is told in detail by Pyarelal, Gandhiji's secretary for long years: "The tragic outbreak of communal frenzy in pre-partition India took Gandhiji to Noakhali and from there to Bihar. Badshah Khan was with him in Bihar. Together they tried to wipe the tears from the eyes of the victims of communal frenzy, instil courage into their hearts and quicken the conscience of the majority community so that both the communities would be able to live together like brothers as before. While Gandhiji was thus occupied, the Congress leaders accepted the partition plan behind his back. The Muslim League demanded a referendum in the North-West Frontier Province as the price of its acceptance of the partition plan for Punjab and Bengal, and the British and the Congress accepted it over the heads of, and without reference to, the Khan brothers or their Khudai Khidmatgars. Badshah Khan was very upset. 'We fought and won the general election in 1946 on this very issue. Why should we have another opinion poll?' he asked. He and his party boycotted the referendum, and the

N.W.F.P. was declared to be a part of Pakistan. As Badshah Khan later put it, they were 'thrown to the wolves'."

Nehru's Marxist Euphoria

Besides Gandhiji's sanyasi self-abnegation, there was a second factor that made the Congress response to the challenge of Muslim separatism confused and ambivalent. It was Jawaharlal Nehru's belief, as a Marxist, that what he called the 'economic approach' would solve the communal problem. He gave expression to his naive optimism at the Lahore Congress of December 1929 over which he presided, and which accepted separate electorates.

The background was that a constitutional scheme had been drawn up in 1928 by the Motilal Nehru Committee, established by an all-parties conference as the nationalist answer to the all-white Simon Commission sent to India by the British Government. The Nehru Report, as it came to be referred to, asserted the democratic principle of territorial constituencies in which citizens of all religious communities would choose their representative. But Jawaharlal Nehru was unhappy with the report known after his father's name because, as a political radical, he was strongly opposed to the Dominion Status which it envisaged. At the Calcutta session of the Congress in December 1928, the Nehru Report was the principal subject of discussion and opinion was divided. A compromise was reached. It was resolved that if the British Government did not give effect to the recommendations of the Nehru Committee within a year, the Congress would launch Satyagraha for complete independence.

Since the British failed to respond, the Lahore Congress of December 1929 passed a resolution which set forth complete independence as the Congress objective.

Mightily pleased with the rejection of Dominion Status, Jawaharlal Nehru threw out the baby of joint electorates along with the bathwater. He said in the course of his presidential address on 29th December 1929: "It is inconceivable to me that in a free India the Hindus can ever be powerless. So far as I am concerned I would gladly ask our Muslim and Sikh friends to take what they will, without protest or argument from me. I know that the time is coming soon when these labels and appellations will have little meaning and when our struggle will be on an economic basis. Meanwhile it matters little what our mutual arrangements are, provided only that we do not build up barriers which will come in the way of our future progress."

But separate electorates were already a formidable barrier. That is what Dr. Saifuddin Kitchlew had said in his welcome address as Chairman of the Reception Committee of the Lahore Congress: "Let there be a general provision in the future Constitution to the effect that any question relating to religion or religious culture should not be decided in the case of objection, unless a fixed number of members professing that religion, and present in the meeting, gave their support." This, in his opinion, would afford better protection than the "vicious and barbarous system" of separate representation on communal lines.

On 1st January 1930, the concluding day of the Lahore Congress, Jawaharlal moved from the chair the following resolution which was adopted without discussion: "In view of the lapse of the Nehru Report it is unnecessary to declare the policy of the Congress regarding communal questions, the Congress believing that in an independent India communal questions can only be solved on strictly national lines. But as the Sikhs in particular, and the Muslims and other minorities in general, have expressed dissatisfaction over the solution of communal questions proposed in the Nehru Report, this Congress assures the Sikhs, the Muslims and other minorities that no solution thereof in any future Constitution will be acceptable to the Congress that does not give full satisfaction to the parties concerned." This was a blank cheque for separatist politics. It amounted to saying: 'Secularism as the ideal, and appeasement of communalism as immediate policy.'

The next major development was the Communal Award handed down by the British Government in 1932. It perpetuated separate electorates and gave Muslims, who formed 25 per cent of the population of British India at the 1931 Census, one-third of the seats in the central legislature.

Elections were held in 1937 to the provincial assemblies under the Government of India Act of 1935 which incorporated the Communal Award as modified by the Gandhi-Ambedkar accord in respect of representation of the Depressed Classes. Nehru, as a Leftist radical, was opposed to acceptance of office in the provinces where the Congress might win a majority; he wanted the elections to be contested only to demonstrate the extent of the support commanded by the Congress. The 1935 Act did not even mean Dominion Status, let alone the complete independence of which Nehru was an ardent advocate. It is a different matter that his radicalism did not last long. In 1946 he accepted office, as Vice President of the Viceroy's Executive Council, under the Government of India Act of 1935. But Nehru's radicalism did quite some damage while it lasted. Though the moderating influence of Gandhiji led to the Congress accepting office, and doing much good work (as Jawaharlal Nehru was to admit later), Nehru's radicalism combined with Gandhiji's pacifism resulted in the Congress committing hara-kiri in 1939 by resigning office in protest against India being drawn into World War II. The Congress during the war oscillated like a pendulum between pacifism on the one hand, and on the other the offer of support to the war effort conditional on a substantial transfer of power. This was to have grave consequences.

Basking under British patronage, Jinnah's Muslim League made giant strides during the war years while Congress leaders were vegetating in Ahmednagar Fort jail following the 'Quit India' resolution of August 1942. Asaf Ali, a culturally rooted nationalist and liberal, who had been a Swarajist and an advocate of Council entry since the 1920's, noted in his jail diary at Ahmednagar on 4th June 1944 that, but for the negative attitude of the Congress to the war and the rejection of the Cripps offer of early 1942, India would have been well on the way to substantive self-government.

In addition to an understandable desire to achieve power as Prime Minister and do some good in a free even if territorially diminished India, a consideration that induced Nehru to accept the partition plan was his belief in centralised economic planning on the Soviet model. An entry in Asaf Ali's jail diary dated 2nd July 1944 reads: "Jawaharlal made it clear that the big economic plan by which he intended to tackle the problem of India's poverty would not be realisable if the communal tangle continued to come in the way. And therefore he would rather agree, of course unwillingly, to let the Muslims separate where they could. He would then have a strong central government in the rest of India, and proceed with his economic programme."

The combined effect of Gandhiji's pacifism and self-abnegation and Nehru's faith in a Marxist solution to India's Hindu-Muslim problem was to make it easy for Jinnah to realise his dream of Pakistan.

When Gandhiji, held in detention at the Aga Khan's Palace in Poona, commenced a 21-day fast on 10th February 1943, the British authorities were unmoved. The Congress having renounced power in the greater part of British India where its Ministries had ruled till September 1939, there was none to check the large-scale shipment of supplies from India—including food of which there was a domestic shortage—to help provision and feed the Allied forces at the war fronts. The Viceroy was not inclined to put at risk the free hand that he enjoyed, thanks to the self-denial of power by the Congress, by setting Gandhiji free. Preparations were therefore made, if the old man should die, to have his body cremated on the grounds of the Aga Khan's Palace.

It was only on 6th May 1944, after the tide had turned decisively in favour of the Allies, that Gandhiji, who was suffering from malaria, was released unconditionally. There was now little risk in setting him free.

Religious Converts as a 'Nation'

The talks which he sought and had with M.A. Jinnah during September 1944 made Gandhiji realise how deep-seated was Muslim separatism. He had always known that "the vast majority of Muslims of India are converts to Islam or descendants of converts". He now felt constrained to tell Jinnah: "I find no parallel in history for a body of converts and their descendants claiming to be a nation apart from the parent stock. If India was one nation before the advent of Islam, it must remain one in spite of the change of faith of a very large body of her children." He who, in 1919, extended support to the pan-Islamic Khilafat movement, now expresses misgiving about pan-Islamism. Gandhiji asks Jinnah in a letter of 15th September 1944: "Is the goal of Pakistan pan-Islam?"

Within a year of Gandhiji's release, with the surrender of Hitler's Germany imminent, the British authorities felt it safe enough to think of freeing the members of the Congress Working Committee from detention. From 28th March 1945, they were gradually dispersed from Ahmadnagar and sent to their respective provinces, and released in June 1945. Several of them perhaps felt regret, as they looked round and saw the bitter harvest of the negative policy they had followed during the war years: Bengal left prostrate by famine and epidemics; the flower of India's freedom-loving youth being partly upbraided, and partly admired for having risen in spontaneous and violent revolt following the arrest of national leaders in August 1942; the Muslim League having made giant strides; and corruption rampant in the administration in the wake of wartime economic controls.

When fresh elections were held in 1945-46 to the provincial assemblies under the 1935 constitution, the Congress was to be confronted with the ultimate mortification of the Muslim League's ascendancy which it had unwittingly promoted through its relinquishment of power and its negativism during World War II. M.R.A. Baig writes: "In the elections to the Central Legislative Assembly in 1945, the Muslim League won every Muslim seat, the Nationalist Muslims forfeiting their deposits in many instances."

In the elections to the provincial legislatures, the Muslim League's record was as follows:

Assam	Almost all the Muslim seats.
Sind	28 seats, Nationalist Muslims and other groups, 4.
North West Frontier Province	Muslim League 17, Congress 19.
Punjab	75 out of 86 Muslim seats, with four independent Muslims joining the Muslim League after the elections.
Bihar	34 out of 60 Muslim seats.
United Provinces	54 out of 66 Muslim seats.
Bombay	All 30 Muslim seats.
Madras	All 29 Muslim seats.
Central Provinces	13 out of 14 Muslim seats.
Orissa	All four Muslim seats.
Bengal	113 out of 119 Muslim seats.

It is evident from the above data that the separatism of the Muslim League found the greatest support from Muslims in those parts of the sub-continent which could not possibly become part of Pakistan, formation of which was the objective of the political party they voted for. Muslim separatists outside the Muslim-majority provinces did not ask themselves how the proposed Pakistan could receive and assimilate the Malayalam-speaking Muslims (distributed at that time over the Malabar district of Madras Province and the princely states of Travancore and Cochin), or the Tamil-speaking and Telugu-speaking Muslims of Madras Province. The problem was to get highlighted later, with the Mohajirs—Muslims who performed the hijrat to Pakistan from Bihar, Uttar Pradesh and elsewhere—finding themselves unwanted in the Pakistan for the creation of which they had applied their energies.

To sum up, the way to the vivisection of India in 1947 was paved not only by M. A. Jinnah with his pernicious two-nation theory but also the two Himalayan blunders of Gandhiji, the saint who dabbled in politics: espousal of Khilafat, and pressing of the Quit India demand during the war when England was battling for survival. A contributory factor was Jawaharlal Nehru's airy-fairy Marxism.

CHAPTER 7

Minorityism after Partition

It is a major irony of India's history during the 20th century that minorityism, a policy instrument of British colonial rule over India, was taken over and continued by the Congress Party which assumed office in post-partition India and remained in power for three decades continuously, and intermittently thereafter for another two decades.

In the ordinary course, nationalist Muslims should have come into their own in free India. They had stood for territorial patriotism and democracy even at the cost of incurring the hostility and contempt of the separatists. Nationalist Muslims should have been encouraged to educate their co-religionists, numbering more than 35 million, who stayed back in partitioned India to overcome their sense of separate identity and to join their fellow citizens in the tasks of building up free India as a strong and progressive nation on the basis of democracy, with equal rights and responsibilities for all citizens.

Mishandling of Kashmir

Instead, a series of developments contributed to perpetuation of the two-nation mentality. First was Jawaharlal Nehru's mishandling of the princely State of Jammu & Kashmir, ruled by a Hindu Maharaja. The majority of the population were Muslims but the principal political party of the State, led by Sheikh Abdullah, stood for the Indian model of democracy as opposed to Pakistan's

Islamism. The Maharaja had not yet acceded to either of the two new Dominions by 15th August 1947. Another State which stood out was Hyderabad, which had a Hindu-majority population but was under a Muslim ruler. Hyderabad was right in the heart of the new Indian Dominion, while Jammu & Kashmir was contiguous both to India and Pakistan. A third problem State was Junagadh, on the western coast, which was surrounded by Indian territory and had an overwhelmingly Hindu population.

In terms of the scheme of partition that was drawn up by Mountbatten and accepted by the Congress and the Muslim League, it was for the ruler of a State to decide which of the two new Dominions he might accede to. Even earlier, Jinnah had made it clear in the course of his talks and correspondence with Gandhiji in 1944 that the Pakistan resolution of 1940 was meant to apply only to British India and not to the princely States.

It suited Jinnah to leave the decision on accession to Pakistan or India to the princes, rather than the will of the people of the princely States. Hyderabad, Bhopal and Junagadh had Muslim rulers while their large population was overwhelmingly non-Muslim. If these Princely States acceded to Pakistan or stayed out of India as independent units, Pakistan would have a considerable augmentation of territory and population, or India would be greatly weakened.

When the Muslim ruler of Junagadh conveyed his accession to Pakistan, Governor General Jinnah had no compunction about accepting it in contrast to Jawaharlal Nehru's conditional acceptance, later, of the Kashmir Maharaja's accession to India. But Pakistan was in no position to govern Junagadh. When the people rose in indignation at the ruler's decision, the Nawab, a wastrel whose chief passion was dogs of which he kept over 150, flew to Pakistan taking with him as many of his dogs as possible. In the chaotic situation that ensued, popular leaders of the State appealed to the Indian Government for restoration of order. It was to legitimise a reversal of the ruler's decision that the Indian Government said it would arrange to hold a plebiscite in Junagadh. The position was quite different in respect of Jammu & Kashmir. After the State was attacked by raiders armed and equipped by Pakistan, the Maharaja sought Indian assistance to repel the aggression and signed the Instrument of Accession on 26th October 1947. The action was supported by Sheikh Abdullah, leader of the principal political party in the State, for whose legal defence in a case launched by the Maharaja's administration Nehru and Asaf Ali had visited Srinagar. And yet the Indian Government announced that acceptance of the accession was provisional and subject to ascertainment of the people's wishes. This meant that the lives of Indian soldiers, and Indian money, were being committed to the defence of Jammu & Kashmir while leaving open the possibility of the State not remaining part of India.

The Indian Government could have refused to accept the J & K ruler's accession and thereby thrown Sheikh Abdullah to the wolves, as had been done earlier in respect of Abdul Ghaffar Khan. The other option was to accept the accession as final. The third course, of conditional acceptance, befitted a college of saints rather than a Cabinet of practical statesmen. There could be no reason other than the religious complexion of the population of Jammu & Kashmir for not accepting the ruler's accession unconditionally. It was as if Jinnah's two-nation theory had rubbed off on the very persons who had resisted it. The primary responsibility for the extraordinary decision, which proved politically and financially costly for India, was that of Jawaharlal Nehru, who as Prime Minister took direct charge of Jammu & Kashmir. The accession, and eventual integration with the Indian Union, of all the other Princely States numbering several hundred were handled, with remarkable success, by Sardar Patel who headed the newly created States Department from 5th July 1947.

The working of the mind of Jawaharlal Nehru, and of the Government of India, regarding J & K is set out in a note of 26th October 1947 from Nehru to Mehr Chand Mahajan, at that time Prime Minister of J & K. (Mahajan became a Judge of the Lahore High Court in 1943 and of the East Punjab High Court following partition, and after his prime ministership of J & K during 1947-48 served as a Judge of the Federal Court from 1948 to 1953 and became Chief Justice of the Supreme Court in 1954. His autobiography, *Looking Back*, brings out how Nehru turned a blind eye to the Sheikh's anti-Hindu bias.)

Nehru said in the note: "The Defence Committee of the

Cabinet of the Government of India considered the situation in Kashmir and the request made by the Government of J & K for help against the raiders who had entered their territory and caused great loss. The suggestion that the Kashmir State should accede to the Indian Union was also considered. The Committee came to the following conclusions, which were subsequently confirmed by the Cabinet:

"(1) In view of the request made by the Kashmir government for help against raiders who have entered their territory, the Government of India have decided to give such help. In furtherance of this decision they are sending troops by air tomorrow morning to Srinagar. They intend reinforcing these troops by air as well as by the land route via Jammu, as the defence of Kashmir has become their responsibility and they intend to discharge it to the best of their ability.

(2) His Highness the Maharaja, in accordance with his wishes and the wishes of a large number of his people, will agree to J & K State acceding to the Indian Union. The Government of India will accept this accession provisionally, subject to their declared policy that such matters should be finalised in accordance with the will of the people. Any reference to the people can only take place when law and order have been fully established.

(3) His Highness will invite Sheikh Mohammad Abdullah to form an Interim Government."

In a further communication dated 31st October 1947, Nehru tells Mahajan: "The Governor General and I are going to Lahore tomorrow for a meeting of the Joint Defence Council... The only point that might arise would relate to the conditions of the plebiscite. It is obvious that a plebiscite cannot take place till complete law and order have been established. I see no chances of this happening for some months so far as the Poonch and Mirpur areas are concerned.

A plebiscite has to be impartial. After full consideration of this problem we are inclined to think that it should be held under United Nations' auspices."

In the words of Surjeet Man Singh, a former Indian diplomat,

Nehru blundered in imparting "a tenuous or conditional character to the accession by unilaterally promising its reaffirmation or legitimisation through reference to the 'will of the people'; and, despite characterising Pakistan's action in sending armed personnel into Kashmir as 'aggression', making a reference of the issue to the United Nations under Article 35, as if Kashmir were merely a political dispute amenable to peaceful resolution through international mediation."

The feeling of self-consciousness at accepting the accession of a Muslim-majority State, combined with his fondness for Sheikh Abdullah who aimed at virtual independence from India, led Jawaharlal Nehru to get a reluctant Constituent Assembly to confer, through Article 370, a special status on Jammu & Kashmir. Unlike other States of the Indian Union, J & K was authorised to have its own Constitution. The head of its government was designated as Prime Minister instead of Chief Minister, and the Governor given the special title of Sadr-i-Riyasat. Citizens from other parts of India had to secure a permit to enter the territory of J& K though its people were not a primitive tribal community requiring protection from culture shock or exploitation. The State remained for years outside the jurisdiction of the Supreme Court and of the Election Commission of India. The people of J & K were thus deprived of the Fundamental Rights guaranteed by the Constitution and the free and fair elections that have been free India's pride. Jawaharlal Nehru turned a blind eye to Abdullah's effort to establish a sheikhdom of his own with the help of Indian money, while enjoying protection by Indian armed forces from being gobbled up by Pakistan.

Islamism has been fostered in J & K by two contradictory tendencies in the Centre's handling of the State. One is the pampering of its Muslim majority through a special degree of autonomy, though the religious composition of the population in any part of a secular republic should be a consideration irrelevant for the purpose of autonomy. At the same time, a feeling of hostility towards the Centre— taking the form of Islamic alienation from 'Hindu India' —has been provoked from time to time by autocratic Central intervention.

Article 356 of the Constitution empowers the President to

dismiss an elected State government and place the State under Central rule. If the Congress Party erred greatly in granting a wrong kind of autonomy to J & K, it erred equally in failing to respect legitimate autonomy. Farooq Abdullah was dismissed by the Centre in July 1985 and replaced by G.M. Shah. When, lacking popular support, the Shah government proved untenable, Farooq was made to agree to an alliance with the Congress in J & K as the price for his returning to power. Farooq Abdullah became Chief Minister again in November 1986, but Kashmiri pride had been deeply hurt and he could not regain his popularity. The situation was comparable to that in Andhra Pradesh, where the Telugu Desam party started by N.T. Rama Rao rose to power on the crest of the hurt pride and anger of Andhras at the removal of Congress Chief Ministers in rapid succession and their replacement by marionettes controlled from Delhi.

Ved Marwah, retired officer of the Indian Police Service who served for a term as advisor to the Governor of J & K, wrote in an article in *Indian Express* of 14th September 1993 about the rampant secessionist activity in the State since 1990: "The Kashmir problem may have not taken this sinister turn if the Farooq government had not been dismissed and replaced with the Shah government in 1984, and the Congress-National Conference alliance had not taken place."

Indira Gandhi as Prime Minister mishandled the Punjab problem equally badly. By dismissing successive Akali governments formed as the result of popular mandate, she alienated Sikh sentiment. The lust for power also impelled the Congress Party to build up the fanatical Bhindranwale in a move to divide the Akalis, resulting in Operation Blue Star launched by Indira Gandhi, in 1984 to destroy the Frankenstein of her own creation, and subsequently her assassination by some of her Sikh bodyguards.This was followed by a gruesome pogrom led by Congressmen in Delhi and elsewhere resulting in the killing of thousands of Sikhs by crowds incited by members of the Congress party which professes secularism. P. V. Narasimha Rao, who was Union Home Minister at the time, did nothing to bring under control the situation in the capital till after more than 2500 Sikhs had been killed.

As in Punjab, elected State governments have been dismissed by the Centre from time to time in Assam, Tamil Nadu and Uttar Pradesh among other States, both to get rid of non-Congress regimes and to sort out inner-party wrangles over which Congress-man or Congresswoman should be Chief Minister. This has been done through misuse of Article 356 which empowers the President (meaning in effect the Union Government) to dismiss a State government and to bring the State under Central rule "if the President, on receipt of a report from the Governor of a State or otherwise, is satisfied that a situation has arisen in which the government of the State cannot be carried on in accordance with the provisions of this Constitution." Article 356 and Article 370 are thus the obverse of each other, the one permitting Central hegemony and the other granting an undue degree of autonomy, both serving to encourage secessionism.

Religious Instruction in Schools

Another major example of minorityism practised in the name of secularism pertains to religious instruction in educational institutions. Articles 28 and 30 of the Constitution treat Indian citizens differently on the basis of their religion. Whereas Article 28 prohibits religious instruction "in any educational institution wholly maintained out of State funds", Article 30 reads: "All minorities, whether based on religion or language, shall have the right to establish and administer educational institutions of their choice." It further provides: "The State shall not, in granting aid to educational institutions, discriminate against any educational institution on the ground that it is under the management of a minority, whether based on religion or language."

The right given to linguistic minorities to run educational institutions of their choice is unexceptionable. But why should religious minorities alone, instead of all citizens, be given the right to establish and run educational institutions? The effect of this provision has been to encourage fanatical indoctrination in Islam and Christianity, the two important minority religions. Neither of these Semitic religions acknowledges the validity of other faiths. Christian educational institutions in India have been receiving aid from churches abroad ever since the establishment of British rule.

The building of mosques and the running of *madrasas* also began to receive foreign aid on a massive scale from the oil-rich countries of West Asia following the oil price boom of 1973. Fanatical indoctrination in Islam in hundreds of schools run by the Jamaat-e-Islami in Kashmir has been a potent factor in stoking the fires of secessionism and insurgency.

It would have been far better to make instruction in the best humanist teachings and insights of all major religions a compulsory part of the curriculum at every stage of education, in all educational institutions by whomsoever run. This is what was recommended by the first Commission on University Education, headed by Dr. S. Radhakrishnan. The Commission observed in its report (1949): "To be secular is not to be religiously illiterate. It is to be deeply spiritual."

It will also be in consonance with the views of Maulana Azad. A month after assuming the Education portfolio in the Interim Government, he said in February 1947: "The religious instruction often imparted in India in private institutions is of a kind which, instead of broadening the outlook and inculcating a spirit of toleration and goodwill towards all men, produces exactly the opposite results. The aim of all religious teaching should be to make men more tolerant and broad-minded. And it is my opinion that this can be more effectively done if the State takes charge of the question than if it is left to private initiative." Returning to the subject a year later, Maulana Azad told the Central Advisory Board of Education: "At first it was considered that religious instruction would stand in the way of the free intellectual development of a child, but now it has been admitted that religious education cannot altogether be dispensed with. If national education was devoid of this element, there would be no appreciation of moral values or moulding of character on human lines."

But the dominant personality in the early years of India's freedom, Jawaharlal Nehru, ignored the advice of his own Education Minister and of the Education Commission headed by Radhakrishnan. A purely secular education was ordained for the great majority of students—Hindus—who attend schools and colleges financed by panchayats, municipal boards and State governments; on the other hand, young people attending institutions run by religious minorities were allowed to be indoctrinated in their respective faiths. This twist given by the Congress under Nehru to the concept of secularism, as obligatory for practice by Hindus on a unilateral basis, came to be accepted by all political parties other than the Jana Sangh which subsequently became the Bharatiya Janata Party.

Deploring the grant of autonomy only to educational institutions run by religious minorities, Atal Bihari Vajpayee said in the course of a discussion on the New Education Policy in the Rajya Sabha on 22nd August 1986: "How ridiculous it is that in West Bengal, schools run by the Ramakrishna Mission had to go to court and say they are minority institutions in order to preserve their autonomy! Hindus have become a minority in this country. The Arya Samaj had to do the same thing in Punjab. How far will this dividing line go?"

The BJP's manifesto for the mid-term elections to the Lok Sabha in May 1991 said, in the section on "Law and Constitution": "Article 30 permits minorities to run their own schools. It will be rationalised and suitably amended to ensure justice and equality to all irrespective of religion." This will improve matters only to a limited extent by giving schools and colleges established by the majority community the autonomy now available only to minority institutions. But the real mischief of Article 30 as it now stands arises in the context of Article 28—which prohibits religious instruction in educational institutions run on State funds. If, as strongly recommended by the Radhakrishnan Commission on Education and by Maulana Azad as India's first Education Minister, instruction in the humanist values common to all the religions of India at their best is to be made compulsory, it will require amendment of Article 28. Article 30 will also call for attention in that context, lest religious minorities should invoke it to claim exemption from compulsory instruction in the ethical values common to all religions. There ought to be no freedom to conduct fanatical indoctrination in a single religion—a freedom which now unfortunately prevails.

There is no reference to Article 30 in the BJP's manifesto for the 1996 elections; and neither the 1991 manifesto nor the latest discusses Article 28. It is to be hoped that leaders of the BJP will give their thought to this important question. Nothing will serve better to put on test those who profess secularism than a non-official resolution in Parliament calling for implementation of the Radhakrishnan Commission's recommendation. If any Muslim or Christian members should oppose the resolution, they will reveal themselves in their true, fanatical and anti-secular colours. Similarly, if the Congress, Communist or casteist parties should oppose the resolution, the hypocrisy of their profession of secularism will be shown up.

Muslim Polygamy left Untouched

The mid-1950s saw a travesty of secularism which matched Articles 28-30 in treating religious minorities differently from the Hindu majority. This was the reform of family laws to enforce monogamy, provide the relief of divorce in the event of failure of a marriage, and to grant to daughters a share of the property of persons dying intestate, i.e., without making a will. The confining of these laudable measures of social reform to Hindus was in violation of the Directive Principle of State Policy in Article 44. It reads: "The State shall endeavour to secure for the citizens a uniform civil code throughout the territory of India." Nehru, despite his vaunted secularism, was obviously not willing to risk the displeasure of Muslim male chauvinists. They zealously cling to the right to have more than one wife which is sanctioned by the Quran and the Shariat.

The confining of family law reforms to one community was criticised in Parliament by several members, among both opponents and supporters of the legislation. N.C. Chatterji of the Hindu Mahasabha, who had been elected to the Lok Sabha from the Hooghly constituency of West Bengal, said while opposing the Hindu Minority and Guardianship Bill on 9th December 1954: "Daily, the Congress leaders are harping on the evils of communalism. The Prime Minister of India is ranting on the menace of communalism. What business has this Congress government to bring up a communal legislation?" Chatterji described the legislation as being violative of Article 14, which guarantees equality before the law, and of Article 15 which prohibits discrimination on grounds of religion.

Sucheta Kripalani of the Kisan Mazdoor Praja Party supported the measure, but condemned its being confined to Hindus. She asked: "Why do we not have one civil code for all the people of India if we want reform? We believe that religion is a personal and individual matter. Our social life should be governed under one law. Therefore, we should have one civil code governing the lives of all citizens of India. One criticism is that such communal legislation is against our Constitution. It is against one of the Directive Principles of State Policy."

Subsequent critics of the confining of family law reform to Hindus include Sarvepalli Gopal, official biographer of Jawaharlal Nehru. He said in the course of a paper read by him at a Seminar on "Jawaharlal Nehru and India's Quest for a Secular Identity" at New Delhi on 12th April 1987: "There are certain steps which, under pressure of circumstances, Nehru took or failed to take, which do not fit squarely with his promotion of secularism as the root of equality and the basis of democracy. Special treatment of minorities is in itself a weakening of the secular ideal. In his keenness to win the confidence of the Muslim community, he failed to provide equality before the law to all Indian women and to promulgate a common civil law. But there is no room in a secular society for inequalities which claim religious sanction. To deny rights to Muslim women which are available to women of other faiths is a violation of the provision in the Constitution that the State shall not discriminate against any citizen on grounds of religion."

Mohammad Currimbhoy Chagla (one-time Chief Justice of the Bombay High Court who was India's ambassador in Washington and later served in the Union Cabinet) wrote in his autobiography: "I have often strongly disagreed with the Government policy of constantly harping upon minorities, minority status and minority rights. It comes in the way of national unity. Of course, it may serve well as a vote-catching device to win Muslim votes, but I do not believe in sacrificing national interests in order to get temporary party benefits. I am horrified to find that in my country, while monogamy has been made the law for the Hindus, Muslims can still indulge in the luxury of polygamy. It is an insult to womanhood, and Muslim women, I know, resent this discrimination between Muslim women and Hindu women."

An advocate of discouraging polygamy among Muslims was Professor M. Mujeeb of the Jamia Millia. Referring to the prohibition of bigamy in the conduct rules for civil servants, he pointed out in the course of his inaugural address at a Seminar on Islamic Law in Modern India in January 1972 that there "has been no opposition from the Muslims against the law which forbids a government servant to have more than one wife." Mujeeb suggested that "the law could be extended to cover those employed in institutions receiving governmental grants and further still to those dependent on government assistance in any form."

Over the four decades since Jawaharlal Nehru got legislation enacted for enforcing monogamy on the Hindu male but left Muslim polygamy untouched, there has been a curious line-up of conservative Muslims and of politicians shrilly professing secularism, against any attempt to enact a uniform civil code.

This line-up has been perceptively analysed by Baharul Islam, a retired Judge of the Supreme Court and member of the Rajya Sabha. He said in the course of the fourth Motilal Nehru Memorial Lecture delivered by him on 9th December 1987: "The Muslim intelligentsia are in a dilemma. They do not have sufficient contact with Muslim masses. The latter do not follow them, but are easily misled by the ulema who talk to them politics in terms of religion. Paradoxically, the Muslim intelligentsia are also not much needed by the political parties unless they are fanatical enough to influence the Muslim masses who constitute the vote banks. The result is that the progressive Muslim leadership is torn between nationalism and communalism, between conscience and convenience."

A mighty blow to the concept of a uniform civil code was delivered in 1985-86, during the prime ministership of Jawaharlal Nehru's grandson, Rajiv Gandhi.

There was a howl of protest from backward-looking, male chauvinist leaders of the Muslim community against a unanimous judgment of the Supreme Court in the Shah Bano Case in 1985, that a Muslim husband, like other Indian citizens, is bound to provide maintenance to a divorced wife who is in need. Bowing before the voices of unreason, the Rajiv Gandhi government brought forward legislation, ironically titled the Muslim Women

(Protection of Rights on Divorce) Bill, to nullify the effect of the Supreme Court's judgment. Enacted early in 1986, the law makes it the duty of everyone except the husband to provide maintenance to a divorced and needy wife. The Shariat was thus placed above the Indian Penal Code. This landmark development deserves to be studied in detail.

Supreme Court Urges Common Code

The Court was called upon to determine whether or not, under the Criminal Procedure Code of 1973, a Muslim husband who has divorced his wife is under an obligation to provide maintenance for her if she is unable to support herself. The Cr. P.C., like the Indian Penal Code and the Child Marriage Restraint Act, is applicable to all citizens irrespective of their religion.

The relevant portions of sections 125 and 127 read:

"125 (1) If any person having sufficient means neglects or refuses to maintain.

(a) his wife, unable to maintain herself... a Magistrate of the first class may, upon proof of such neglect or refusal, order such person to make a monthly allowance for the maintenance of his wife.... at such monthly rate not exceeding five hundred rupees in the whole, as such Magistrate thinks fit....

Explanation

For the purpose of this Chapter..... 'wife' includes a woman who has been divorced by, or has obtained a divorce from, her husband and has not remarried.

(2) Such allowance shall be payable from the date of the order or, if so ordered, from the date of the application for maintenance.

(3) If any person so ordered fails without sufficient cause to comply with the order, any such Magistrate may, for every breach of the order, issue a warrant for levying the amount due in the manner provided for levying fines, and may sentence such person, for the whole or any part of each month's allowance remaining unpaid after the execution of the warrant, to imprisonment for a term which may extend to one month or until payment if sooner made... . Provided further that if such person offers to maintain his wife on condition of her living with him, and she refuses to

live with him, such Magistrate may consider any grounds of refusal states and may make an order under this section notwithstanding such offer, if he is satisfied that there is just ground for so doing.

Explanation

If a husband has contracted marriage with another woman or keeps a mistress, it shall be considered to be just ground for his wife's refusal to live with him... .

127. (1) On proof of a change in the circumstances of any person receiving under section 125 a monthly allowance, or ordered under the same section to pay a monthly allowance to his wife... the Magistrate may make such alteration in the allowance as he thinks fit...

(3) Where any order has been made under section 125 in favour of a woman who has been divorced by, or has obtained a divorce from, her husband, the Magistrate shall, if he is satisfied that—

(a) The woman has, after the date of such divorce, remarried, cancel such order as from the date of her remarriage;

(b) The woman has been divorced by her husband and that she has received, whether before or after the date of the said order, the whole of the sum which, under any customary or personal law applicable to the parties, was payable on such divorce, cancel such order...."

In the Shah Bano Case, it was argued on behalf of the husband Mohammad Ahmad Khan, a well-to-do advocate who had divorced her and who came in appeal against an order by the Madhya Pradesh High Court for payment of maintenance, that under Muslim personal law a husband who divorces his wife is under no obligation to pay maintenance beyond the period of *iddat* (three months, or until delivery of the child if the woman is pregnant). It was also contended that the *Mahr* which the husband undertakes, at the time of marriage, to pay to his wife is the sum payable on divorce, referred to in section 127 (3) (b), and that there can be no further claim on the husband even if the divorced wife is indigent.

The case was heard by a five-member bench of the Supreme Court comprising Chief Justice Y.V. Chandrachud, Justice D.A. Desai, Justice O. Chinnappa Reddy, Justice E.S. Venkataramiah and Justice Ranganath Misra. They held unanimously in the judgement delivered on 23rd April 1985 that:

(i) Section 125 contains no words of limitation to justify the exclusion of Muslim women from its scope. Therefore a divorced Muslim woman, so long as she has not remarried, is a 'wife' for the purpose of section 125. The statutory right available to her under that section is unaffected by the provisions of the personal law applicable to her.

(ii) The Explanation to the Second Proviso to section 125 (3) confers upon the wife the right to refuse to live with her husband if he contracts another marriage— leave alone three or four other marriages. It shows, unmistakably, that section 125 overrides the personal law, if there is any conflict between the two.

(iii) In fact there is no conflict. Muslim personal law which limits the period of responsibility to *iddat* does not contemplate or countenance the situation envisaged by section 125. It is only if the divorced wife is able to maintain herself that the husband's responsibility is limited to the *iddat* period.

(iv) Any deferred part of the payment of *Mahr* becomes payable on dissolution of the marriage contract by the death of either of the parties or by divorce. *Mahr* is not the amount payable 'on divorce'. A man settles a sum on his wife as a mark of respect. He does not divorce her as a mark of respect. Therefore a sum payable to the wife out of respect cannot be a sum payable on divorce. Section 127 (3) (b) was apparently drafted on the basis of the misconception that dower is an amount payable 'on divorce'.

(v) The true position, is that if the divorced wife is able to maintain herself, the husband's liability to provide maintenance for her ceases with the expiration of the period of *iddat*. If she is unable to maintain herself, she is entitled to take recourse to section 125.

The judges cited English translations of relevant *Aiyats* of the *Quran* in Arabic, specially 241 and 242 which say that "in addition to her dower", adequate provision should be made for a divorced woman.

The judges noted with 'deep regret' that some of the interveners who supported the appellant took up an extreme position: "...the All India Muslim Personal Law Board have gone to the length of asserting that it is irrelevant to inquire as to how a Muslim divorcee should maintain herself. The facile answer of the Board is that the Personal Law has devised the system of *Mahr* to meet the requirements of women and if a woman is indigent, she must look to her relations, including nephews and cousins, to support her. This is a most unreasonable view of law as well as life."

The Supreme Court's judgement concluded with these significant observations on the subject of a common civil code: "It is also a matter of regret that Article 44 of our Constitution has remained a dead letter. It provides that 'The State shall endeavour to secure for the citizens a uniform civil code throughout the territory of India'. There is no evidence of any official activity for framing a common civil code for the country. A belief seems to have gained ground that it is for the Muslim community to take a lead in the matter of reform of their personal law.... No community is likely to bell the cat by making gratuitous concessions on this issue. It is the State which is charged with the duty of securing a uniform civil code for the citizens of the country, and unquestionably, it has the legislative competence to do so. A counsel in the case whispered, somewhat audibly, that legislative competence is one thing, the political courage to use that competence is quite another. We understand the difficulties involved in bringing persons of different faiths and persuasions on a common platform. But, a beginning has to be made if the Constitution is to have any meaning. Inevitably, the role of the reformer has to be assumed by the courts because it is beyond the endurance of sensitive minds to allow injustice to be suffered when it is so palpable. But piecemeal attempts of courts to bridge the gap between personal laws cannot take the place of a common civil code. Justice to all is a far more satisfactory way of dispensing justice than justice from case to case."

The Supreme Court reiterated its commendation of the enactment of a uniform civil code in the course of a judgement in another case the same year. It concerned a well educated tribal woman of Meghalaya, a Christian who had married a Sikh and sought divorce from him. Christian women are governed by the Indian Divorce Act of 1869 which has no provision of divorce by mutual consent. The Act provides different grounds for the seeking of divorce by men and by women. For example, it is adequate for the husband to prove the commission of adultery by the wife in order to divorce her. But a wife seeking divorce has to prove incestuous adultery, or bigamy with adultery, or adultery with cruelty, or adultery with desertion. The Supreme Court pointed out that there is no provision in Muslim law, either, for divorce by mutual consent (such as is provided in the Hindu Marriage Act and the optional Special Marriage Act). "We suggest," the Supreme Court said, "that the time has come for the intervention of the legislature in these matters to provide for a uniform code of marriage and divorce and to provide by law for a way out of the unhappy situations which couples like the present have found themselves in."

'Secularists' for Shariat

It is a measure of the cynical indifference of the shrill advocates of secularism to the features of the Shariat that are unjust and cruel to Muslim women that they have all either explicitly disowned, or keep silent on the issue of, a common civil code. These pseudo-secularists include the Congress, political parties like the Janata Dal headed by ex-Congressmen, and the two Communist parties.

Elections to the ninth Lok Sabha were held in 1989, after the disgraceful surrender of the Congress government headed by Rajiv Gandhi to Muslim chauvinists. Yet, the election manifestos of the CPM and the CPI made no reference to the subject of a common civil code. It is doubtless because both West Bengal and Kerala, where the Communists have been in power continuously in the first case and intermittently in the latter, have a substantial Muslim population. The Marxists are as keen on influencing the Muslim vote in their favour, through the Mullahs and Imams who shape Muslim opinion, as other pseudo-secularists are.

The Congress manifesto, 1989, was silent on the subject of a common civil code. In the section on Women, the manifesto claimed credit for sponsoring several items of legislation pertaining to women like those dealing with dowry, Sati and indecent representation—but mercifully did not list the Shah Bano Act among its 'achievements': it kept silent on the disgraceful law.

As for the National Front, spearheaded by V. P. Singh's Janata Dal and including three powerful regional parties of Tamil Nadu, Andhra Pradesh and Assam, its manifesto promised "complete non-interference" in the personal laws of the religious minorities.

On the curious spectacle of secularists including Marxists showing exaggerated respect for the personal laws of religious minorities in India, O. V. Vijayan, who is a satirical sage as writer and cartoonist, has the following comment: "We have ingested the Magna Carta and the Westminster model. We have taken on other people's histories. We might, in secular ecstasy, defend Henry the VIII's right to behead more of his queens, his personal law."

The only party to display the courage of conviction was the BJP. Its manifesto for 1989 said that a commission would be appointed to examine the various personal laws in vogue in the country (Hindu, Muslim, Christian, Parsi, Civil, etc.) to identify the fair and equitable ingredients in these laws and "to prepare a draft with a view to evolve a consensus for a uniform civil code." The approach was thus persuasive and not combative, though the conviction was strong.

BJP adhered to its commitment to a common civil code in the manifestos for subsequent elections. The programme put forward by it in the manifesto for the mid-term elections to the tenth Lok Sabha, held in May 1991, said: "We will appoint a Law Commission to study various Civil Laws—ancient, medieval and modern—to evolve a Common Civil Law for the whole country to give all our citizens a feeling of unity and brotherhood."

And in the 1996 manifesto the party pledged itself, in the section on 'Our agenda for women', to: "Introduce a Uniform Civil Code that will (i) Give women property rights; (ii) Ensure women's right to adopt; (iii) Guarantee women equal guardianship rights; (iv) Remove discriminatory clauses in divorce laws; and (v) Put an end to polygamy."

The reaction of right-thinking people against the intellectual dishonesty of the professedly secular parties reached a climax when, on the eve of the 1996 elections to the eleventh Lok Sabha, Prime Minister Narasimha Rao publicly ruled out a Common Civil Code and went to the extent of saying that the subject should not even be discussed. Rao thus made what is ordained as a Directive Principle of State Policy, in the Constitution, sound like something bad, if not obscene and unfit for mention in polite society.

Pseudo-secularists have lately spoken of the prohibition of cow slaughter in similar terms, as if it is something terribly improper and exhibits Hindu communalism at its worst. They would like the people to forget Article 48, which reads: "The State shall endeavour to organise agriculture and animal husbandry on modern and scientific lines and shall, in particular, take steps for preserving and improving the breeds, and prohibiting the slaughter of cows and calves and other milch and draught cattle." Those who decry a ban on cow-slaughter forget that the Supreme Court examined the question forty years ago and upheld such a ban as a reasonable restriction.

Voice of Enlightened Muslims

Over the decades, there has been a steadily growing reaction against the amoral pursuit of power by the pseudo-secularist political parties, who have allied themselves with Islamic fundamentalists in order to woo Muslim votes. This revulsion is not confined to Hindus but has been felt and expressed by several morally sensitive Muslims, Christians, Sikhs and others.

Dr. Moazzim Ali Beg, a Reader in the Department of Psychology, Aligarh Muslim University, saw in the Jana Sangh a vehicle for reviving, and carrying forward in contemporary conditions, the heritage of Bhakti-Sufism. In the course of a newspaper article in 1974, he said: "Repressive capitalism, socialism and communism are all expressions of an evolving spiral of nihilism which is self-destructive. Unfortunately the Congress-I which is presently handling the government machinery in open alliance with the communists seems to be wedded to these nihilistic disciplines. On the contrary, the ideology to which the Jana Sangh is committed is a contradiction of nihilism and throws out a formidable challenge to it. It has its philosophical moorings in the preachings, writings and sayings of Krishna, Shankaracharya, Ramanuja, Chisti, Nanak, Vivekananda, Ram Tirtha and Iqbal of 'Hindustan Hamara' fame... I am convinced through my experience of the past decade and a half that the tag of 'minority character' can never save the Aligarh Muslim University from the defacement of its identity which is going on under the increasing pressures of nihilism, communism, anti-religious and anti-patriotic forces... The Jana Sangh wants to replace nihilism with integral humanism which definitely guarantees a safe place to religion, to Indian culture, to ethical and spiritual values, and above all to a stable framework of morality."

Aizaj Rizvi, another early Jana Sangh member, was a Minister in the BJP Government of Uttar Pradesh in the early 1990s. He was earlier practising before the Lucknow bench of the Allahabad High Court as a criminal lawyer. Asked by a newspaper representative how he kept company with the BJP which is considered by other political parties as anti-Muslim and communal, Aizaj Rizvi said: "I joined the BJP in 1974 because I found it to be better than other parties. To dub the BJP as communal is wrong. Such propaganda is carried out by pseudo-secularists to hoodwink the gullible electorate for votes. The BJP is not communal. It is pro-India and wants all citizens to be pro-India."

One of the Vice Presidents of the BJP is Sikander Bakht. He is the most prominent nationalist Muslim outside the loudly secular parties. Sikander Bakht had the courage to say during the Ramjanmabhoomi-Babri Masjid controversy, in the accents of the Sufi saints: "I am a Ram Bhakt before I am a Sikander Bakht." He was speaking at Hisar, a town near Delhi, on 3rd April 1991 on the eve of a BJP rally in the capital in support of the construction of a temple at the birthplace of Rama. In the spirit of the early Iqbal, Sikander Bakht hailed Rama as part of a glorious Indian heritage which is shared by Muslims. He said that Muslims in post-1947 India should feel grateful that they have been granted equal rights even though most Muslims had backed the demand for partition of the sub-continent. On another occasion Sikander Bakht deplored the fact that the Constitution of India, a secular republic, takes note of and makes special provisions regarding 'religious minorities'.

Opportunism Right and Left

Vote seeking pseudo-secularists have turned a deaf ear to the voice of enlightened Muslims. The tendency to woo Muslim votes through the conservative leaders of the community is not confined to a single political party, or to the Right or the Left. The two Communist parties and the Congress have had no compunction about forming coalition governments in Kerala from time to time with the patently communal Muslim League, while inveighing against the 'Hindu communalism' of the BJP among whose members are Indians professing all faiths. In 1969, the then Communist-led coalition government of Kerala, in which the Muslim League was a partner, carved out a new Muslim-majority district of Malappuram amidst protests from those who feared that such actions might generate a movement for the separation of new 'Muslim homelands' from an already partitioned India.

On the eve of the 1989 elections to the Lok Sabha, an emissary of Congress president Rajiv Gandhi and V. P. Singh of the Janata Dal alternately called on the Imam of the Jama Masjid to beg his support.

The 1991 elections to the Lok Sabha were remarkable for the competitive wooing of the religious minorities by all the major political parties other than the Bharatiya Janata Party, which declared itself, as it had done earlier in its manifesto for the 1989 elections, in favour of equal rights for all citizens and appeasement of none. The Congress (I), on the other hand, promised protection to minorities, and measures to "remove the prevailing sense of insecurity and fear among minorities and infuse confidence in them." The manifesto promised to provide a statutory basis for the Minorities Commission. (The BJP envisaged its replacement by a Human Rights Commission to look into complaints of injustice against any section of society—as recommended by the Minorities Commission itself in 1982 when it had as its chairman Mirza Hameedullah Beg, former Chief Justice of the Supreme Court.) The National Front (of which the Janata Dal was the main constituent) also promised statutory status for the Minorities Commission. Additionally, it said that *wakf* properties would be exempted from rent control laws.

The Communist Party of India (Marxist) promised "protection of life and property of minorities during riots", thus suggesting that minorities never provoke but are always the victims of communal riots. Wittingly or unwittingly, the major political parties except the BJP have thus tended to create an impression, which has no basis in fact, that Indian Muslims are an endangered species. The proportion of Muslims in the total population of post-partition India has grown steadily from Census to ten-yearly Census, from 9.91% at the 1951 head count to 11.35% in 1981 and 12.12% in 1991. The decadal (1981-91) growth rate of Hindus was 22.78%, and of Muslims 32.76%. This is due in part to a higher rate of natural increase in the Muslim population, and partly to a net excess of in-migration over out-migration—apart from conversions. The biggest inflow of Muslims into India has been from Bangladesh, which has the unhappy distinction of having an even lower per capita income than India. This has generated the fear, in some quarters, of Muslim predominance in districts of India's West Bengal which adjoin Bangladesh and the demand for their separation as yet another 'Muslim homeland'.

A major instance of the professedly secular political parties keeping alive and strengthening the sense of a separate Muslim identity is the conferment of statutory status, and the powers of a civil court (summoning of witnesses including officials, documents, etc.) on the Minorities Commission. On 12th May 1992 the Union Welfare Minister Sitaram Kesri, treasurer of the Congress for thirteen years, said with unabashed candour during a newspaper interview (*Indian Express*, Delhi, 21st May 1992) that the empowerment of the Minorities Commission was designed to win back the Muslim vote bank for the Congress.

Foreign-funded Proselytism

First Christianity and then Islam came to India peacefully to begin with, and their adherents were hospitably received because the Hindu religion does not believe in a single path to salvation or a single or final prophet. In contrast, the monotheistic faiths that came from abroad were fervently proselytising. When various parts of India came to be subjugated by West Asian and subsequently European conquerors, Islam and Christianity gained adherents on a large scale through the exercise of force or the offer of inducement.

The close connection between foreign rule and the spread of foreign religions is brought out by reports on the decennial Indian Censuses. E.A. Gait, member of the Indian Civil Service and Fellow of the Royal Statistical Society, supervised the 1911 Census. He notes the reduction of Hindus to a minority along the "route of invading Muslim hordes". Hindus were few in the North West Frontier; they formed one-eighth of the population in West Punjab; 22 per cent in Kashmir; less than a quarter of the population in Sind; and 45 per cent in Bengal. The Census Commissioner goes on to say: "Though there is at present no organised proselytism by the Mullahs, here and there individuals are constantly attorning (turning) to Mohammedanism, some few from real conviction but more for material reasons such as the desire to escape from an impossible position when outcasted or, in the case of widows, the allurement of an offer of marriage . . . At the present time, however, the defections from Hinduism are chiefly the result of conversions to Christianity."

The report notes that the number of Indian Christians had increased three-fold since 1872, and by 32.6 per cent over 1901. It says: "Missionaries find it easier to convert depressed castes of Madras and Punjab, and hill tribes of Chota Nagpur and Assam than to convert high caste Hindus or Muhammadans." It was easy to recruit tribal animists for Christianity since they were free of caste and therefore conversion entailed no cutting off from relations and friends. Other groups vulnerable to conversion, the report adds, were the low caste Mahars of Central Provinces and Berar, Chuhras of Punjab and Shamans of Madras in the southern districts. That most of the conversions were skin-deep is brought out by the statement that "in Kaira, many converted during famine returned to ancestral beliefs". (This helps to explain the term 'rice Christians'.)

The 1911 Census Report includes the following observation: "Hindus have no fanatical opposition. Many send children to missionary schools and colleges. In this way Christian thought influences large numbers who remain Hindus, and Christian ideals and standards are everywhere gaining vogue. The European reader of Indian newspapers is often astonished at the writers' familiarity with the Bible."

British and American evangelical industry in India during the colonial era was supported on a considerable scale by funds from foreign Christian churches. After 1947, religious conversion of Hindus from their mother religion should have been few and far between, and only as the result of a genuine conversion of mind and soul. But, even after independence, large-scale and obviously manipulated conversions—no longer through naked force, but through inducement—have continued. To examine why is to discover how very little changed in India after independence under the leadership of Jawaharlal Nehru, though he was a professed radical. (There was, for example, no change from governmental control of radio—and subsequently television—or from the irrational electoral system of first-past-the-post inherited from the British days.)

In 1931, the Karachi session of the Indian National Congress adopted a resolution on Fundamental Rights and on the socio-economic objectives which should be included in any future Constitution. This resolution envisaged that every citizen would enjoy "the right freely to profess and practise his religion." Curiously, however, the 1950 Constitution of free India added, in Article 25(1), the right also to 'propagate' religion. Considering that the religion of the great majority of Indians is non-proselytising, this meant in effect the grant of a Fundamental Right to Christian and Muslim missionaries to continue their work in India. It was a triumph of minorityism over Jawaharlal Nehru's professed secularism.

Whereas Christian churches have for two centuries received substantial funds from abroad, following the oil boom in the Muslim countries of West Asia since the early 1970s Islam, too, became a well-endowed multinational religious corporation. Tensions have been generated from time to time by money-induced conversions to Islam and Christianity in certain parts of the country. Notable among such instances were the conversion to Islam of many Harijans in 1981 in and around Meenakshipuram in Thanjavur district, and subsequently elsewhere in Tamil Nadu including North Arcot district.

Worthy of the attention of our legislators, jurists and opinion-makers are the observations made on the subject of proselytism by Justice Baharul Islam, a former Judge of the Supreme Court. He said in the course of the fourth Motilal Nehru Memorial Lecture under the auspices of the Institute of Constitutional and Parliamentary Studies in New Delhi on 9th December 1987: "In my opinion, guarantee of the right to propagate religion was excessive and unnecessary, if propagation of religion includes conversion of a person from one religion to another.

"There should be no objection if a person voluntarily renounces his or her religion and accepts another, but propagation of religion and conversion by persuasion or lure creates, and has created, a lot of misunderstanding between different communities, and often creates considerable tension. I believe it will be more conducive if Article 25(1) is amended to the extent indicated above."

An all-India enactment with a bearing on proselytising activity is the Foreign Contribution (Regulation) Act of 1976. Its provisions are not stringent with regard to religious associations compared to political parties, the press and those in public employment. Whereas acceptance of foreign contributions by the latter categories is prohibited, there is no total bar on receipt of foreign money by associations having a "cultural, economic, educational, religious or social programme". The good faith of religious associations will be assumed until and unless it comes to the knowledge of the government that such an association has failed to furnish information, or furnished wrong information, about foreign funds received by it and the purposes for which they were utilised. (For a detailed analysis of the provisions of this Act, see the present writer's *Development and Communication in India*, Gyan Publishing House, 1992.)

There is no uniformity in the regulation by the State of the use of their funds by religious institutions of the different faiths, whether the funds are derived from abroad or from within the country. Statutory control over the utilisation of the funds of

Hindu temples has a long history. It is the most stringent, compared to the laws for regulating the use of the funds of Muslim wakfs and Sikh gurudwaras, which too date from pre-independence days. There was no separate legislation in the British period for regulating the use of the funds of Christian churches, nor is there any now. This is yet another instance of minorityism in a supposedly secular State.

Christian missionaries have, over the centuries, been most active among the simple, unlettered tribal folk of India. Three States with large tribal populations have found it necessary to enact legislation making conversion through force, fraud or inducement an offence. They are Orissa, Madhya Pradesh and Arunachal Pradesh. The legislation in all the three States defines force to include the threat of social excommunication. There is no information on the working of these Acts, the number of prosecutions launched, and the number of conversions—through permitted means—reported by the proselytising agencies each year. It is strange that legislators, social science researchers and the press have shown little interest in eliciting information on the working of the three Acts, and the situation with regard to conversions in other parts of the country.

The continuance of proselytising activity in free India on a large scale has entailed reaction thereto in the form of the Shuddhi movement. This movement gained public notice following forced conversions to Islam in the wake of Khilafat. Gandhiji disapproved of all conversion including reconversion or Shuddhi, saying: "In my opinion there is no such thing in Hinduism as proselytism as it is understood in Christianity or to a lesser extent in Islam. The Arya Samaj has, I think, copied the Christians in planning its propaganda... It has done more harm than good." Gandhiji was powerless to stop the activity of Christian and Muslim proselytisers; nor could he prevent Hindu reaction to it. After independence, the constitution-makers committed the mistake of making the propagation of religion a fundamental right; and successive governments thereafter have not corrected the mistake.

Those who feel concerned about preserving Hindu society from corrosion have therefore been working to facilitate the return to their mother religion of those proselytes who wish to come home. M. S. Golwalkar, head of the RSS, organised the Vishwa Hindu Parishad in 1964 with the object of bringing together the heads of the religious institutions of various sects and castes of the Hindu family. At the first national conference of the VHP held at Prayag in 1966, a resolution was put before the assembled *dharma-charyas* for removing the taboo against admission of proselytes. This was necessary because, over the millennia, Hinduism has been an ethnic religion into which one is born, unlike the transnational and proselytising religions of Christianity and Islam with their ceremonies of baptism and circumcision to mark the admission of converts. Pandit Madan Mohan Malaviya (1861-1946), the patriot and social reformer who was a leader both of the Congress and the Hindu Mahasabha, devised simple modes of Shuddhi. In the 1920s he persuaded the pandits of the Oriental Faculty of the Banaras Hindu University, founded by him, to agree to reclamation of those members of the Depressed Classes who had been converted but wanted to return to their native faith. He himself conducted the Shuddhi by making them recite the mantra 'Shri Ram, Jai Ram, Jai Jai Ram'. At the turn of 1928 he braved the opposition of the orthodox pandits of Calcutta, some of whom resorted to hooliganism, and twice conducted the *mantra deeksha* (initiation) of some members of the Depressed Classes with the words 'Namah Shivaya'.

Most of the religious heads assembled at Prayag in 1964 were willing to endorse the resolution, but it was opposed strongly by the then Shankaracharya of the Puri Govardhan Peeth. He held that there was no provision in the Shastras for the return of converts; once a person relinquished his mother religion he became *bhrasht* (defiled). Guru Golwalkar succeeded in bringing the Shankaracharya round by pointing out how the continuous depletion of the Hindu population in some parts of the country was at the root of India's partition, and of the unhappy situation in Kashmir. The Shankaracharya eventually told the conference that just as it is not wrong to take back one's money that has been stolen, it should not be wrong to take back former Hindus, who had been misled, into the Hindu fold. This was a landmark development comparable to the 'Harijan fast' of Gandhiji in 1932 when he risked his life to prevent separate electorates for the Depressed

Classes, and thereby helped to preserve the integrity of Hindu society.

Hindu Poverty, Muslim Poverty

Appeasement of Muslims in the competitive wooing of their votes by professedly secular parties reached a climax when the Congress government headed by P. V. Narasimha Rao made a distinction between Hindu poverty and Muslim poverty.

A news release by the Press Information Bureau on 16th March 1995 said that the National Minorities Finance and Development Corporation would extend assistance to members of religious minorities if the annual family income is below double the poverty line as defined by the Planning Commission from time to time. No explanation was furnished as to why members of religious minorities need to be only half as poor as poor Hindus to qualify for assistance from public funds on concessional terms. Nor as to how this discrimination on the ground solely of religion squares with Article 15(1) of the Constitution which prohibits discrimination against any citizen on grounds only of religion.

According to the annual report of the Union Ministry of Welfare for 1994-95, Government has notified five communities as religious minorities at the national level. These are: Muslims, Sikhs, Christians, Buddhists and Zoroastrians. It is obvious that the plural term 'minorities' is a euphemism for a singular community—the Muslims, who constitute the largest minority and are an attractive vote bank in our electoral system of first-past-the-post.

It is ironic that the post-independence rulers of India should play on and accentuate religious differences, in order to buttress themselves in power, exactly as the British did. In pre-independence days the British authorities took every opportunity to highlight and aggravate social divisions. Thus the annual report of the Railway Board for 1939-40 set out in detail the number of 'Hindu only' and 'Mussalman only' refreshment rooms at major railway stations. The report also said that there was a 'Christian' refreshment room at Mormugao harbour, and that there were "Indian restaurant cars (for lower class passengers) with separate kitchens for Hindus and Mohammedans" on certain trains. And the platforms at railway junctions where drinking water was served would resound with the cry, 'Hindu Pani, Muslim Pani'.

Gandhiji utilised the formation of the Interim Government on 22nd September 1946, headed by Jawaharlal Nehru, to press for abolition of the obnoxious two-nation cry. He wrote in *Harijan* under the title 'Hindu Pani', 'Muslim Pani' that its continuance "would be repulsive, now that the government at the Centre is wholly national, and a well-known Indian in the person of Asaf Ali Saheb is in charge of transport and railways. It is to be hoped that we shall soon have the last of the shame... Thanks, we still breathe the same air, walk on the same mother earth. All communal cries, at least at the railway stations, should be unlawful."

It fell to the former Prime Minister Narasimha Rao to extend the two-nation distinction from the drinking water of pre-independence days to post-independence poverty.

Effect on Foreign Policy

The Islamic factor in the Indian sub-continent's politics has not been without its effect on external relations. The new State of Pakistan, like most of the Muslim countries of West Asia, aligned itself with the Anglo-American camp in the Cold War. And the West, during consideration of the Kashmir issue in the United Nations, equated Pakistan the aggressor with India the victim of aggression. This reinforced the pro-Soviet inclination of the Nehru Government, which turned to the USSR for support. Part of the syndrome of India's foreign policy during the Cold War, and specially in relation to Israel, was a strongly pro-Arab stance, sometimes in contrast to and sometimes in competition with Pakistan. But India has not secured the expected gain from pro-Arabism. The Organisation of Islamic States comprising 51 countries has been backing Pakistan on the Kashmir issue.

The Gulf War of early 1991 saw a resurgence of pan-Islamic sentiment which coincided with the anti-Americanism of the Communists and some others. In scenes that called to mind the Khilafat movement, members of the Jamia Millia Teachers Association demonstrated at the US Embassy in New Delhi demanding stoppage of the hostilities against Iraq (Saddam Hussein seemed to many Muslims a modern counterpart of the Khalif based in Turkey during World War I). After a Friday prayer gathering at the Jama Masjid in the third week of January 1991, a crowd of about 500 Muslims, joined by workers of the Janata Dal (principal constituent of the National Front), which is stridently 'secular', burnt effigies of President Bush of the USA. On the same day there was a protest rally at the US Embassy in which activists of the two Communist Parties and their front organisations participated. The Khilafat analogy was heightened by a report on 12th February from Washington, by the United News of India news agency, that a group calling itself the United American Muslims for Peace had advised young Muslim citizens of the US to seek 'conscientious objection' status if they were drafted for military service. "We are loyal to nobody except Allah", the group said.

Early in 1992, four decades after India's recognition of the new State of Israel in September 1950, the Government decided to establish diplomatic relations. This provoked criticism by the Muslim League. Ibrahim Sulaiman Sait, president of the Indian Union Muslim League, said that the decision was wrong and went against the aspirations of the Palestinian people and the Arabs. (The Muslim League was an ally, in the Indian Parliament, of the ruling Congress Party which did not command as absolute majority.) Other critics included the Communists, as also Prof. M.S. Agwani, the Muslim vice-chancellor of Jawaharlal Nehru University (a Central university funded by the Union Government). He said in the course of an article in the *The Times of India* that the Government's decision was a sequel to the Indian vote in the U.N. on 16th December 1991 reversing the 1975 General Assembly resolution equating Zionism with racism, and warned that America was seeking to "pit India against the Muslim world." The pan-Islamist and anti-Zionist reactions during 1991-92 were reminiscent of the Muslim League's criticism of Asaf Ali's plea in the UN, at its special session in April 1947, that the Jewish side be heard along with the Palestinian and other Arab spokesmen.

CHAPTER 8

Reaction against Appeasement

The formation of the Bharatiya Jana Sangh in 1951 was in the tradition of sturdy nationalism which first found expression in the popular movement against the partition of Bengal in 1905.

Bengal's partition was designed by the British to placate Muslims and to insulate them from the then nascent Indian nationalism. During the anti-partition movement, of which 'Vande Mataram' was the rallying cry, were forged the weapons of Swadeshi and Boycott which Gandhiji was to adopt later.

The anti-partition movement was led by such eminent sons of Bengal as Surendranath Banerjee and Bepin Chandra Pal, Rabindranath Tagore and Aurobindo Ghose. Outside Bengal, the movement attracted the support of radical nationalists like Lala Lajpatrai of Punjab and Bal Gangadhar Tilak of Maharashtra. As a reaction to the harsh measures adopted by the British rulers to crush the anti-partition movement arose revolutionaries who believed in replying to violence with violence. Earliest among them were Shyamji Krishna Verma, Vinayak Damodar Savarkar and Lala Hardayal.

The Indian National Congress, founded in 1885, had little to do with these stirring developments. At that time a petition-making body, the Congress did not initiate or organise the anti-partition movement. Indeed, so muted was its criticism of Bengal's partition that when the Congress held its annual session at the close of December 1905 in Calcutta, there was a parallel gathering of Hindu leaders under the presidentship of B.N. Mahajan of Berar.

The Mahasabha

This Hindu Sabha was a forum of robust nationalism that was an alternative to the Congress with its weak-kneed response to British-aided Muslim separatists. An Akhil Bharatiya Hindu Sabha was formed in 1914. Such forces of uncompromising nationalism eventually joined hands to form the Akhil Bharatiya Hindu Mahasabha. Its leaders were unyielding in their opposition to the pernicious principle of separate electorates for Muslims incorporated in the Indian Councils Act of 1909—the first to provide for a significant elected component, though on an extremely limited franchise, in provincial legislatures. Separate electorates were subsequently created in a systematic application of the strategy of divide-and-rule, for Sikhs in Punjab and Indian Christians in Madras Presidency under the Government of India Act of 1919. The 1919 Act, moreover, created reserved seats for non-Brahmins in Madras Presidency and for Marathas (also non-Brahmins) in Bombay Presidency. The Government of India Act of 1935 extended the principle of reserved seats to the Depressed Classes. The British Government had wanted to go further and to introduce separate electorate for the Depressed Classes but had to give up the more consequent on Gandhiji's fast and Dr. Ambedkar's humane response thereto.

The Congress began by opposing separate electorates but accepted them under the agreement it entered into with the Muslim League, known as the Lucknow Pact, in 1916. As noticed earlier, the Motilal Committee Report of 1928 re-asserted the principle of joint electorates, only to be discarded at the Lahore Congress of December 1929.

In contrast, the position taken by leaders of the Hindu Mahasabha was clear and steady. It was summed up in Veer Savarkar's message to Indian Muslims: 'We shall fight for freedom along with you if you will join us, without you if you do not, and despite you if you stand in the way.' Savarkar's successor as President of the Hindu Mahasabha was Dr. Syama Prasad Mookerjee, widely respected scholar and educationist.

Typical of the Congress readiness for appeasement, and the Mahasabha's rejection of this policy are the contrasting reactions of the two organisations to a proposal made by the Viceroy, Lord

Wavell, in June 1945. He offered to reconstitute his Executive Council with an equal number of members to represent the 250 million Hindus and the 90 million Muslims. The Congress was willing but the Mahasabha objected. The plan fell through only because of Jinnah's insistence that all Muslims in a reconstituted Executive Council should be nominees of the Muslim League.

Syama Prasad and Jawaharlal

Syama Prasad Mookerjee represented the Hindu ethos at its best—tolerant, liberal and humane. Though as a leader of the Mahasabha he had differed from the Congress, he entertained high regard for Jawaharlal Nehru. It is not widely known that it was Dr. Mookerjee who sowed in 1941 in Nehru's mind the idea of *The Discovery of India* which got written in 1944. As Vice-Chancellor of Calcutta University, Syama Prasad Mookerjee wrote to Jawaharlal, then in Gorakhpur prison, inviting him to deliver the Kamala Lectures at Calcutta University whenever it might suit him in the future. (The lectures were instituted by Asutosh Mookerjee, father of Syama Prasad and a distinguished educationist and jurist. A social reformer who campaigned against untouchability, he gave his daughter Kamala, who had become a child widow, in remarriage in 1908 in defiance of opposition from the orthodox. Kamala died young, and the lectures were in her memory.)

Jawaharlal at first declined politely. But, as he says in a prison diary note of 26th November 1941, "He has written again a very decent letter and I have agreed. The subject I have suggested—Syama Prasad made a similar suggestion—is *The Discovery of India.*" In the second letter of 23rd November 1941, Syama Prasad had said: I am most eager that you would please reconsider your decision. Your penetrating analysis of world's history and the background of the Indian struggle has placed you in the front rank of political thinkers. So far as the Indian situation goes, specially the future of the Hindus, there may be honest differences of opinion on some points between men of your view and mine. But all of us believe that India through her ages contributed an imperishable message of the freedom of the soul of man, which alone can save civilisation from destruction and elevate it to a higher and nobler order...At this critical time you are one of the limited few who can worthily rise above narrow party considerations, appreciate different standpoints and hold out, amidst the crumbling heaps of modern civilisation the picture of a future India worth living in. Do please say 'yes' to my request." This was a handsome tribute, coming from one who was of a different political persuasion. Jawaharlal could not fulfil the engagement because of the sweep of events, but Syama Prasad's suggestion led on to the writing of Jawaharlal's last major work while in detention at Ahmadnagar Fort.

Syama Prasad was elected to the Constituent Assembly by the West Bengal legislature. He was included in the first, broad-based, government of free India formed by Jawaharlal Nehru and held the portfolio of Industries. Mookerjee soon became unhappy with what he regarded as Nehru's weak handling of problems with Pakistan where the lives and property of the Hindu minority were in jeopardy in contrast to the firm steps by the Indian Government to protect the 35 million Muslims who had stayed behind. Mookerjee wanted to promote a political party as an alternative to the Congress, but it was to be a nationalist and not a Hindu party.

A Hindu organisation to resist British-inspired Muslim separatists and their Congress appeasers was in order till partition and the emergence of a free though diminished India. Was a Hindu party any longer necessary or appropriate in an independent India with a democratic Constitution that did away with separate electorates and introduced adult suffrage?

Atmaram Kulkarni in his biography of L.K. Advani (Aditya Prakashan, 1995) recalls: "Mookerjee suggested that the Hindu Mahasabha should either open its door to non-Hindus or become a socio-cultural organisation. He believed that over eighty per cent Hindus in independent India do not need an exclusive political party."

The suggestion made by Mookerjee to his own organisation was in the spirit of a resolution that was adopted by the Constituent Assembly on 3rd April 1948 but was not implemented through a suitable constitutional provision. The resolution said : "Whereas it is essential for the proper functioning of democracy and the growth of national unity and solidarity that communalism should be eliminated from Indian life, this Assembly is of the opinion that no communal organisation which by its Constitution or exercise of discretionary power vested in any of its officers or organs admits or excludes from its membership persons on the ground of religion, race or caste or any of them should be permitted to engage in any activities other than those essential for the *bona fide* religious, cultural, social and educational needs of the community, and that all steps, legislative and administrative, necessary to prevent such activities should be taken."

As his suggestion was not accepted, Mookerjee resigned from the Hindu Mahasabha on 23rd November 1948. He continued to press from inside the Nehru Cabinet for stronger pressure to be brought to bear on Pakistan to assure protection to its minorities. Not satisfied with the terms of an agreement signed on 8th April 1950 by the Prime Ministers of India and Pakistan, popularly known as the Nehru-Liaquat Pact, Mookerjee resigned from the Cabinet on 15th April 1950. On the eve of the first general elections that were to be held on the basis of adult franchise under the Constitution of free India, Syama Prasad Mookerjee launched the Jana Sangh on 21st October 1951.

It is significant that the Rashtriya Swayam Sevak Sangh lent its support to the new party, which was nationalist and secular. Formed in 1925 to organise Hindus for self-defence in the wake of the outbursts of Muslim violence set off by the pan-Islamic Khilafat movement, it was as though the RSS was the answer to one of Gandhiji's two desires expressed in the course of his article of 29th May 1924 on the causes of Hindu-Muslim tension, cited earlier. The Mahatma had said that he would prefer Hindus to take recourse to violence in self-defence rather than be cowardly and run away when set upon by Muslim bullies. Among the aims of the RSS was to organise Hindus to defend themselves.

Formed but a few weeks prior to the beginning of polling during the winter of 1951-52, the Jana Sangh could not make much of a showing in the first general elections. But Mookerjee himself won the South Calcutta seat, securing 45 per cent of the popular vote as against 30.5 per cent secured by his nearest rival, Mriganka M. Sur of the Congress.

Syama Prasad was in full sympathy with the agitation launched on 17th November 1952 by the Praja Parishad, a party based in the Jammu province of J & K, for complete integration of the State with India. In March 1953, the Jana Sangh joined the agitation. Mookerjee decided to assert his right, as an Indian citizen, to enter J & K without a permit. He was arrested by the J & K police after he had crossed the artificial political border between the State and the rest of India. Denied proper medical care, he died while in detention, in June 1953. How right he was in warning that Abdullah was creating his own Sheikhdom in Kashmir at India's cost, and how wrong had been Nehru's policy of pampering Abdullah, became clear when, within weeks of Mookerjee's death, Abdullah was dismissed from office, and put under arrest, in August 1953. But Nehru's heart was not in this operation. The removal of Abdullah was master-minded by Rafi Ahmed Kidwai, a nationalist Muslim and a Cabinet colleague of Nehru's who was more realistic than the Prime Minister.

When Jawaharlal Nehru, accompanied by Asaf Ali and Diwan Chaman Lal, went to Kashmir in June 1946 via Lahore and Rawalpindi to defend Abdullah in a trial on the charge of sedition, Nehru was detained on the way and held in detention at the Uri dak bungalow. But there was a British Viceroy in Delhi who quickly brought to heel the Maharaja's administration, and Nehru flew back to Delhi by a special plane to assist the Congress President, Maulana Azad, in the negotiations for the transfer of power. When Syama Prasad Mookerjee crossed into Jammu seven years later, he was detained by Sheikh Abdullah's police as Nehru had earlier been detained by the Maharaja's minions. But Nehru did not act as the British Viceroy did. Having allowed Dr. Mookerjee to enter J & K without a permit (required by regulations sanctioned by Article 370), Nehru let him meet whatever fate awaited him at the hands of the Lion of Kashmir. Syama Prasad had said at a public meeting in Jammu, in August 1952: "I will get you the Indian Constitution, or lay down my life for it." The words proved tragically prophetic.

Critics of the BJS/BJP make the debating point, to this day, that Syama Prasad Mookerjee was a member of the Cabinet that approved Article 370 at Prime Minister Nehru's urging. But we all live and learn. Did not Jawaharlal Nehru learn to his cost that his trust in Communist China was misplaced? Syama Prasad's acquiescence in Article 370 at the time of its adoption by the Constituent Assembly in 1949 is like L.K. Advani's acquiescence, as a member of the Morarji Desai Cabinet, in the establishment of a Minorities Commission by the Janata Party Government. Advani has acknowledged more than once that this was a mistake, and that a Human Rights Commission should have been formed instead, to safeguard the rights of all citizens.

Syama Prasad was quick to recognise the danger of Article 370 of which he was himself to become a notable victim. It has, over the years, promoted autocratic misgovernment, religious fanaticism and secessionism in Kashmir culminating in the forced migration of hundreds of thousands of Hindus from the Valley. It is ironic that Jawaharlal Nehru, whom Syama Prasad had rated so highly in a letter quoted earlier, refused the demand for an inquiry into the circumstances of the BJS leader's death, as a prisoner, at Srinagar.

Though Syama Prasad's membership of the first Lok Sabha was brief, he made a mark as a parliamentarian. He brought together the members belonging to the Ganatantra Parishad of Orissa, Akali Dal of Punjab, the Hindu Mahasabha and several independents to form, along with the three BJS members, a National Democratic Front. As leader of the Front and by virtue of his stature as an eminent educationist and orator, he functioned as the virtual Leader of the Opposition. With his impressive personality and ringing voice, he commanded the attention of the House when he rose in his seat, much as Atal Bihari Vajpayee has done in recent years.

First Elections: The Godse Factor

There were three reasons for the poor showing of the BJS in the first Lok Sabha elections. One was the very short time it had—a matter of weeks—to prepare for the polls conducted during the winter of 1951-52. Another is the British electoral system of first-past-the-post which was retained, without critical examination, after independence. The BJS won only three seats as against 14 to 15 which it might have got under proportional representation.

The most important reason, however, was that the Congress, which basked in the reflected glory of Mahatma Gandhi, sought in its propaganda to foist on the head of the Hindu Mahasabha and the RSS and, retrospectively, on the Jana Sangh, the blame for the assassination of Gandhiji on 30th January 1948.

It was a brutal and revolting crime of political passion, committed by Nathuram Vinayak Godse of Maharashtra. He was indignant at Gandhiji's role in India's partition and at his last, 'pro-Muslim' fast. Godse had been at one time attracted by the RSS, and later took part in the political work of the Hindu Mahasabha. But he fell out of sympathy with both the organisations following the country's partition. Unable to accept the fact of partition, he was angry with Veer Savarkar for saying that the government formed in its wake should be accepted as the National Government of India. Godse was also shocked at Savarkar permitting Syama Prasad Mookerjee to join the Nehru Cabinet. The assassination of Gandhiji was thus the deed of a maverick individual.

Godse offered a detailed explanation of why he killed Gandhiji. This was in the course of a statement he read out in the court of the Special Judge, Atma Charan, at the Red Fort in Delhi on 8th November 1948. Only scrappy accounts of the statement appeared in newspapers at the time, and publication of the full statement was banned. Nathuram Godse did not deny the charge of murdering Gandhiji, and appealed to the High Court at Simla only against the charges of conspiracy including conspiring with Veer Savarkar. The High Court acquitted Veer Savarkar, sentenced five persons to transportation for life, and confirmed the death sentence on Nathuram Godse and Narayan Apte. The two were hanged in Ambala jail on 15th November 1949.

In a letter to his younger brother Dattatraya Godse a day prior to the execution, Nathuram Godse expressed the following wish: "My ashes may be sunk in the holy Sindhu river when she will again flow freely under the aegis of the flag of Hindustan. That will be the sacred day for us. It hardly matters even if it takes a couple of generations for realising my wish. Preserve the ashes till then, and if that day does not dawn in your life time, pass on the remains to posterity for translating my desire into reality. If and when the Government lifts the ban on my statement made in the court, I authorise you to publish it." He added in a postscript written at 7.15 a.m. on the day of execution: "I have donated Rs. 101 on this day for utilisation for the dome (*kalasha*) of the sacred Somnath temple which is now under construction."

The statement made by Nathuram Godse in the court of the special judge on 8th November 1948 was eventually published in English in 1977, nearly three decades after the event. Given below are some extracts from Nathuram Godse's political testament which should be of interest to serious students of India's political history in the first half of the 20th century culminating in partition and the creation of a Muslim State of Pakistan. The extracts are from a 1993 reprint, published under the title 'May It Please Your Honour' (Surya Bharati Prakashan, Delhi):

"When Gandhiji finally returned to India at the end of 1914, he brought with him a very high reputation for courageous leadership of Indians in South Africa. His simplicity of life, his self-sacrifice and earnestness in fighting against racial arrogance, had raised the prestige of Indians. When he returned here to serve his countrymen, he had legitimately hoped that, as in South Africa, he would command the unchallenged confidence and respect of all communities. But in this hope he soon found himself disappointed. In South Africa, Indians had claimed nothing but elementary rights of citizenship. Hindus, Muslims and Parsis therefore stood united like one man against the common enemy. We were intent on overthrowing an imperial power which was determined to continue its sway over us by all means including the policy of 'Divide and Rule', which had intensified the cleavage between Hindus and Muslims. Gandhiji was thus confronted at the very outset with a problem the like of which he had never experienced in South Africa.

"By 1919 Gandhiji had become desperate in his endeavours to get the Muslims to trust him, and went from one absurd promise to another. He backed the Khilafat movement and was able to enlist the full support of the Indian National Congress to that policy. He made much of the Ali Brothers, but what he wanted never happened. Very soon the Moplah Rebellion showed that the Muslims had not the slightest idea of national unity on which Gandhiji had set his heart and had staked so much. Like the proverbial gambler Gandhiji increased his stake. He agreed to the separation of Sind and to the creation of a separate province in the North West Frontier. The Congress continued to support the Communal Award under the hypocritical words of neither supporting nor opposing. In April 1940, within six months of the war, Jinnah came out with the demand for Pakistan on the basis of his two-nation theory. The Muslims did not obstruct the war effort and the Congress sometimes remained neutral and sometimes opposed. On the other hand the Hindu Sabha realised that this was an opportunity for our young men to have military training, which is essential for our nation and from which we were kept away intentionally by the British. But due to the War the doors of the Army, Navy and Air Force were opened to us, and the Mahasabha urged our countrymen to militarise Hindus. The result was that nearly one to two millions of Hindus learnt the art of war and mastered the mechanised aspect of modern warfare. The Congress Government are enjoying the fruits of the Mahasabha's foresight because the troops they are using in Kashmir, and had employed in Hyderabad, would not have been there ready-made.

"The Congress in 1942 started the Quit India Movement. It completely failed. Britishers had triumphed in the war and the Congress leaders decided to come to terms with them. Indeed, in the subsequent years the Congress policy can be quite correctly described as 'Peace at any Price' and 'Congress in Office at all Costs'. The Congress compromised with the British, who placed it in office, and in return the Congress surrendered to the violence of Jinnah, carved out one-third of India to him—an explicitly racial and theocratic State—and destroyed two million human beings in the process. Pandit Nehru now professes, again and again, that the Congress stands for a secular State. His vociferous adherence to a secular State is nothing but a case of 'my lady protests too much'.

"Gandhiji is being referred to as the Father of the Nation. He has proved to be the Father of Pakistan. It was for this reason that I as a dutiful son of Mother India thought it may duty to put an end to the life of the so-called Father of the Nation.

"Laik Ali, the Prime Minister of Hyderabad, had an interview with Gandhiji during the last week of January 1948. It was evident from the manner in which Gandhiji looked at the Hyderabad affairs that he would soon start his experiments of non-violence in the State of Hyderabad and treat Kasim Razvi as his adopted son, just like Suhrawardy. It was not at all difficult to see that it was impossible for the Government to take any strong measures against a Muslim State like Hyderabad so long as Gandhiji was there. Had the Government decided to take any military or police action against Hyderabad, it would have been compelled to withdraw its decision just as was done in the case of the payment of Rs. 55 crore to Pakistan.

"I do say that my shots were fired at a person whose policy and action had brought rack and ruin to lakhs of Hindus. I felt that this man should not be allowed to meet a natural death, so that the world may know that he had to pay the penalty of his life for his unjust, anti-national and dangerous favouritism towards a fanatical section of the country.

"I had no respect for the present Government owing to their policy which was unfairly favourable towards the Muslims. But at the same time I could clearly see that this policy was entirely due to the pressure of Gandhiji in that behalf. In the absence of such pressure, the way is now open for the establishment of a secular State in the true sense of that word.

"May the country properly known as Hindustan be again united and be one, and may the people be taught to discard the defeatist mentality leading them to submit to aggressors. This is my last wish and prayer to the Almighty."

When Gandhiji embarked on his last fast to secure the safety of Muslims in Delhi and the payment of Rs. 55 crore to Pakistan, some among the million refugees who had poured into Delhi (out of the total of seven million Hindus and Sikhs who fled West Pakistan) raised the slogan:

Gandhi ko Marne do
Ham ko Mākan do
'Let Gandhi die. Give us shelter.'

With searing memories of the murder, rape and loot from which they had escaped, some of the refugees who occupied Muslim houses or mosques in Delhi felt outraged when they were thrown out by the police. Their mood, and that of very many others in Delhi and elsewhere in India, was not in consonance with Gandhiji's. In the words of Manohar Malgonkar in *The Men Who Killed Gandhi* (Macmillan, 1978): "The truth was that Gandhi's non-violence had lost out to violence; no one else believed in his ahimsa any longer, inside or outside the Congress. Whatever its force in normal times, these were not normal times; and to censure the refugees for having fled from Pakistan and to exhort them to go back was to many a form of perversity if not madness; or the action of a saint bent on martyring his flock in a grand gesture of idealism."

Jana Sangh/BJP: The Hindu Bogey

The assassination of the Mahatma was perceived, or deliberately painted, by some as an anti-Muslim outrage rather than simply as an outrage. The British had in their time dubbed the Indian National Congress as an organisation of Hindus, more especially of the upper castes of the Hindu community. The colonialists did not accept the claim of the Congress to be a 'national' forum. It suited the Congress after independence to label the Bharatiya Jana Sangh and subsequently the Bharatiya Janata Party as narrow-minded Hindu communalists, hostile to Muslims.

When Prime Minister Indira Gandhi split the Congress party in 1969 on a populist plank, she accused Neelam Sanjiva Reddy—whose nomination for election as President of India she had filed—of seeking the support of Jana Sangh members of the electoral college. She secured the defeat of Sanjiva Reddy, and emerged as leader of the majority faction of the Congress.

Six years later, when Indira Gandhi's election to the fifth Lok Sabha was set aside by the Allahabad High Court on the ground of corrupt electoral practice, she persuaded President Fakhruddin Ahmed to proclaim a state of internal emergency which entailed suspension of the citizens' Fundamental Rights. She justified the step by citing a threat to the nation from alleged forces of destabilisation—prime among them, according to her, the RSS—the acknowledged backbone of the Jana Sangh. She jailed the leaders of all opposition parties, and imposed censorship on the

Press. The newspapers could not report freely even court judgments and the proceedings of Parliament and the State legislatures. Propaganda material brought out by the Emergency regime concentrated its fire on the RSS. Two pamphlets were brought out by the Directorate of Advertising and Visual Publicity: one, in October 1975, calling RSS the 'Indian version of Fascism', and the second, in December 1975, on the RSS as 'Bulwark of militant Communalism'. Some non-Congress political groups, which were victims of Indira Gandhi's repression during the Emergency, now employ the same words of abuse against the BJP and the RSS.

Having begun to believe her own propaganda about the huge popularity of the measures taken by her during the Emergency, Indira Gandhi relaxed the censorship in January 1977 and held elections to the Lok Sabha in March. The Congress was swept out of power by the Janata, a hastily formed conglomerate of which the BJS was an important unit and which included among others the Socialists and the post-1969 minority faction of the Congress known as the Congress (Organisation). Morarji Desai leader of the erstwhile Congress (O), replaced Indira Gandhi as Prime Minister of India.

It now became the turn of some non-Congress political parties to bait the Bharatiya Jana Sangh for its RSS connection. The real reason for the fall of the government headed by Morarji Desai was the gang-up against him by others who wanted to replace him as Prime Minister. But the power struggle was sought to be given an ideological, anti-communal and 'secular' cloak. Charan Singh formed a new Janata Government in July 1979 with Congress support from outside, only to resign when the support was soon withdrawn. In the elections that followed, in January 1980, the BJS which had been the main constituent of the Janata Party fared badly for no fault of its. Having put up with RSS-baiting long enough, the BJS left the Janata Party in April 1980 to emerge under a new name as the Bharatiya Janata Party.

Effect of Further 'Gandhy' Murders

The BJP met with no better luck at the start of its career than its predecessor the BJS at the start of its. The reason had to do with an assassination in both cases.

Salman Rushdie says in his Introduction to *The Nehrus and the Gandhis: An Indian Dynasty* by Tariq Ali (Pan Books, 1985) that the first edition of *The Times*, London, to report Indira Gandhi's murder on 31st October 1984 carried a picture of hers with a caption which described her as daughter of Mahatma Gandhi. On the error being noticed, the caption was changed in the second edition to 'disciple'—not a much more accurate description.

It is not only the sub-editors of *The Times* who were misled by the spelling of the surname of Jawaharlal Nehru's daughter. When word of her engagement to get married to a Parsi young man named Feroze got round early in 1942, the *Leader* of Allahabad published the news. It spelt his surname as 'Gandhy', in the usual Parsi fashion and in accordance with Feroze's own practice. Facsimiles of letters written by Feroze and by Jawaharlal Nehru (a letter of 16th August 1935 from Feroze to Swami Abhayananda of Belur Math at Calcutta, and a letter from Nehru to Agatha Harrison, dated 16th December, 1935) establish that Feroze's surname used to be spelt in the Parsi style as 'Gandhy'. 'Gandhi', on the other hand, is the spelling of the similar-sounding name of Gujarati Hindus of the Modh Bania caste into which the Mahatma was born.

Feroze had been brought up and educated in Allahabad by his considerably older sister, Tehmina Kershasp Gandhy, in whose care he had been left by his father who worked in the merchant navy and led an itinerant life. 'Gandhy' is the spelling of the surname that Feroze's sister continued to employ; she used it, for instance, in an article contributed by her to a volume of tributes to Indira Gandhi brought out in 1975 under the title *The Spirit of India*.

The change of the spelling of Feroze's surname occurred first in a statement issued by Jawaharlal Nehru, and published by the *Leader*, saying that he had received numerous enquiries and confirming that his daughter Indira Priyadarshini was engaged to wed 'Feroze Gandhi'. The change and the resultant confusion was to have profound consequences, entirely beneficial to Indira because the surname seemed to suggest a family relationship with the Mahatma.

News of Indira Gandhi's assassination on 31st October 1984 had an electrifying effect on the country comparable to that of the Mahatma in 1948. Without waiting for the election of a new leader by the Congress Parliamentary Party, President Zail Singh swore in, the same day, Indira Gandhi's son Rajiv Gandhi as Prime Minister almost as if the office had become hereditary. (Indira Gandhi did not succeed her father at once but after an interregnum during which Lal Bahadur Shastri was Prime Minister.) The former aircraft pilot had been reluctant to enter politics. But he left Indian Airlines and became Congress general secretary because his mother pressingly requested his help after the death of her younger son Sanjay Gandhi in an air crash. Rajiv virtually waded to the Prime Minister's chair through a sea of blood of Delhi Sikhs —more than 2500 to whom were butchered by mobs, led by Delhi Congress leaders, wanting to take revenge for the killing of Indira Gandhi by her Sikh bodyguards. It was strange behaviour on the part of leaders of a political party which claims to be 'secular' in outlook. Equally strange was the masterly inactivity observed by the then Union Home Minister as the rioting went on for days in early November. He was P.V. Narasimha Rao. (Now, as Congress president, he is supporting, from outside, and in the name of secularism, a United Front Government comprising a number of political parties who say they are against the BJP because they are pledged to secularism.) Rajiv Gandhi cashed in on the sympathy generated by his mother's assassination by immediately calling fresh elections to the Lok Sabha. In these elections, held in December 1984, the emotional wave in favour of the Congress swept away all the opposition parties, including the BJP which got merely two seats.

Rajiv Gandhi was in turn assassinated on 21st May 1991 when, having lost the 1989 Lok Sabha elections on account of corruption scandals concerning the purchase of foreign guns and submarines for India's armed forces, he was campaigning for the Congress party in the mid-term polls. While in office, the politically inexperienced Prime Minister had agreed to send an Indian Army force to Sri Lanka to help maintain peace in the face of insurrection by the Liberation Tigers of Tamil Eelam (LTTE). The assassination was carried out in south India as retaliation for Rajiv Gandhi sending Indian armed forces to fight LTTE. The wave of sympathy for the Congress that swept the country following Rajiv's death was strong, but it did not affect the BJP significantly. The Congress share of the popular vote was 32.90% in the pre-assassination phase of the polling; it went up to 40.65% in the post-assassination phase.

In 1989, without the benefit of an assassination-generated sympathy wave, the Congress strength in the Lok Sabha had come down to 194 seats as against the 415 seats (all-time high) bagged by it in 1984 following Indira Gandhi's death. Similarly in 1996, with no fortuitous help from an assassination, the Congress strength came down to 136 (all-time low) compared to the 226 won by it in 1991 when Rajiv Gandhi was killed after the polling process had started but before its completion.

A Flawed Electoral System

In addition to political developments such as those discussed above, the outcome of Indian elections has been affected—one might say, distorted—by the electoral system of first-past-the-post in which the winner takes all.

The table on the next page giving the percentage of seats and the percentage of the popular vote secured by the Congress and the BJS/BJP respectively in the eleven elections to the Lok Sabha, brings out vividly the distortion caused by the electoral system. It will be seen that in six elections the Congress won two-thirds and more of the seats with less than half of the popular vote. Contrariwise, the BJS secured, during the first five elections, and again in 1984, a percentage of Lok Sabha seats far less than its percentage share of the popular vote. The pattern changed in the last three elections, the BJP securing a higher percentage of seats relative to its share of the popular vote. In 1989 and 1996 it was the turn of the Congress to get a smaller percentage of seats than its share of the popular vote.

It is to the credit of the BJP that it has consistently advocated a reform of the electoral system even though it has been lately benefiting from the flawed system now in force. It said in its 1991 manifesto: "BJP will examine the feasibility of introducing the list system." Again, in the 1996 manifesto, it pledged itself to examining the introduction of the list system.

Results for a party in terms of seats are determined to a large extent by the number of opponents it has to face in a given constituency. The fewer the number of opponents, the greater is the challenge for a party: it must gain a majority or a near-majority of the popular vote in order to win. On the other hand, a candidate opposed by a large number of contenders can get through, under the first-past-the-post system, with a ridiculously small percentage of the votes cast in his constituency. Under the Indian election law, a candidate loses his deposit if he polls less than a sixth (16.6%) of the votes cast. There has been an instance of a candidate who lost his deposit but was declared elected, because each of his numerous opponents secured even fewer votes than he did.

CONGRESS AND BJP IN LOK SABHA
Share of seats and votes: 1952-96

Year of election	*Total seats for which election held*	*Seats Won*		*% of Votes Polled*	
		Cong.	*BJS/BJP*	*Cong.*	*BJS/BJP*
1952	489	364 (74.4%)	3 (0.6%)	45	3.1
1957	494	371 (75.1%)	4 (0.8%)	47.8	5.9
1962	494	361 (73%)	14 (2.83%)	44.7	6.4
1967	520	283 (54.4%)	35 (6.73%)	40.9	9.4
1971	516	342 (66.02%)	22 (4.24%)	43.7	7.4
1977	542	154 (28.41%)	93[1] N.A.	34.5	N.A
1980	529[2]	353 (66.8%)	16 N.A.	42.7	N.A
1984	542	415 (77%)	2 (0.36%)	48.1	7.4
1989	524[3]	194 (37.02%)	86 (16.4%)	39.53	11.49
1991	538[4]	226 (42.01%)	117 (21.75%)	37.57	20.95
1996	534[5]	136 (25.47%)	161 (30.15%)	28.2	20

[1] BJS identity was merged in the Janata Party at the time of the 1977 and 1980 elections. The figures given are of the successful candidates owing allegiance to the BJS.

[2] Elections were not held for 12 out of 14 seats in Assam.

[3] Elections were postponed in Punjab.

[4] Elections were not held in Jammu & Kashmir.

[5] Results in respect of some more seats were declared later. The figures of seat and vote share are provisional.

The present electoral system enabled the Congress, during the long years of its dominance at the Centre, to amend the Constitution virtually at will with its two-thirds majority, and to enact obnoxious legislation such as the Muslim Women's Act which nullified the effect of the Supreme Court's judgment in the Shah Bano case. By normal standards, a political party which was on the way to replacing the Congress as the ruling party at the Centre would have been tempted to retain the system so as to reap the same kind of benefit. The BJP has resisted the temptation.

It is not surprising that, as the premier political party in India for over a century, the Congress secured a higher percentage of the popular vote in the 1996 elections than the BJP though the latter secured a larger number of seats in the Lok Sabha. With a substantial organisational presence in almost all parts of India, the Congress has been putting up a larger number of candidates than any other party. What is significant is that the BJP's share of both seats and votes has been going up. In the case of the Congress, its share of the popular vote has been steadily going down since 1989 despite its all-India presence and larger number of candidates.

The BJP having emerged as the front-running political party, its prospects seem bright. But only if it can avoid infiltration of its ranks by seekers of pelf through power who are likely to place their bets on what promises to be the winning horse.

PART III

NATION'S IDENTITY AND DESTINY

CHAPTER 9

Fifty-year Search for Identity

It has been said that the American civil war (1861-65) defined a nation. Before the war, the United States of America used to be spoken of in the plural: "The United States are....' After the war, it became: "The United States is ....'

The Indian civil war of 1946-47, touched off by the Muslim League's 'direct action' on 16th August 1946 divided the sub-continent to create Pakistan as a Muslim State. But post-partition India was left in a crisis of identity.

Was it Hindustan that remained, after the separation of Pakistan? The term had long been in use to denote the land of the river Sindhu and its people. Mohammad Iqbal in his early, patriotic phase had composed a song celebrating Hindustan as the fairest country in the world. But 'Hindustan' was unacceptable to westernised Hindu secularists like Jawaharlal Nehru. The reason was that it carried also the suggestion of Hinduism as a religion—though Nehru and the Congress had agreed to partition of the sub-continent precisely on the basis of religion. The English name India (from the Greek 'Indos') was preferred, with 'Bharat' being mentioned in the Constitution as an additional name of the country. This was meant as a sop to those, not wholly Anglicised and westernised, who took pride in the cultural heritage of ancient India.

What is Secularism?

Nehru would often speak of India as a secular State. This was understandable as a way of distinguishing our democratic, non-theocratic polity from Islamic Pakistan. Nehru was aware of what 'secular' meant in English as ordinarily understood. *The Concise Oxford Dictionary* gives these meanings: 'concerned with the affairs of this world; not sacred or monastic or ecclesiastical'; sceptical of religious truth or opposed to religious education.' He would therefore clarify that India's secular State had a special meaning: it was not opposed to religion as such but was not identified with, or partial to, any one religion. Nehru gave the word another dimension of meaning when he said in the course of a letter to Chief Ministers of States in 1956: "We call our State a secular one. The word 'secular' perhaps is not a very happy one. And yet, for want of a better, we have used it. What exactly does it mean? It does not obviously mean a state where religion as such is discouraged. It means freedom of religion and conscience, including freedom for those who may have no religion. The word 'secular', however, conveys something much more to me, although that might not be its dictionary meaning. It conveys the idea of social and political equality. Thus, a caste-ridden society is not properly secular."

He might have done well to add that the description of India as a secular State did not mean denial of the validity of transcendental experience, as when we lose the sense of individual identity and experience the bliss of communion with the cosmos or God, or when we are deeply moved by music or by relating profoundly to an infant or a lover. We then touch eternity and feel infinity within ourselves. T.S. Eliot had this supra-natural experience in mind when he condemned secularism in a passage quoted by R.K. Das Gupta in the course of an article (*Indian Express*, 25th January 1976) on *Ramacharitamanasa* of Tulsidas. Das Gupta wrote: "The modern reader may find the poem too supernatural to be acceptable to his reason. But all art is essentially a form of supernaturalism, and if our secular humanism obliges us to discard supernaturalism we would one day be obliged to discard art. T.S. Eliot warned us against this when he said that 'the whole of modern literature is corrupted by what I call secularism. It is simply unaware of, simply cannot understand the meaning of, the primacy of, the supernatural over the natural life; of something which I assume to be our primary concern.' All sacred poetry is the story of a miracle, a divine history which demands belief in the supernatural; without this belief there is no insight into man's moral and spiritual nature. Tulsidas is committed to the supernatural as the poet of the Incarnate Deity. And who has been a witness to the Truth without appearing absurd? The greatness of Tulsidas is in his genius for presenting that Truth through an old myth which he could make his own. And those who accept that myth as the poetry of their faith would repeat the words of Tertullian: 'It must needs be believed because it is absurd. It is certain because it is impossible'."

Though as an anglicised agnostic and socialist Nehru was a spiritual child of Macaulay and of Karl Marx, he had flashes of insight which increased in their frequency and profundity in the closing years of his life. Even in his first work, the autobiography (1936), he quotes approvingly a passage in which Romain Rolland speaks of "many souls who are, or who believe they are, free from all religious belief, but who in reality live immersed in a state of super-rational consciousness which they term Socialism, Communism, Humanitarianism, Nationalism and even Rationalism. It is the quality of thought and not its object which determines its source and allows us to decide whether or not it emanates from religion. If it turns fearlessly towards the search for truth at all costs, with single-minded sincerity, prepared for any sacrifice, I should call it religious; for it presupposes faith in an end to human effort higher than the life of existing society."

In 1959, in the course of the first Maulana Azad Memorial Lecture, Nehru spoke of the need for religion as well as science, and of the threat to ethical values from the consumerist culture bred by industrialism: "We see the effects of rapid technological changes more especially in young men and women today. Parents and educators and social workers are troubled because of the divergence between young people and adults. The patterns of behaviour which were held by the adults are no longer accepted, and there is a tendency to criminality, alcoholism, destructiveness, eroticism, in addition to a cynical and negative attitude towards life and work... Four great religions have influenced India—two emerging from her own thought, Hinduism and Buddhism, and two coming from abroad but establishing themselves firmly in India, Christianity and Islam. Science today challenges the old concept of religion. But if religion deals not with dogmas and ceremonials, but rather with the higher things of life, there should be no conflict with science, or *inter se* between religions. It might be the high privilege of India to help in bringing about this synthesis."

Clearly, Jawaharlal Nehru saw secularism as a desirable attribute of the State, and not as in itself a value system or a religion or Dharma for people to live by. Yet, in later years Indian leaders and intellectuals espousing secularism began to speak of religion and secularism in the same breath, and to describe men of God as secularists! In April 1987, a gathering at Simla of Establishment intellectuals of such government-funded bodies as the Indian Council for Social Science Research, the Institute for Advanced Studies and the Indian Institute of Mass Communication adopted a resolution which said: "Secular values should be actively promoted by judges, teachers and religious teachers." On 22nd November 1991, Prime Minister Narasimha Rao said in the course of his convocation address at the Sathya Sai Institute of Higher Learning that Sai Baba's "emphasis on five universal values of Sathya, Dharma, Shanti, Prema and Ahimsa is truly secular in character, and these constitute the major bedrock of all the religions of the world." President Shanker Dayal Sharma went one better and described Guru Teg Bahadur, who put his religion above his life, as a secularist. In a statement on the anniversary of the Guru's martyrdom President Sharma said in December 1993: "May his shining example of service and secularism, and the glory of his sacrifice, inspire each one of us to work for national unity."

The virtual meaninglessness of the term secularism, because of the variety of meanings attributed to it, is brought out by the Supreme Court's decision of 11th March 1994 upholding the dismissal, by the President, of the governments in four BJP-ruled States following the demolition of the disputed Babri structure at Ayodhya in December 1992. Justice Ahmadi (now Chief Justice) in the course of his order quoted the following words of Mahatma Gandhi from an article published in *Harijan* in 1946: "I swear by my religion. I will die for it. But it is my personal affair. The State has nothing to do with it. The State will look after your secular welfare, health, communication, foreign relations, currency and so on, but not my religion. That is everybody's personal concern." Having quoted these words, Justice Ahmadi went on nevertheless to say: "It was with the weapons of secularism and non-violence that Mahatma Gandhi fought the battle for independence against the mighty colonial rulers." Justice Ahmadi said further: "The term 'secular' (in the Preamble to the Constitution) has advisedly not been defined, presumably because it is a very elastic term not capable of a precise definition, and perhaps best left undefined." (*Supreme Court Cases*, 1994, Vol. III, p. 77.)

Another judge on the same bench of the Supreme Court which decided the above case, Justice B.P. Jeevan Reddy, remarked in the course of his order: "Both the expressions—'socialist' and 'secular'—by themselves are not capable of precise definition." Yet the two judges joined the seven others on the nine-member bench in holding that secularism is a basic feature of the Indian Constitution.

Remarking that all political parties profess secularism—whatever it may mean—and accuse each other of communalism, Aruna Asaf Ali said in the course of an article in *National Herald* of 2nd October 1993: "Is it not time to drop the term from the vocabulary of our political discourse? If what we want to advocate is equal goodwill on the part of the State towards all citizens of India irrespective of their religion, and civilised and humane treatment of each other by the citizens themselves, I would suggest that we find another word. Perhaps it could be humanism."

Unilateral Dharma for the Majority

Not only has secularism, which really means non-theocracy, become a Dharma along with other religions, it is a Dharma which is prescribed by its exponents mainly, if not solely, for the majority community.

The prescription of right conduct for Hindus on a unilateral basis, irrespective of the behaviour of other sections of Indian society, has its roots in Gandhiji's teaching. He held that it was for the Hindu majority to educate the Muslim minority into good sense by turning the other cheek, and by returning good for evil. Gandhiji virtually exempted the religious minorities from citizenship obligations, holding that it was for the 'strong' majority to set an example to the 'weak' minorities.

"We want", Gandhiji wrote in *Harijan* of 29th May 1924, "to do away with the communal spirit. The majority must, therefore, make the beginning and thus inspire the minorities with confidence in their *bona fides*. Adjustment is possible only when the more powerful take the initiative without waiting for response from the weaker." Are the numerically larger necessarily more powerful? And is a minority section of society incapable of launching aggressive action?

The answer may be surmised from what Gandhiji himself said in the course of the same article: "There is no doubt in my mind that in the majority of quarrels the Hindus come out second best. My own experience but confirms the opinion that the Mussalman as a rule is a bully, and the Hindu as a rule is a coward. I have noticed this in railway trains, on public roads, and in the quarrels which I had the privilege of settling. Need the Hindu blame the Mussalman for his (the Hindu's) cowardice? Where there are cowards, there will always be bullies. They say that in Saharanpur the Mussalmans looted houses, broke open safes and, in one case, a Hindu woman's modesty was outraged. Whose fault was this? Mussalmans can offer no defence for the execrable conduct, it is true. But I as a Hindu am more ashamed of Hindu cowardice than I am angry at the Mussalman bullying .... Those Hindus who ran away to save their lives would have been truly non-violent and would have covered themselves with glory and added lustre to their faith and won the friendship of their Mussalman assailants, if they had stood bare breast with smiles on their lips and died at their post. They would have done less well, though still well, if they had stood at their post and returned blow for blow. If the Hindus wish to convert the Mussalman bully into a respecting friend, they have to learn to die in the face of the heaviest odds."

Jawaharlal Nehru, too, used to speak of the 'greater responsibility' of the majority community for maintaining communal harmony. Though he did not subscribe to Gandhiji's doctrine of turning the other cheek, Nehru advanced the dangerous doctrine that religious minorities have a lesser responsibility as citizens than members of the majority community. He did so even though the Muslim League had demonstrated, in 1947, that a determined and aggressive minority can hold the majority to ransom.

After Gandhi and Nehru, much of the espousal of secularism became part of opportunist political rhetoric, aimed at securing Muslim votes. The Indian government was quick to ban Salman Rushdie's *Satanic Verses* since the book had angered Muslims. When Prof. Mushirul Hasan, Pro Vice Chancellor of Jamia Millia (a Central university funded by the Government) said in the course of an interview to a journal that reasoned discussion is a better way of countering views with which one disagrees, he was hounded out of Jamia Millia by furious Islamic mobs. He continues to be holed up in the campus of Jawaharlal Nehru University where his wife teaches.

The pulling down of the disputed Babri structure in December 1992 by a section of *Karsewaks* (volunteers for token construction of a temple) who got out of hand was followed by acts of violence by Muslims in several parts of India. These retaliatory acts included the destruction of Hindu places of worship in Kashmir Valley (as in Bangladesh and Pakistan). The retaliation for the destruction of a disused mosque culminated in a series of bomb explosions in Bombay as the result of which more than 250 innocent persons, including several Muslims, lost their lives. While the Ayodhya incident continues to be condemned to this day, there has been no matching condemnation, by secularists, of the retaliatory violence that followed.

Nor has there been serious investigation of the truth behind the suggestion that the happening of 6th December 1992 at Ayodhya was engineered by Pakistani *agents provocateur*. This possibility, which is not incredible in the context of Pakistan's implacable hostility towards India, was pointed to by no less a person than Arjun Singh, a senior Congress leader and former Cabinet colleague of Prime Minister Narasimha Rao. In a letter of 1st December 1992 to the Cabinet Secretary, Arjun Singh said: "There is indication that some *agents provocateur* from Pakistan have been able to infiltrate into Ayodhya and would try to damage the Babri masjid if the VHP *Karsevaks* fail in their mission to do the same. The resulting civil strife as a consequence of this incident is what Pakistan would very much like to happen."

Diffidence of Westernised Hindus

A factor which has made for the continuation, and even accentuation, of minorityism after independence is the feeling of inferiority felt by many of the westernised among English-educated Indians about their Hindu lineage. Reference has been made earlier to the aims of Thomas Babington Macaulay in introducing English medium education in India. The hopes entertained by him have been substantially realised, more so—paradoxically—after independence.

English education received a spurt after 1947 because English is the language that opened for the middle and upper classes the gate to material advancement. Idealism used to animate many among these classes during the freedom struggle and in the early years of independence. It has been displaced by the materialism, consumerism and sexism associated with the affluent countries of the world which enterprising Indians want to imitate. While a half or more of the population continue to live in poverty and illiteracy, the size of the English-knowing middle and upper strata of Indian society has been growing. Estimates of the number of English-knowing Indians vary widely, from about two per cent going up to ten per cent in a population that stands now at some 900 million. Each estimate could be right, depending on the rigour of the definition. There is no doubt, in any case, that the study of English in India has increased after the end of British rule. This is evidenced by the rise in the circulation of English-language daily newspapers from 697,000 in 1952 to about 3.8 million in 1993—a growth rate much higher than of the country's population.

In an encounter between two cultures of which one happens to be more advanced in material terms, there will inevitably be two kinds of effect. Those among the materially less advanced who are strong in mind and spirit will accept from the new culture only its best elements, and will in their turn point to, and commend, what is best in their own heritage. Such were Swami Vivekananda, Rabindranath Tagore and Mahatma Gandhi. Vivekananda called for a combination of Vedanta brain and Islam body. Rabindranath said of the international university which he established at Santiniketan: "Visva Bharati represents India where she has her wealth of mind which is for all. Visva Bharati acknowledges India's obligation to offer to others the hospitality of her best culture, and India's right to accept from others their best." Gandhiji said: "I want the winds of all cultures to blow free about my house. But I do not want to be blown off my feet by any."

On the generality of Indians, however, the effect of English education has been to make them feel inferior. Unlike stalwarts of the renaissance of India in the modern period, who were rooted in their country's culture and literature, an increasing proportion of the English-educated, specially during the second half of the 20th century, know little of the literature of their regional language and less of Sanskrit. They look at India's history through Western spectacles, and feel apologetic because of the unflattering picture.

A language is more than a set of words with specific, denotative meanings. Words carry connotative associations pertaining to religion, philosophy, life style and all of the gamut of human experience. Therefore, an Indian who has learnt English becomes a bit of a Christian and is westernised in his values to some extent.

The English-educated Hindu began to regard as funny the symbols of religion worn by his parents and his neighbours, such as the marks on the forehead, or the tuft of hair on the back of the head, but not the cross worn round the neck by Christians or the robes of priests. He learnt that there were some Hindu mendicants wearing saffron who led licentious lives; he did not know that the word 'nepotism' is from the practice of Popes—supposed to be celibates—appointing their illegitimate sons, whom they called nephews (*nepote*) to profitable positions in the church. He was taught to believe that the monotheism of Christianity and Islam is superior to Hindu polytheism, but neither the teacher nor student knew Vedantic monism as a transcendence of both monotheism and polytheism. The westernised Hindu did not appreciate the co-existential ethos of polytheism compared to the burning of heretics practised in the name of the one and only true God by fanatics of the monotheistic faiths (including the modern variant known as Marxism while it was the State religion in the former Soviet Union and in Maoist China). He felt ashamed of the old Hindu ban on widow remarriage, and of some verses in the *Manusmriti*, compiled between 200 B.C. and 200 A.D., which say that a woman is dependent in turn on father, husband and son, and cannot therefore be independent. But he did not know that the Bible says in the Old Testament: "Thy desire shall be to thy husband, and he shall rule over thee" (Genesis, 3.16); and in the New Testament: "I would have you know that the head of every man is Christ and the head of the woman is the man" (I Corinthians, 11.3). Or that the Quran sanctions the taking of women as war booty by the conqueror, sanctions a man having four wives at a time, and paints a picture of paradise full of sensual delights for the Muslim warrior who dies in the course of *jihad*.

The fact is that the scriptures of every religion contain much that is ennobling and humane, as well as much that is inhumane. It is for us to choose what we shall try to live by: the humane and egalitarian, or the dogmatic and anti-humanist side of a religion. The Hindu heritage contains humane elements including reverence for nature and for all forms of life, and awareness of ecology, in higher proportion than other religions.

The same Manu Smriti that is derided by those who denounce the BJP for its alleged 'Manuvaad' contains the following: "Where women are honoured, there the gods rejoice; where they are not honoured, there, all sacred rites are fruitless." If some Hindu Puranas speak of Brahmin superiority, and prescribe differential punishment for the same offence, with the most severe penalties ordained for the lower castes, Hindu scriptures also affirm: "It is not our religion, still less the colour of our skin, that produces virtue; virtue must be practised. Therefore, let no one do to others what he would not have done to himself." (Yagnavalkya, about 700 B.C.). In the Chandogya Upanishad, Svetaketu is advised by his father: "Live the disciplined life of a student of sacred knowledge. No one, indeed, belonging to our family is unlearned in the Vedas and remains a Brahmin only by family connections as it were."

Much of this is beyond the ken of most Indian students in schools and colleges today. They acquire skills, but not values to live by. This is partly because the Constitution prescribes purely secular education for the great majority of students, while the mass media, in particular government-run television, are promoting a consumerist life style with a heavy dose of sex, imitative of the least admirable aspects of contemporary western culture.

Misleading 'National' Calendar

An outstanding instance of the lack of pride of the westernised Hindu in his national heritage is the official calendar of independent India.

A committee was formed by the Nehru Government in November 1952 to suggest a unified national calendar in place of the numerous traditional almanacs that were in vogue in different parts of the country. The committee was headed by a renowned physicist, Meghnad Saha. He was, like Jawaharlal Nehru, an admirer of the Soviet Union.

The committee came up with a proposal that would make Indian civilisation, which began three millennia before the Christian era, appear junior to the Christian civilisation of the West. The Saka era recommended by the Meghnad Saha Committee, and accepted by the Government, has for its zero year 78 A.D. (the 78th Year of the Lord).

The Sakas, or Scythians, began their incursions into India around 140 B.C. from Central Asia. Vikramaditya of Ujjain, in Central India, is believed to have repelled a Saka attack around 57 B.C. He founded what is known as the Vikram era, to commemorate his success. Among the suggestions received by the M.N. Saha Committee was adoption of Vikram Samvat. Those who made this recommendation suggested also that Ujjain be made the standard 'Greenwich' of India and that astrological observatories with modern equipment be established there.

Why did the committee prefer an era commemorating foreign conquest of India to an era celebrating resistance to foreign attack? Incidentally, the Saka era was not inaugurated by those who led the initial influx into India. The Sakas were followed by a kindred tribe, the Kushans. It was a Kushan monarch, Kanishka I, who began to reckon the years from his ascent to the throne in what is now known as the Saka era.

A national calendar should reflect and strengthen national identity. India would have had no national calendar if Muslim rule, with the Hejira calendar of the Islamic world, had continued. If British rule had not ended, we would still be using the Gregorian as the sole 'national' calendar. It is so called because Pope Gregory XIII, in 1582, prescribed for the faithful the (pre-Christian) Julian calendar as corrected by him. Neither the Saha Committee nor Jawaharlal Nehru advanced cogent reasons why the national era of India could not be based on Emperor Ashoka (3rd century B.C.); or the Buddha (4th century B.C.); or the time of composition of the Vedas (1500 B.C.); or the Sindhu River Civilisation which was already in full bloom in 2500 B.C.; or the surmised date of the Mahabharata War and of the Kali Yuga, around 3100 B.C.

M.N. Saha, chairman of the Calendar Reforms Committee, died soon after the submission of the committee's report in 1955. A member of the committee, Gorakh Prasad, acknowledged in the course of a talk on radio on 19th March 1957, shortly before the coming into force of the new unified 'national' calendar (on 22nd March 1957): "The recommendation which has been criticised the most is the one which desired the Saka era to be universally used. The reason for this recommendation is that the Saka era is already in use in most parts of India, and in the remaining parts of India is used at least as a second alternative to the Vikram era. People have objected to it on sentimental grounds, chiefly because it is not as old as the Vikram era. Some have even suggested the introduction of the Buddha era on the ground that this would be older still. Scientifically considered, there is no harm in using any era, but uniformity is desirable throughout India."

Though the central recommendation of the M. N. Saha Committee proved controversial, its report contains information that throws a flood of light on India's history, political and cultural. The centre-piece, on page 258 of the report, is a chart giving the name, the starting year translated into the Christian era, and other details of some thirty Hindu calendars that were, and continue to be, prevalent in various parts of the country. A survey of the major Indian eras detailed in this chart affords a panoramic view of the chequered course of India's history.

The earliest of the traditional Indian eras is the Kali Yuga. The thinkers of ancient India had concepts of time and space of mind-boggling vastness, like those of modern astrophysics. The sweep of their vision is in contrast to the calculation made by an Irish bishop and incorporated in the Bible published by the Watch-tower Bible and Tract Society of New York—that God created the world in 4004 B.C.!

Another symbol of inadequate national self-esteem is the presence of a statue of V. K. Krishna Menon in front of Sena Bhavan (Army House) in New Delhi. Menon was Defence Minister when the Indian Army was instructed by Jawaharlal Nehru to 'clear the North East Frontier Agency of the Chinese'—a task for which the Army was totally unprepared. The humiliating reverses suffered by India in the 1962 hostilities compelled Nehru to shift his dear friend Menon from the Defence Ministry to Defence Production and soon thereafter to drop him from the Cabinet. That Indira Gandhi should have unveiled Krishna Menon's statue outside Sena Bhavan was thoughtless, to say the least. That the statue has not yet been removed to some museum speaks for the low level of national self-respect among the political leaders who have subsequently been in power.

A manifestation of the diffidence of westernised Indians, accentuated by the deference to Islam which has become synonymous with secularism, is the great emphasis on the 'composite' nature of Indian culture. The term refers to such developments during Muslim rule in India as the emergence of Urdu as a language distinct from both Persian and Hindi; of the ghazal and qawwali in semi-classical Hindustani music, Mughal painting, and Indo-Islamic architecture.

Indian political leaders who are Hindu by birth keep lauding the contribution made by Islam to the country's 'composite' culture, and they compete with each other in holding Iftaar parties during the month of Ramzan to show their friendliness towards Muslims. The contribution made by Christianity to India's cultural life is also similarly lauded. But there is no corresponding acknowledgement by Muslim and Christian leaders of the contribution of the age-old Indian heritage, pre-Islamic and pre-Christian, to the country's composite culture. Nationalist Muslims like M. Asaf Ali, who took pride in the Sanskrit literary heritage and advocated the popularisation of a 'Basic Sanskrit', have been exceptions to the rule.

The subservience to Islam on the part of some exponents of 'composite' culture is illustrated by Jawaharlal Nehru's culturally rootless and politically witless grandson, Rajiv Gandhi. Speaking as Prime Minister at the Red Fort in Delhi on 15th August 1988, he said: "We have to consider what kind of India we would like to make. We shall remove poverty and we shall eliminate unemployment, but in what image shall we mould our country? Our endeavour should be to take the country to the heights to which it belonged about 250-300 years ago, before people from different corners of the world set out to discover India." (English rendering published by Directorate of Advertising and Visual Publicity).

What is the image in which Rajiv Gandhi wanted India to be moulded? During the period referred to by him, India was under the rule of a fanatical and ruthless Muslim emperor, Aurangzeb. Guru Teg Bahadur was executed in 1675, and the Jazia tax on non-Muslims re-imposed in 1679. Aurangzeb reached the zenith of his power in 1691 after defeating the Jats, and died in 1707 in the midst of conflicts with the Marathas and the Deccan Sultanates. This is the 'golden period' to which Rajiv Gandhi would have liked to take India back.

Corrupt Polity, Creolised Culture

By the time of the elections to the eleventh Lok Sabha in April-May 1996, the Indian polity had touched the nadir. Prime Minister Narasimha Rao himself is widely believed to have bribed some members of the tenth Lok Sabha in order to survive a no-confidence motion in July 1993. There were charges of corruption against some half dozen of his Cabinet colleagues, all of whom had to resign one after the other when the evidence came to light.

Doordarshan, the government-owned television system, has become a pervasive influence on urban middle class life. Eager to multiply advertisement revenue by putting out more and more programmes appealing to the lowest common denominator of taste, the authorities who run Doordarshan have brought cabaret-type entertainment into Indian drawing rooms.

A paper prepared by B. G. Verghese, Dilip Padgaonkar and N. Bhaskara Rao analysed the situation thus: "Programming is increasingly determined by reach rather than relevance. Its central aim is the generation of revenues rather than the rejuvenation of cultural and social life. Advertising and sponsorship now compete for prime-time slots. Hence the dominance of serials, soaps, film-based programmes and a variety of talk shows... The exceptions to the rule cannot detract attention from the fact that the broadcasting system is embarked on an emotional and intellectual trajectory deviating from the values and aspirations enshrined in the Preamble of the Constitution, in its articles on the rights of citizens and in many of its Directive Principles. The programmes aired at present satisfy only those elements of the middle class and mass who yearn for titillation." (*Social Effects of Mass Media in India*, Gyan Publishing House, 1996).

As far back as in 1984, a Working Group on Software for Doordarshan, of which the present writer was a member, cautioned against the increasing trend towards meretricious entertainment and the display of sadistic violence on the television screen. Its report said: "The problem of India is that the new middle class has turned acquisitive and hedonistic, and is aggressively trying to utilise the agencies of the State, including the communication network, for pursuit of 'play, fun, display and pleasure'. The vast masses, on the other hand, have still to fight for their economic and social survival at the level of elementary and basic needs. Will the greed of the new middle class have precedence over the basic needs of the vast masses? Will the Communication Revolution aid the masses in their uplift and emancipation, or become an instrument of the upper-middle classes for their self-aggrandisement? This is how perhaps Gandhi would have posed the issue if he were alive today."

The Working Group, of which the chairman was P.C. Joshi—an economist with wide interests in mass communication and the arts—offered many suggestions for making television socially relevant. The suggestions have been ignored. The combined effect of Doordarshan's filmy entertainment and of the foreign satellite TV channels brought to Indian homes by cable operators is to promote a Creole culture imitative of American pop music and dance.

In a report presented in August 1994, the Parliamentary Standing Committee on Human Resource Development expressed its "serious concern over the ever increasing and reckless exhibition of violence, anti-social activities and obscenity through the cinema, the worst sufferers of which are the younger generation whose finer sensibilities are being coarsened and creative faculties dulled." Calling for a proper response to the threat to our cultural traditions from the mass media, both indigenous and foreign, the committee said: "There is every danger of India succumbing to an imitative culture and losing its indigenous creative genius. It will avail us nothing if we attain material progress but lose our soul in the bargain."

CHAPTER 10

BJP's Alternative Model

The significance of the Bharatiya Janata Party replacing, in 1996, the Congress as the largest political party in the Lok Sabha is as much cultural as political. It is a landmark in the process of recovery of national identity and of self-confidence.

Sustenance from Cultural Roots

The BJP's manifesto for the 1996 elections (see Appendix III) brings out in these words the importance of national development drawing its sustenance from cultural roots rather than borrowed ideas and foreign models: "We hold that it is necessary to emphasise the linkage of development elements to cultural elements, including local relevance, relevance to geographical and environmental factors, historical traditions, traditional knowledge and skills. We believe that cultural factors play an important role in energising a nation."

The threat to Indian culture from certain trends in the mass media, including and specially Doordarshan, has been discussed in the previous chapter. Though it was little noticed at the time, the BJP even in its 1991 manifesto pledged itself to "implement the P.C. Joshi Report on television software to improve the quality of TV programmes". The 1996 manifesto deals with the cultural scene in greater detail.

Respect for womanhood, basic to Indian culture, has been undermined in recent decades by the depiction of women in films and on television as nothing but sex objects. This has had the effect of tempting some urban women as well as men of the younger generation to imitate the dress and deportment of the meretricious models depicted in the film and television media. This has created a vicious circle of cause and effect between 'reel' life and real life. Newspapers, specially in English, have made their own contribution to cultural degradation, with space generously applied by them to bare-bodied women in 'beauty' contests, and to models sporting bizarre dresses or displaying their limbs in fashion shows. Some newspapers regularly tickle their subscribers with sexy fare, not only pictorial but also verbal in the guise of sex education and counselling. It is as if Doordarshan and a section of the press are in competition to benumb the social conscience of Indian youth and to advertise, instead, a vision of human life as an endless round of cosmetics and party dresses, soft-drink guzzling, fast driving and public fondling. Particularly to blame is government-run Doordarshan, which has reduced itself to an extension agency of the Indian film industry.

"Popular cinema", the BJP manifesto says, "has played an important role in promoting social harmony and nationalism, apart from providing inexpensive entertainment to the masses. But in recent years, popular cinema, increasingly funded by the underworld, has had a negative impact on society, especially impressionable young minds. Sex and violence on the silver screen are beginning to gnaw at the moorings of our cultural ethos." Among the steps proposed for checking the unhealthy trends in the film industry is to enable film-makers to secure resources from financial institutions to curb the influence of underworld financiers and mafia dons; appointment of women as members of the Censor Board and Censor Panels to the extent of at least fifty per cent; and exemption of quality films from entertainment tax. The manifesto also pledges that the BJP will "discourage indecent representation of women in advertisements and publications."

Evidence of the BJP's earnestness in this regard was provided by Sushma Swaraj, who was Minister of Information and Broadcasting in the brief-lived Vajpayee Government during May 1996. She spoke as no Minister had done before about the vulgarity and potential danger of the advertisements at bus stops and hoardings on Delhi's roads which promote 'safe sex' in the name of AIDS awareness. She also came down on those TV programmes in which, in order to maximise audience size and advertisement revenue, some women presenters display their limbs.

Symbolic of the neglect of India's cultural identity by the governments headed by Congressmen and ex-Congressmen over the last fifty years is that Jawaharlal Nehru University, a Central university located in the country's capital, teaches numerous languages Indian and foreign but not Sanskrit. In contrast, the BJP manifesto promises to "encourage the study of Sanskrit".

An important contribution already made by the BJP to the restoration of national identity and self-respect is the revival of 'Vande Mataram', the song that inspired the anti-partition movement—the first militant expressiòn of Indian nationalism in the 20th century. It was a BJP member of the tenth Lok Sabha, Ram Nayak, who, by raising half-an-hour discussion got introduced the practice of each session commencing with the playing of 'Jana Gana Mana' and concluding with 'Vande Mataram'.

The significance of this in the process of the recovery of national self-respect cannot be exaggerated. Gandhiji with his saintly self-abnegation, as noticed in an earlier chapter, said that the song should not be sung even if a single Muslim raised objection. Jawaharlal Nehru, after independence, threw his weight behind the adoption of 'Jana Gana Mana' rather than 'Vande Mataram' as the National Anthem. He was well aware of the objection to the latter song that used to be raised by M.A. Jinnah. In a letter of 13th February 1938 to Nehru, Frances Gunther narrated how her husband John Gunther and she had spent three hours talking to Jinnah: "For two and three-quarter hours John listened politely while Jinnah talked and talked. Finally I could stand it no longer and shouted, 'But for God's sake, what in hell does the Muslim League want?' Well, believe it or not, he brought up the Vande Mataram. . . . It's just one verse they object to, I understand. Why don't you get them to offer a substitute verse? Challenge Jinnah publicly to a poetical duel?"

While acknowledging that Vande Mataram "is obviously and undisputedly the premier national song of India, with a great historical tradition, and intimately connected with our struggle for freedom", Jawaharlal Nehru told the provisional Parliament on 25th August 1948: " In regard to the national anthem tune, it was felt (by the Cabinet) that the tune was more important than the words, and that this tune should be such as to represent the Indian musical genius as well as the Western, so that it might be equally adaptable to orchestra and band music, and to being played abroad. The real significance of the national anthem is perhaps more abroad than in the home country." Nehru was looking forward to the ceremonial welcomes he would receive in foreign capitals during his tireless peregrinations as India's Prime Minister.

The partial restoration of 'Vande Mataram' to the status that is its due as the original national anthem of India is symbolic of the dedication to national freedom and territorial integrity which has earned BJP the respect and support of patriots. The Unity March led by Murli Manohar Joshi as President of the BJP was a landmark event. Starting from Kanya Kumari, the southernmost tip of the Indian peninsula, on 11th December 1991, he reached Srinagar to hoist the national flag at Lal Chowk on 26th January 1992 in defiance of dire threats by Pakistan-abetted terrorists. It is no wonder that among those attracted to the BJP are retired Lt. Gen. Jacob, former G.O.C., Eastern Command, and retired Major Gen. Khanduri, who was elected to the Lok Sabha in 1996 from Uttarakhand.

Also drawn to the BJP over the years have been such distinguished men in public life as the late M.C. Chagla, judge and diplomat; Jethmalani the eminent jurist; and T.N. Chaturvedi, former Comptroller and Auditor General of India. Such instances have served to dispel the notion of BJP as a party of the trading class—the picture painted by Leftists and the Congress establishment. In any case, trading is a socially useful and honourable profession, unlike the influence peddling which has become the occupation of many leaders of the Congress and some other parties.

Compassionate Gandhian Economics

It is likely that, in the years to come, Gandhiji will be remembered and valued more for the caring and compassionate economics which he advocated, than for his ideals of Brahmacharya and Ahimsa which are impossible for most human beings. His saintly self-abnegation was admirable on the personal plane, but when mixed with politics led to unfortunate results as discussed earlier. In contrast, his economic philosophy of giving first importance to the last and least among India's masses, by providing gainful employment, has proved superior to the pursuit of industrialism for its own sake, whether through private or state capitalism. The BJP's approach to India's economic problems is close to the Gandhian.

Though the fact has not come to be widely noticed, even Jawaharlal Nehru became a convert to Gandhian economics towards the close of his life. In the sphere of economic policy, therefore, unlike in other spheres, the BJP's policy provides a continuity and link with the best in the Gandhi-Nehru legacy.

Prior to independence Nehru used to scoff at Khadi as a means of regeneration of India's rural economy, and advocated large-scale industrialization. As Prime Minister and Chairman of the Planning Commission he thought he could replicate in India with its democratic political system and civil liberties the Stalinist model of heavy industries as well as cooperative joint farming as in Communist China. The measures of nationalisation and State control over private investment, production, distribution and pricing introduced in his time were further extended by his successors as means for extracting donations from industrialists in return for conferring patronage. Both at the Centre and in the States, chairmanship of public sector enterprises became substitutes for the emoluments, perquisites and power of patronage carried by ministership. With a staggering debt, domestic and foreign, accumulated over the decades as the price for statism, populism and corruption, the Congress under Narasimha Rao's leadership went over to the other extreme of the World Bank-IMF model.

It is useful to recall the self-critical remarks on economic policy which Jawaharlal made in the closing months of his life.

In modification of his earlier views on Khadi, Nehru in the course of an address on the social aspects of development in September 1963 referred to the spinning wheel, revived and popularized by Gandhiji, as being important both in itself and as a symbol. Rebutting the notion that the Mahatma was against all machinery, Nehru said: "Gandhiji did not want machinery except in the context of the well-being of the mass of our people. What he suggested—cottage industry—was something which immediately benefited the people, not only in regard to employment but also in production."

Nehru voiced his disillusionment with the model of development based on heavy industries while addressing the National Development Council on 8th November 1963. He said: "One of our States which in comparison to others is more prosperous is Punjab where there is hardly any big industrial plant, but there are plenty of small industries. Some states which are full of big plants are low down in the scale of per capita income." He was referring to Bihar, where "the average farmer lived as he did a thousand years ago."

Finally, in the course of his reply to a debate on planning, in the Lok Sabha on 11th December 1963, Nehru said: "One thing that distresses me very greatly is that there are a good number of people in India who have not profited by planning, and whose poverty is abysmal and most painful. I begin to think more and more of Mahatma Gandhi's approach."

One finds here an echo of the memorable 'talisman' commended by Gandhiji on the eve of independence in August 1947: "Recall the face of the poorest and the weakest man whom you may have seen, and ask yourself if the step you contemplate is going to be of any use to him."

While India's first Prime Minister moved away from Marx towards Gandhi, Nehru's successors have moved away from both Marx and Gandhi, towards the World Bank with its gospel of the global pursuit of maximum profit by the financially powerful. Over the three decades since Nehru's death, the pattern of India's development became increasingly elitist. It serves the upper crust of society, and is symbolised by the Maruti car and by the commercial advertising on government-run Doordarshan which spreads the hedonistic culture of consumerism.

An echo of Gandhiji's 'talisman' can be heard in the series of lectures on 'Integral Humanism' delivered by Deen Dayal Upadhyaya, president of the Bharatiya Jana Sangh, in April 1965. The distinction made by him between human wants that are basic, and needs that are stimulated; his warning against heedless industrialism for its own sake; and his emphasis on first priority for providing full employment are in consonance with Gandhiji's approach. Following are excerpts from Deen Dayal Upadhyaya's lectures:

"The economic system must achieve production of all the basic things essential for the maintenance and development of people, as well as the protection and development of the nation. Having satisfied the basic minimum requirements, the question arises whether there should be more production for greater happiness. The western societies consider it most essential to go on continuously and systematically increasing the desires and needs of man. People are induced to desire and use the things that have been and are being produced, instead of producing to meet the demand.

"The present economic system and system of production are fast disturbing the equilibrium of nature. It is essential to use only that portion of the available natural resources which nature will be able to recoup easily. In the effort to take a greater harvest from the land, chemical fertilisers are used which in a few years render the land altogether infertile. How long can this dance of destruction go on?

"To import machinery from western countries, where shortage of manpower was the guiding factor in the design of machines, will be a serious mistake. Full employment must be a primary consideration."

The question needs to be considered whether there is a contradiction between the Gandhian economic approach and the 'protection of the nation', i.e., defence, which Deen Dayal Upadhyaya referred to as a basic requirement. In contrast to the insistence on Brahmacharya—with which the Mahatma remained obsessed till the end—Gandhiji was flexible in his views on Ahimsa and on the use of machinery. Amritananda Das in his *Foundations of Gandhian Economics* (Allied, 1979) argues for decentralised and small-scale production of "people's defence" equipment alongside limited import of high-technology weaponry for interdiction of aggressors. The author cites in support Gandhiji's praise of Switzerland's 'grand example' in preserving the country's neutrality during the First World War: "They have trusted to the heroism of their own armed people." Again, during the Second World War, Gandhiji wrote in *Harijan* of 3rd August 1941: "If a nation is unprepared for such sacrifices (i.e. to perish in totally non-violent non-cooperation) it can still adequately defend itself by determined armed popular resistance."

The influence of Gandhian economics can be seen also in the BJP's 1996 manifesto. It promises to "implement Antyodaya schemes throughout the country, because we hold that sustainable employment is at the core of poverty eradication. These Antyodaya schemes will be targeted at the poorest of the poor. Five crore families will be selected for immediate relief.

"In outlining our strategy, we recognise that the post-Cold War world has adopted the market place for fast economic growth. However, the market may ensure growth but it cannot ensure redistributive equity and justice. The State continues to have a role to play. The poor and deprived have to be helped by the State to attain a sustainable minimum quality of life.

"A society such as ours has to innovate its own strategy, to adapt itself to the high-tech challenges of a supposedly borderless world, without the abandonment either of its identity or of its own socio-cultural ethos. This is the essence of our Swadeshi approach: a self-reliant India, asserting its national economic interests, not as autarchy, but as a pre-requisite to meeting the challenge of globalisation; of preserving our identity; and not compromising our sovereignty or self-respect. We reject unbridled consumerism and believe in adherence to sustainable consumption and growth."

The BJP's economic philosophy was summed up succinctly by Atal Bihari Vajpayee in the course of an address at a gathering of industrialists on 17th April 1996: "The policies a BJP Government will follow will dismantle further the licence-quota-permit raj without ushering in a licentious regime. Our policies will free business and professions from State control, without bringing in anarchy.

"The BJP's policy of Swadeshi has often been misrepresented by its political opponents with the intention of painting us as anti-reforms and anti-free market. This is far from the truth. When we talk of Swadeshi we stress our abiding faith in the creative genius of every Indian and the ability of our entrepreneurs to compete with the best in the world. Our policy of Swadeshi makes it imperative for us to ensure the protection of local industry and enterprise, especially the small-scale sector. By Swadeshi we also mean that the benefits of liberalisation should not be limited to a few but reach the last man in the last row."

Here is an approach which is neither that of state capitalism nor unbridled free enterprise. It is close to the Gandhian approach. Recalling Nehru's late awakening to the virtue of the approach, Aruna Asaf Ali said in the course of her speech on the occasion of receiving the Jawaharlal Nehru Award for International Understanding in November 1992:

"In the early years of our independence India used to be looked upon by many countries emerging from colonial bondage as a model for self-reliant growth free of the evils both of early capitalism and of Stalinist collectivism. However, over the decades India's development has become lop-sided. Neglecting the basic needs of the many, we have been applying scarce resources, including foreign exchange, to providing more and more luxury goods and services to the well-to-do. Alongside a culture of consumerism which has contributed to corruption, there is a persistence of mass poverty and mass illiteracy. It is a pity that many countries of what is called the Third World have followed a similar pattern of development. I do feel that if we in India correct our course, we will not only extricate ourselves but set an example to other developing countries. It will help us to reorder our priorities if we hold fast to the guideline that Gandhiji gave us."

It may well be that, on receiving a stable mandate to govern, it becomes the privilege of a BJP government to demonstrate to the world that a third alternative to the Stalinist and the World Bank models is available, and that it is the best course for recently free countries seeking economic development with social justice.

Social Justice with Harmony

The third major feature of the BJP's alternative model is that it seeks the correction of social inequalities without fomenting social discord through caste war. The 20th century has seen that class war is neither necessary nor desirable, since trade unions flourish better in a democracy than in a totalitarian system even if it calls itself a dictatorship of the proletariat. Similarly, it has been possible for the women's movement in India to secure voting and property rights without resort to the violent methods of the suffragette movement in the West. If the inequities in class and gender relations can be resolved amicably in a democracy, so can caste inequalities.

The British rulers in their time deliberately fanned conflict between castes. It suited the colonial authorities to create discord between Brahmins and non-Brahmins on the one hand, and between the Depressed Classes (now known as the Scheduled Castes) and the rest of Hindu society on the other. Since Brahmins were to the fore in taking to modern English education, they were conspicuous by their preponderance in the modern professions during the pre-independence years. They also happened to be conspicuous in the leadership of the Indian National Congress. The British therefore encouraged the emergence of non-Brahmin political leaders as against the Congress, specially in the Madras and Bombay Presidencies. With the Congress following a negative policy of boycott of the councils (as legislatures were known in the early part of the century), non-Brahmin political parties entered the councils, formed ministries and framed rules for college admission and for recruitment to public services which would favour non-Brahmins.

The very first amendment of the post-independence Constitution, in 1951, was designed to protect the rules framed in Madras Province, in favour of non-Brahmins, from being struck down on the grounds of being violative of the Fundamental Rights to equality and to non-discrimination. It was felt by the Congress which was in power at the Centre and in most of the States that, with universal adult suffrage, the benefits given to the non-Brahmin castes (much larger in their population strength than the Brahmins) could not and should not be withdrawn. The reservations in their favour had served to secure non-Brahmins a better social status, even if at the cost of a certain decline in standards in the public services.

Over the decades, the non-Brahmin castes became powerful lobbies competing with each other for political power, with the competition sometimes resulting in inter-caste violence. The conflict has been promoted by the economically powerful in each caste, aspiring for political power. They have not at all liked the Supreme Court's ruling that the creamy layer in each caste classified as 'Other Backward Classes' should be excluded from the benefits of reservation. This ruling has remained largely unimplemented, with State governments prescribing extremely high levels of income in the definition of 'creamy layer'. There has been increasing conflict between the leaders of different caste groups, both *inter se* and with the Scheduled Castes who are often the victims of social and economic oppression by some of the OBCs.

As against encouragement of caste alliances and of caste conflict by most other parties, the BJP seeks social justice along with social harmony. Its manifesto says:

"The BJP believes in one nation, one people, one culture. We are, therefore, committed to promoting social reconciliation rather than conflict. We are resolved to put an end to the politics of competitive communalism, of appeasement, and of casteism. The politics of pitting caste against caste, community against community and class against class has torn asunder our social fabric. The BJP will reweave this fabric into a harmonious pattern."

"The BJP is committed to providing both social and economic justice to the socially and educationally backward classes (Other Backward Classes) through the instrument of reservations. At the same time, we hold that the path to progress of all sections of our people lies not through social divisions brought about by casteist politics but through social harmony. The BJP advocates:

1. Continuation of reservations for the Other Backward Classes till they are socially and educationally integrated with the rest of society;
2. A uniform criteria for demarcating the 'creamy layer';
3. Flow of reservation benefits in an ascending order so that the most backward sections of the OBCs get them first;
4. Ten per cent reservation on the basis of economic criteria to all economically weaker sections of society, apart from the Scheduled Castes/Scheduled Tribes and the Other Backward Classes; and,

5. Special programmes to provide education and vocational training as well as awareness campaigns."

It testifies to the active work done by RSS and BJP volunteers among the tribal groups and Harijans, through such organisations as the Vanavasi Kalyan Ashram and Seva Bharati, that the number of members of these categories elected to the eleventh Lok Sabha on the BJP ticket is as much as 30.

Also noteworthy is that the number of women members on the BJP benches is 14 out of the total of 38 women members. Sixteen were elected on the Congress ticket, and eight were sponsored by other political parties. The quality of women's representation being more important than its quantity, the Congress tally is of questionable significance. A Congress woman MP, Dr. Najma Heptullah who has been Deputy Chairman of the Rajya Sabha, joined male chauvinists of the Muslim community when she said in connection with the Shah Bano Case: "Islam was not made by Parliament or the Supreme Court. They have no right to interfere." Sheila Kaul of the Congress is among the former Cabinet colleagues of P.V. Narasimha Rao who are facing charges of making money through corrupt means.

CHAPTER 11

The 1996 Watershed

As a hung Lok Sabha, with no political party commanding an absolute majority, the eleventh Lok Sabha that was constituted following the May 1996 elections was not unique. It was the third hung House in a row.

What has made 1996 a watershed is that no political observer gives the Congress any chance of recovering its position as the largest single party in the Lok Sabha, let alone winning an absolute majority. The Congress share of the popular vote, despite its fielding the largest number of candidates, has been going down steadily: from 39.53% in 1989 to 37.57% in 1991 and now to 28.2%. And dissensions within the Congress are acute.

In the ninth Lok Sabha, elected in 1989, the Congress had only 194 members in a House of 524. (This number was better than in 1977, when the Congress won only 154 seats and for the first time sat in the opposition.) But whereas the Janata Party secured an absolute majority and formed the government in 1977, in 1989 there was no party in a position to form the government on the basis of its own strength. The Janata Dal was second in seat strength with 27.1% of the seats as against 37.02% of the Congress. It was able to form a government with V.P. Singh as Prime Minister because it was backed from outside by the BJP with 16.4% of the seats and the Communist Party (Marxist) with 6.1% of seats, plus some minor parties.

The BJP withdrew its support when V.P. Singh, without consulting the friendly parties, suddenly resurrected the ten-year-old report of the Mandal Commission on Backward Classes and touched off a caste war. He did this in order to stave off a threat to his chair from the then Deputy Prime Minister, Devi Lal. After V.P. Singh, Chandra Shekhar heading a small party became Prime Minister on the basis of Congress support from outside, which did not last long. Mid-term elections had, therefore, to be held in 1991. This time, too, the Congress failed to secure an absolute majority: only 226 seats in a House of 538. But P.V. Narasimha Rao formed a government and secured the necessary backing through questionable means. He managed to last a full term of five years, though as the head of a government with the largest number of members—including himself—facing credible charges of corruption.

For the second time in the history of free India, the Congress failed in 1996 to emerge even as the largest single party. It secured only 136 seats in a House (as of May) of 534. The BJP emerged as the largest single party, with 161 seats. However, even after adding the seats won by its allies during the elections, it had no majority. When the President, adopting the constitutionally correct course, invited the BJP as the largest party to try and form a government and to prove its majority on the floor of the Lok Sabha by the end of May, Atal Bihari Vajpayee accepted the invitation in the hope that some of the other political parties not already BJP's allies might extend their support. But he and his party did not resort to the offer of bribes, whether in cash or in kind through ministerships.

Instead, the BJP formulated a minimum programme—leaving out some items put forward in its election manifesto—on the basis of which other political parties could, if they were willing, offer principled support to the BJP government. The minimum programme set out in a broadcast to the nation on 19th May 1996, left out of the immediate agenda certain contentious items: enactment of a uniform civil code; abrogation of Article 370 of the Constitution pertaining to Jammu & Kashmir; and the construction of a temple at Ayodhya. As significant as these omissions was the reaffirmation by Atal Bihari Vajpayee of the BJP's commitment not to misuse Article 356 for dismissal of duly elected State governments. The text of the broadcast is reproduced below.

Prime Minister Vajpayee's Broadcast

I am grateful to you for giving me this opportunity to address the nation as Prime Minister.

Rashtrapatiji invited me to form the Government since the Bharatiya Janata Party, and its allies, won the largest number of seats. This decision of Rashtrapatiji is entirely in tune with established democratic norms, in fact it strengthens them. I have accepted this responsibility in all humility. That, I believe, is the will of the people; the essence of the electoral mandate of 1996. I am dismayed, and I am sure that most of you share this sentiment, that this decision has been unfairly criticised by some groups. Those that have undergone many splits, have come together only to fragment, who have formed conflicting combinations but failed to win more seats than the BJP, are now prepared to join hands, without any hesitation, even with those whom they opposed in the polls with great vigour. This can only be termed as politics without any principles, motivated by the sole aim of coming to power by any means.

During the last week we have not heard them say even a word about that they would do for you or for the country. They seem to have a single-point agenda: Stop the Bharatiya Janata Party at any cost. To achieve this, a determined campaign has been launched to paint us in adverse colours. This has only one purpose: to defeat the mandate given by the people.

Instead of entering into a debate on 'communalism', or the true meaning of secularism, a determined effort is being made to obscure issues, to avoid on honest and meaningful debate.

India is an ancient civilisation. It has always had different sects and religious practices. We do not limit ourselves to one God or one Prophet or a single book. We are a multi-religious country, and we believe in the equality of all religious faiths. It is because of this that we have never had any tension, leave alone a violent struggle, on the correct path to achieve a realisation of God. "Sarva panth samabhav", or equal respect to all faiths, is part of our civilisational consciousness. Secularism thus is integrated into our lives. India never was, and never will be, a theocratic State. My Government is committed to creating an environment of social harmony and peace.

What happened in Ayodhya on 6th December 1992 was not the result of any pre-planned conspiracy. If problems related with religion are not resolved for long periods of time, then the result is what happened at Ayodhya. Every society has two methods of solving Ayodhya—like disputes—by discussions and dialogues or through legislation. In the case of Ayodhya, neither of these two approaches was pursued seriously. The dispute was before the Courts for decades and remains there.

It is hardly necessary to recall that immediately after the advent of Islam in West Asia, the first mosque was built in Kerala, then ruled by a Hindu Raja. In like manner, soon after the crucifixion of Jesus Christ, the first church was established in India. These manifestations of different faiths are living symbols of our secular traditions. We will maintain these traditions.

Eleven successive General Elections, and scores of them to State Assemblies have clearly demonstrated that we are a mature democracy, an enlightened nation. It is necessary that we do not allow irrelevant issues to cloud our national vision and to shroud the real issues.

What are they? Before the electorate was the question of development, of elimination of corruption, transparency and accountability in all spheres of government—in short, good governance. They remain entirely relevant today.

The primary challenge before us is the upliftment of the poor. Despite possessing adequate natural resources, the majority of our countrymen remain poor. They are deprived of opportunity and avenues of growth. I know their condition, I have lived it.

Immediately after the 1996-97 Budget, my Government is committed to announcing, and implementing, a revolutionary 10-year plan focussed on providing nutrition for the children of the poor, their health care, and facilities for education, so that they are brought at the same level as other children. In the first year itself we will mobilise adequate resources for this. Along with rationalisation and simplification of the tax structure, and our revenue regime, we will take steps for their strictest compliance. My Government will ensure that funds allocated for the upliftment of the poor actually reach them, so that we are able to achieve our goal of economic and social equality within the next decade.

You are, of course, aware that there are certain prerequisites for achieving such major plans. These are: political will, honest administration and determination to spend money for the purposes for which it is allocated. As a first concrete step towards bringing about honesty in the administration, from top to bottom, my Government will make public the income and assets of all members of my Cabinet within 30 days from today.

We will not hesitate to take the sternest measures to see that corruption is eradicated from public life, that there is no misuse of funds allocated for development schemes, that they are utilised with care and diligence.

Creation of productive and sustainable employment, especially in the rural areas, is the most important facet of poverty eradication. My Government pledges to allocate 60% of Plan funds for agriculture and rural development. Towards that end, we will soon begin the process of identifying five crore poorest of the poor families for immediate relief. In addition to this, we will protect the needy sections of society, especially in the tribal areas, by better targeting of the Public Distribution System and ensuring price stability.

My Government will give primacy to enacting, in cooperation with other political parties, legislation to secure 33% reservation for women in State Assemblies and in the Lok Sabha.

My Government will not misuse Article 356 of the Constitution to achieve political ends. Immediate steps will be taken to restore the balance of resources in favour of the States. Steps will also be taken, very speedily, to convene and activate the Inter-State Council, to settle inter-State and Centre-State disputes.

My Government will very quickly assess deficiencies in the physical infrastructure, especially those that are hampering the growth of the economy and of exports. Towards this end, we will form a committee of economic Ministers under the Chairmanship of the Prime Minister to implement several stalled projects in a time-bound manner. All such projects will be cleared speedily for implementation.

The new Government is committed to quick enactment of comprehensive electoral reforms, keeping in mind the Goswami Committee Report as well as the recent judgment of the Supreme Court.

This Government will pro-actively pursue a foreign policy based on peace, equality and cooperation. Our immediate goal is to improve our relations with all our neighbours including Pakistan.

My Government will not relent in its efforts to establish peace in the State of Jammu and Kashmir. Elections will be held on schedule. The territorial integrity of our country will be preserved and protected at all costs. I salute the dedication, sense of duty and the valour of our Jawans and officers of our Armed Forces. Our soldiers, sailors, airmen, our scientific community that helps in our national endeavour, are the true sentinels of India. I am committed to upholding their honour, dignity and welfare.

My Government will very quickly introduce administrative reforms, to simplify procedures so that in those Departments which interact frequently with the public, there is no scope for arbitrariness and discretion.

We have already begun identifying areas where simplification of rules and regulations will deliver just and prompt responses to the common people. Directions will be issued to the Civil Services, all along its chain, to dispose off, at the earliest, matters relating to the day-to-day problems of the people. The power to say 'No' to simple routine requirements of life will be reduced drastically. Scope for arbitrary conditionalities will be minimised.

Many of the new things I have said tonight may not carry conviction because previous Governments have had a dismal record in this regard. Some of them may even appear to be dreams, in the light of the past record of unkept promises. Despite that, I pledge that we will carry out the assurances that we give today. Hasn't somebody said: if you don't dream, how will dreams come true?

In one of my poems, I have prayed:

Mere Prabhu!
Mujhe itni unchai kabhi mat dena
Gairon ko gale na laga sakun
itni rukhai
kabhi mat dena.

(Freely translated, the lines will read in English:

My Lord,
Elevate me not so high
That I cannot fraternise with others;
May I be spared
Such a barrier.)

That prayer is now a pledge. I conclude by leaving this pledge and this dream with you.

Jai Hind!

Typical of the general public reaction to Atal Bihari Vajpayee's broadcast to the nation as Prime Minister was the following editorial comment in the *Indian Express*:

"If the yardstick of success in politics is measured purely in terms of survival, it is possible that the BJP-led government of Atal Bihari Vajpayee may yet be found wanting on the day the Lok Sabha votes on the motion of confidence. However, if popular endorsement is a consideration, the new Prime Minister appears to have surged ahead of his two challengers, H.D. Deve Gowda and P.V. Narasimha Rao. Vajpayee's broadcast to the nation on Sunday evening did not break new ground in terms of policy prescriptions, but it did establish the BJP leader's reputation as a sober, responsible politician capable of shouldering the responsibilities of the highest political office. Always a cut above the rest for oratorical skill, Vajpayee distinguished himself this time by puncturing his opponents' claim that both he and his party are extremists whose continuation in office will endanger social harmony. His forthright contention that theocracy is alien to the Indian inheritance is not new, but it acquired more meaning because it was said in his capacity as Prime Minister. The spirited attempts by the Third Front and the Congress to cobble together an anti-BJP majority will not run aground after Vajpayee's address, but it will now be seen for what it actually is: an ideological cover for humdrum power politics. To that extent, Vajpayee appears to have successfully diluted BJP's untouchability among the people, even if he has not been able to translate that mood for the political classes.

From the viewpoint of the BJP, this constitutes a spectacular advance. The great healing touch advocated by Vajpayee is little different from V.P. Singh's prescription for the Third Front-Congress understanding. Where Vajpayee scores is on two points. First, his insistence that the single largest party in a fractured Lok Sabha has a legitimate claim on the governance of the country. Second, his simultaneous admission that the BJP does not have the requisite mandate to press for the more contentious features of its election manifesto. In spelling out a liberal, conciliatory and federalist agenda, the Prime Minister has made it that much more difficult for the anti-BJP forces to claim the moral high ground. Using his agreeable image to full advantage, he has shown that whereas he has a vision, they have a target. Even if he loses the battle, he may end up winning the war."

Like Prime Minister Vajpayee's broadcast to the nation, President Shanker Dayal Sharma's address to Parliament on 24th May 1996 set out a non-contentious programme on which there could be a consensus for cooperation among many political parties. Following is the text of the President's address:

President's Address to Parliament

"It gives me great pleasure to address both Houses of Parliament at this first session after the eleventh general election to the Lok Sabha. I extend my warm felicitations to the Members of the new Lok Sabha.

The general election, just concluded, has demonstrated the democratic credentials of the country. The nation and the world have witnessed the majesty of the democratic process in India. The recent general election was organized with efficiency and despatch. Our people participated in large numbers and exercised their sovereign right in electing their representatives. Once again, India has demonstrated the strong, vibrant and enduring nature of her democratic ethos. Government will fully honour the mandate implicit in the result of the election. The present session of Parliament should enable the House of the People to determine whether it has confidence in the Council of Ministers.

The country stands at the crossroads of history. As the century comes to a close and the millennium turns, our destiny as a strong and a powerful nation beckons us. The Government is conscious of our common responsibility to fulfil these historic tasks. Our endeavour should be to strive for a wholesome consensus on all vital national issues.

Among our primary tasks is that of ensuring to the State its due honour, prestige and strength. The basic institutions devised by the founding fathers with a view to providing good governance have to be strengthened. This may necessitate appropriate reforms in our polity and governance.

Providing clean and efficient administration is the need of the hour and the Government must commit itself to this goal. Probity and accountability have to be the key norms of public administration. Due propriety, promptitude and effectiveness should characterize every measure: administrative, legislative and political.

The deficiencies in our electoral processes are to be attended to. The matter has been pending for long and we can ill-afford any further delay. A large number of suggestions have been made from time to time. On the basis of the wealth of material available and otherwise, necessary reforms will be taken up urgently. The prime objectives would be that the use of money power in the electoral process is eliminated, accountability of political parties is ensured and unfair practices are removed.

An in-depth review of our decision making processes is another field which requires immediate attention. The primary task is to reduce as much as possible the scope of arbitrary decision making by ensuring that our processes are made simpler and more transparent. For a meaningful implementation of such a programme, we will have to provide expeditious means for speedy disposal of public grievances.

Government is committed to uphold the prestige and independence of the judiciary. A comprehensive examination of the work methods and environment, emoluments and conditions of service of the subordinate judiciary is being undertaken by the First National Judicial Pay Commission. Government will facilitate its work with a view to ensuring speedy submission of its report.

Every effort will be made to reduce the arrears in the Courts through the spread of modern management techniques and expeditious filling of the vacancies of judges.

Government is conscious of the need to improve the welfare of Central Government employees. The Fifth Pay Commission is currently looking into their emoluments, structure and service conditions. Since the final report of the Commission is likely to take some time, Government have requested them for their interim recommendations as early as possible, on the basis of which appropriate relief would be given.

The Government has a deep and abiding commitment to the freedom of the press and media. The electronic media are acquiring increased importance in our daily lives as a result of their pervasive presence and Government are determined to free All India Radio and Doordarshan from governmental control by finally implementing the Prasar Bharati Act, 1990. In 1995, the Supreme Court had even directed the Government to set up an independent authority to regulate the airwaves. The Government would take all necessary steps to establish a truly autonomous Prasar Bharati Corporation which would strengthen national identity, integration, credibility in dissemination of information and provision of quality education and entertainment.

The vastness of our country, its diversity and the underlying unity are our basic strengths. India is one people, one nation with her unique culture. Government will do all that it may to ensure that harmonious relations are maintained between different communities and groups. Government is committed to provide security and protect the life and property of all people, particularly the weaker sections and minorities. Violence manifesting itself in separatist, extremist, criminal and anti-social activities has no place in any civilized society and would be effectively dealt with by the Government. In doing so the Government cannot forget that political, social and economic measures are equally necessary in resolving these problems.

The North Eastern region of our country continues to suffer from violence, insurgency and ethnic strife. There is need to check the inflow of foreign arms and terrorists from across the border by strengthening the security apparatus and the intelligence network. Illegal immigration which has an unsettling effect will be curbed through comprehensive measures. Effective administration for acceleration of economic development and providing for a prompt grievance redressal system, are also urgent requirements.

Jammu & Kashmir is an inalienable part of India. No attempt to interfere with our internal affairs there will be tolerated. We are keen to restore the democratic functioning of the State for which all efforts are being made to ensure free and fair polls in the State. Side by side, efforts for socio-economic development of the different regions will be intensified.

Government is anxious to improve Centre-State relations. The report of the Sarkaria Commission and other extensive studies provide ample material on the various facets of this problem. Government will ensure that there is increased consultation with the State Governments and that there is no misuse of Article 356. The role and status of the Inter State Council envisaged under Article 263 of the Constitution will be reviewed in depth and action taken to make it an effective mechanism to resolve disputes between States and for better coordination of policies and action in matters of common interest to States.

In order to fulfil the aspirations of the people of Uttaranchal and Vananchal, the Government will take such steps as are necessary to give them full statehood. The various problems connected with the grant of full statehood to Delhi will also receive our serious consideration.

Our vision of India's economy is one which enables India to achieve its destiny in the forefront of the nations of the world. We have an abiding faith in the creative genius of every Indian. Our task is to release their energies by shedding out-dated structures of controls and regulations and re-equipping Government for its new role of providing a supportive framework for free market operations for growth, while strengthening programmes for poverty eradication and building of social infrastructure.

The economic reforms of the past five years did achieve some measure of success. Government will invigorate the growth impulses in the economy and control inflation by accelerating the process of economic reforms, providing much greater support and impetus to infrastructure development, and maintaining a sound framework of fiscal and monetary policies.

Today, high interest rates and scarce credit are inhibiting the growth of industry, trade and agriculture. The root cause of the problem is the continued recourse to high levels of borrowings by Government, to meet its ever-expanding expenditures. Government will prune non-development expenditure and accelerate tax reform to reduce the fiscal deficit and thus release resources for more productive activities. Government will identify areas from which it needs to withdraw. In taxation, we will ensure that not only levels and rates of taxation are such that growth is not constrained, but that the burden-sharing is equitably distributed among all affluent sections of the society. Government will also devise a suitably structured value added tax.

To deal with the massive overhang of past public debt and to ensure a higher return to assets in public enterprises, the Government will constitute a Disinvestment Commission to accelerate the process of disinvestment in a systematic and transparent manner. Part of the proceeds will be earmarked for retiring public debt and the balance to finance capital expenditure. While disinvesting, care will be taken so that the workers' interests are not harmed. The National Renewal Fund will be realigned towards retraining and redevelopment of workers that may be necessary in a fast growing economy.

Public savings will increase and private savings will be stimulated to finance the much higher levels of national investment necessary to accelerate economic growth and eradicate poverty. Foreign savings and investment will be welcomed to supplement the national savings effort. A country of India's size and potential can easily double the flow of direct foreign investment, especially in the critical infrastructure areas of power, roads, ports and telecommunications.

The Government will draw up an integrated time bound programme to increase capacities and release bottlenecks posed by insufficient infrastructure in energy, especially power, coal and petroleum, roads, ports, railways, irrigation and telecommunications. The policy framework for inducting private, including foreign, investment will be revamped and made transparent.

Government is committed to bring about long pending reform of the corporate laws which will ensure their functioning as instruments of economic growth, rather than merely regulatory mechanisms. The laws must promote entrepreneurship and freedom of industry from all avoidable inhibitions and disincentives. Necessary legislative action in this direction will be speedily undertaken.

The Government fully recognizes the importance of the small scale sector for production and employment in the economy. The difficulties faced by this sector will be carefully reviewed and the obstacles to rapid progress will be eliminated.

The construction industry is one of our largest sectors, providing jobs to millions. A major constraint to growth of this sector has been the Urban Land Ceiling Act. Government will review the rationale of this Act.

All this will be necessary to restore the competitive edge of our producers, large and small, so that they can effectively win the challenges of the international market place. Our export growth has to be stepped up to meet the import needs of a more dynamic economy. For the short and medium term viability of our balance of payments, Government will ensure policies for rapid and sustained export growth and for attracting adequate inflows of non-debt creating capital. Government will review and simplify the regime of foreign exchange controls in line with the needs of a modernizing economy.

To strengthen our financial and capital markets, Government will provide for greater accountability and competition for public financial institutions, including banks. To promote healthy development and avoid scams and irregularities, the Government will undertake a programme to modernize the infrastructure of capital markets, including swift passage of enabling legislation for depositories.

Three quarters of our citizens live in rural India, and agriculture is the life-blood of rural society. Rapid broad-based development of agriculture is vital for ameliorating rural poverty, ensuring self-sufficiency in food, strengthening the domestic market for industry and services and building mutually beneficial links between agriculture and industry. The Government will allocate more funds for rural infrastructure, ensure remunerative prices to farmers, free agro-based industries such as sugar from licensing controls and strengthen and Public Distribution System in rural areas. Optimal utilisation of scarce water resources is critical for agricultural development. Government will give special priority to completing ongoing irrigation projects.

Water is our most precious resource and its conservation and effective utilisation is of paramount importance. The Government attaches high priority for watershed-based development of drought prone areas and waste land reclamation through adequate technical support and people's involvement.

In order to ensure cow protection, and to impose a total ban on the slaughter of cows and cow progeny, Government will take up suitable measures.

The Government will pursue policies aimed at the real empowerment of women, so as to ensure that their dignity and rights are not violated and their full potential is realized. The Government will take necessary legislative and other steps to provide for reservation of 33% of the seats for women in all elected bodies, including State Assemblies and Parliament.

The disabled and all those who are placed in a position of undeserved want for reasons beyond their control, are the primary responsibility of the State. Simultaneously trade and industry will be sensitized as to their social obligation in this respect. Our senior citizens also deserve special care. Government will consider their problems and take measures which would make their lives easier in their old age.

The Government is painfully aware of the extensive levels of poverty in the country. The needs of the poorest sections in the country require the most urgent, sympathetic attention. We shall strengthen the programmes which contribute substantially to their social and economic upliftment. These would provide them with gainful employment and income generating assets. In doing so our endeavour would be to ensure that the present disparities in socio-economic conditions are eliminated. Special attention would therefore be given to the Scheduled Castes, Scheduled Tribes, the Backward Classes, the other deprived sections of the society and to the problems of bonded and child labour. Programmes for poverty alleviation and other welfare measures for weaker sections of our society need to be accurately focussed on those who really need support from the Government. Government will soon begin the process of identifying the five crore poorest of the poor families for immediate relief. The role of the State Governments in implementing these programmes is crucial and it would be our effort to give necessary flexibility to them and enlist their active support in the task of promoting greater economic and social justice.

Growth cannot be measured in economic terms alone. The problems of poverty, disease and hunger require a multi-dimensional approach. In fact, no improvement in the quality of life, which is the real index of growth, is possible without social inputs like education, health and other welfare measures. Government would initiate a pioneering ten-year plan focussed upon providing nutrition for the children of the poor, their health care and facilities for education so that they are brought at the same level as other children. Adequate resources for this plan would be made available.

The Government attaches high priority to education as an instrument for the material, physical and spiritual development and enrichment of society and the individual. We witness today the old economic order based on comparative advantage of labour and resources giving way to a new order being built on the foundations of human resource, skills and technology. The changing economic scenario and rising social aspirations require significant modifications in our educational programmes. We have not yet been able to provide free elementary education to our children as enjoined by our Constitution. This requires urgent rectification. Government will encourage vocational and technical education. Government recognizes the need for special efforts for the spread of education amongst women. Programmes in vocational and technical education to enable them to be eligible for suitable employment opportunities would be given emphasis. Higher education would be revamped so as to facilitate India emerging as a major economic power in the international arena. In this sphere, the existing centres of excellence require urgent attention to be strengthened. Such centres in new areas are also called for.

We believe in increasing state investment in health and nutrition programmes as this is essential for raising the quality of life of our people. Our goal will be health for all. Reduction of the infant mortality rate, immunisation of children against killer diseases, improvement of the primary health care systems will be the corner stones of these programmes. In this we will make full use of Ayurveda, Unani, Homoeopathy and other Indian systems of medicine.

The Government will give due priority to population related issues, especially family planning, in the national agenda. The long-term objective is to stabilize population by the first decade of the next century. The Government will devise a system of incentives and disincentives for encouraging adoption of family planning norms.

It is unfortunate that even safe drinking water is still scarce or unavailable to a large number of our habitations. There are 1.6 lakh habitations with no drinking water facilities and 1.4 lakh habitations where such water is badly contaminated. The Government is committed to providing drinking water facilities to all our people in a time-bound manner. We shall consult the State Governments and extend necessary support to them in achieving this goal. In areas where drinking water is chemically contaminated, available technologies would be harnessed for making it safe and potable. The Government considers community participation in this programme necessary and would take action to encourage this.

The Government recognizes the important role that science and technology has in transforming society. Steps would be taken to harness the latest advances in the service of the people. Special attention will be paid to the needs of the rural areas. Measures will be taken to see that national interests and intellectual property rights are adequately protected. Government will continue to support the country's space programme which has demonstrated its high potential and utility for the overall development of the country.

Our foreign policy is governed by our national interests and reflects India's position as a major player in the world arena, responding to the possibilities and challenges of the post-Cold

War situation and rejecting all forms of hegemonism or dominance. In this process, our political, economic, security and other concerns, will be pursued in a clear and unambiguous manner.

The Government's foremost priority in the area of foreign policy will be the improvement of relations with all our neighbours in South Asia including Pakistan, bilaterally and in the SAARC forum. We will foster mutually beneficial partnership with all countries. We will strengthen our broad-based ties with Russia. We look forward to the further strengthening and diversification of our relations with the USA. We will utilize the opportunities offered in India-China relations to enhance friendship and cooperation. In keeping with our commitment to Asian solidarity, we look forward to reinforcing our friendly relations with the ASEAN member states.

India's role in the multilateral field has always been constructive. Our policy on issues such as a Comprehensive Test Ban Treaty and a Fissile Material Cut-Off Treaty will be governed by our traditional commitment to a nuclear weapons-free world. While our commitment to the peaceful uses of nuclear energy is well known, where necessary in the light of our national interests, our nuclear policy will be re-evaluated.

The situation in some parts of India's immediate neighbourhood continues to be uncertain in security terms. It is regrettable that Pakistan continues to instigate terrorism against India. We call upon Pakistan to respond constructively to our repeated offers to resolve all outstanding issues bilaterally.

There will be no compromise on our country's vital security concerns. The programme of indigenous development of our defence capability in terms of research and acquisitions will continue and be reinforced in the light of our security needs. We will stress a coordinated approach to national security by revitalising the structure and enhancing the status of the National Security Council.

We repose full confidence in the capability of the Indian armed forces to defend the nation and will do whatever is necessary to maintain and enhance this capability. I am sure honourable Members join me in commending the armed forces for their professionalism and dedication. Recognizing their invaluable contribution,

Government is committed to taking all possible steps to promote their welfare. We cannot forget the large community of our ex-Servicemen. They have rendered valuable service to the nation and deserve our special consideration. The Government will establish a Sainik Kalyan Foundation with a suitable endowment to take care of their rehabilitation and welfare.

The country is faced with a number of crucial challenges as we stand on the threshold of the next century. The eleventh Lok Sabha will have the honour of contributing to the task of piloting the country to the next century.

My good wishes are with you in this historic task.

Jai Hind!

Comments on Anti-BJP Front

There was no positive response to Atal Bihari Vajpayee's conciliatory offer of a non-contentious programme. On the contrary, more than a dozen parties, large and miniscule, which had fought the elections against each other, ganged up against the BJP. This drew caustic comments from many newspapers. Three English-language dailies of the capital—none of them attached to any political party and often sharply critical of the BJP—were forthright in condemning as unprincipled the 'United Front', earlier known as the Third Front, of disparate political groups.

In a signed front-page editorial in *The Hindustan Times* of 13th May 1996, V.N. Narayanan wrote under the caption 'Respect the Voter':

"If the anti-untouchability law is still in force in this country, leaders of an assortment of political parties which want to be part of the government in Delhi should be chargesheeted under it. For the past few days we have been incessantly told that the Bharatiya Janata Party should be kept out of power and any stratagem can be employed and any unprincipled alliance can be forged to achieve this purpose. As a political objective, there is nothing objectionable about this. But the manner in which it is sought to be achieved smacks of the very fundamentalism in thinking that these politicians and parties are objecting to. True, the BJP has not received a mandate to rule from the people of India. But neither has the

Congress nor the NF-LF combine. The point is that a party which has been voted to power in many States and which has totted up millions of votes from the length and breadth of the country to emerge as the single largest party in the next Lok Sabha deserves its place in democracy.

"The parties clamouring to keep the BJP out need to show a modicum of respect for the electorate which has voted for it. It is not as if the nation went to the polls on a referendum to choose between communalism and secularism. In fact, in most of the States where the BJP was fighting the secularist parties and forces, the people seem to have given their support to it in greater measure than to the parties opposing it. To say all this is not to argue for a government by the BJP at the Centre. It is merely to point out that Indian democracy as well as its basic culture do not permit the treatment of a party as a political pariah. Even from the point of view of expediency it would be a folly of great magnitude to isolate the BJP. Instead of moderating its attitude this could have the opposite effect of pushing the BJP into the clutches of those very extremist elements which are seen as the ugly face of the BJP.

"The Congress party has contributed its own mite though it has not resorted to the pernicious course of being a partner in the so-called alternative seeking to form government at the Centre. It would have been a travesty of democracy and against all canons of political morality if the Congress had tried to be a part of the non-BJP government sought to be formed by NF-LF combine with the help of miscellaneous groups. The Indian voter may not have provided a clear mandate to rule for any party but there certainly was a mandate against the outgoing Congress government. In trying to exist on the support of this very party rejected by the people, the National and Left Fronts would be serving neither the cause of secularism nor of democracy. Perhaps politics does not permit serving the cause of democracy; it is all about capturing power by hook or crook—hook, if possible and crook, if necessary.

"The worst part of all this is that the parties are trying to subvert the constitutional options that the President has in arriving at his own conclusion on what is in the best national interest. If he does not have the discretion, he has the experience of the past to go by in deciding whether the experiments of the so-called support from outside of parties had succeeded in ensuring stability of minority governments. V.P. Singh (1990) and Chandra Shekhar (1991) and to a lesser extent the Charan Singh interregnum of 1979 are examples enough to warn the President as to how credible are the pledges of parties in the matter of supporting minority governments from outside."

Tavleen Singh, a columnist known for vitriolic attacks on 'the saffron brigade', said in her 'Fifth Column' published on 19th May 1996, under the caption 'Pot calls the kettle black':

"A funny thing has happened to me since the election results came out. I have discovered that I am communal. I made this startling discovery when I said to fellow hacks and some of my politician friends that I believed that the Bharatiya Janata Party had more right to form the government in Delhi than anyone else and that the spectacle of the Congress Party trying to do a deal with a caboodle of Marxists, regional parties and lower caste leaders was unprincipled and dishonest. 'What do you mean?' they gasped. 'How can you want a communal party like the BJP to rule India? Can't you see that it would be much better for even Narasimha Rao to become Prime Minister again than for this to happen?'

No, I cannot see it. And, to tell you the truth, I do not think that the BJP is any more communal than the Congress Party or, for that matter, more casteist than the likes of Messrs Laloo and Mulayam Yadav whose entire politics rests on caste. Let me make it clear that I do not like the BJP, and some of the scum it harbours like its various *sadhvis* and *swamis* makes my blood run cold but are they really more communal than H.K.L. Bhagat or Sajjan Kumar? Was it a BJP government that allowed the pogroms of 1984? Was it a BJP leader who justified the killings on the grounds that when 'a big tree falls, the earth shakes'?

"Let us also remember that it is the Congress Party, not the BJP, which has presided benignly over some of the worst Hindu-Muslim riots in Indian history. Meerut, Maliana, Bhagalpur, Bombay. It was also a Congress Prime Minister who sat like a wooden Buddha throughout the demolition of the Babri Masjid. So, it should not surprise us that the majority of Muslims in this country also do not see the Congress as the great secular alternative to the BJP.

"If you say this to 'secular' Congress leaders they tell you that we must not forget that it was a BJP-Shiv Sena government in Maharashtra who cancelled the inquiry into the Bombay riots. True, and it was an outrageous thing to do even if Justice Shrikrishna looked as if he would take till the next century to give us his report, but what difference did it really make when you consider the futility of other riot inquiries. Not one of them has amounted to anything more than an academic exercise. Not one of them has resulted in killers being punished or guilty administrations being brought to book. So, are Muslims and other minorities any worse off under BJP governments than under those led by our smug secularists?

"Perhaps, it is time that we looked again at both communalism and secularism. My understanding of the word secular is that it should prevent the state from associating itself with any particular religion and, as far as we know, we have never had a BJP government in any of our states which does not fit this description. On the other hand we have seen at least two Congress prime ministers who had unusually close relations with Chandraswamy and Dhirendra Brahmachari. Was it secular for these 'religious' gentlemen to have the kind of access to PM House that they did?

"Is it secular for the Indian Prime Minister to be constantly seen making obeisance in some temple or shrine? And, was it secular for a Congress government to involve itself in laying the foundation stone of a Ram temple in Ayodhya?

"Besides, it is now more than time that we looked beyond the secularism-communalism debate at more important things. We need a government in Delhi that can govern. A government that puts on its list of priorities such things as literacy, health care and development. We need a government that recognises the importance of cutting down the size of government and of doing something about the drain on our meagre resources that the public sector has become. We need a government that understands the importance of decentralising power to enable our states to develop. We do not need a government that bangs on endlessly about caste and communalism.

"We have seen in our cities that many of the evils of the caste system disappear with sanitation and municipal water. Similarly, all we really need is an economically prosperous and literate India for people to stop killing each other in the name of religion. More importantly, if killers in communal riots were treated as killers and punished we would see few rioters.

"The shameless jockeying for power that went on in Delhi last week had nothing at all to do with a serious concern about communalism. It had to do with the fears most of our other political parties have about seeing their bastions demolished by the BJP. It was a power struggle, pure and simple, so can we cut the garbage about who is communal and who is not."

The Times of India said in the course of an editorial on 21st May 1996, under the caption 'Opportunism knocks':

"Delhi has a way of grabbing attention, even when tranquillity reigns supreme in the Capital. This is hung Parliament time—time to raid the opposition, round up allies and muster a majority, the stuff of which mystery thrillers are made. It is no surprise, therefore, that keeping track of the numbers game being played out at the Centre has become something of a national pastime. In these past weeks, thousands of column inches of media space and an equal amount of television time have been devoted to the shenanigans of our major political parties at the Centre, while such matters as the escalating ethnic violence in Assam and the group clashes in Arunachal Pradesh have gone unnoticed. Politicians too are happily playing to the gallery, knowing that this is one occasion when every word they utter would be lapped up. For the range of parties forming the Third Front, the banishment of the BJP has become a mission in itself. If the Front's constituents have thrashed out a minimum common programme on policy, they have done a good job of keeping it a secret because the only minimum common programme that has come upfront is the one aimed against the BJP. And towards that end, they appear willing to adopt any means, even go with the Congress which they once condemned as being no different from the BJP and which they swore to oust from power. Given this backdrop, it was inevitable that Prime Minister Atal Bihari Vajpayee should have charged the combine with adopting double standards on the whole communal-secular debate."

The Indian Express of 22nd May 1996 said in an editorial

captioned 'United Farce':

"The only positive outcome of the "Save India from Communalism" day observed by the National Front, Left Front and some regional parties on Monday is that the leadership has finally realised that the people remain sceptical over their claim of providing the country with a purposeful and cohesive government. Unfortunately, the acquisition of a new, and more positive, brand name—United Front—has contributed little by way of reassurance. Ramakrishna Hegde's outburst in Bangalore against 'opportunistic' post-election alliances seems a foretaste of things to come. With the Congress still hedging its bets and rampant confusion over what are the underlying conditionalities of the 'unconditional' support of Deve Gowda, it is hardly surprising that India is looking to the future with some trepidation. The anxieties are partly on account of the fact that the United Front has been crafted on a negative plank—a shared antipathy to the BJP. This means that once the short-term goal of defeating the BJP-led coalition in the vote of confidence is achieved, the United Front will begin to resemble a united farce. It is not a question of ideological divergence—V.P. Singh has just asserted that beliefs are negotiable instruments in coalitions—but temperamental differences among the leading players and the unfulfilled ambitions of Prime Ministers-in-waiting that make the United Front very fragile from the outset. Perhaps a strong leader could have papered over the cracks, but Jyoti Basu has already indicated his desire to opt out of the mess. Nor is V. P. Singh willing to reconsider his extended holiday from politics.

"Equally worrying is the fact that neither the Congress nor the Left Front, the stable groupings in an otherwise ramshackle combine, are going to be part of the proposed Deve Gowda government. Considering that the Janata Dal itself is a loose coalition of regional shoguns, each one passionate in his dislike of the others, a Deve Gowda government will be lacking a solid core support. The very heterogeneity of the Treasury benches will make it a yo-yo government. If the Chandra Shekhar government was pulled down by the farcical incident of four Haryana policemen prying on Rajiv Gandhi, the United Front could collapse on account of a reckless minister jumping a traffic light!"

Shyam Khosla, in his column published on 26th May 1996, saw the country heading for another general election, from which the BJP was likely to emerge with a clear majority:

"The nation celebrates the installation of the first saffron Government headed by Atal Bihari Vajpayee. The spontaneous elation is not unmixed. There is a tinge of anxiety about the durability of the BJP Government. And for good reasons. The verdict though unambiguously against the Congress and the so-called NF-LF, is not decisively in favour of the BJP. The Communists, the sectarians and the regional satraps have ganged up with the decimated and defeated leaders of the Congress to usher in era of uncertainty in the country. The popular goodwill and unequivocal endorsement of the new regime by the common man is sought to be off-set by pseudo-secularists among the media and the elite. Whatever the outcome of the trial of strength in the Lok Sabha later this month, one thing is clear: the saffron brigade is leading in the battle for the hearts and minds of the voter.

"President Dr. S.D. Sharma acted strictly in accordance with the spirit of the Constitution and established conventions by inviting the leader of the single largest party to form the Government. The BJP was in two minds. One view in the party was that the ramshackle 'third force' should be allowed to form an unstable Government with the help of the Congress and wait for the collapse of this unprincipled alliance. The other view was that the mandate was for the BJP and it should not appear to be running away from its duty by declining to form the Government.

"The Communists and the sectarian parties struggled for three days but could not elect a leader. Their first choice was Jyoti Basu which nearly provoked a revolt in the Congress. CPM realised the folly of the leader of a party with less than three dozen members assuming the office of the Prime Minister. In the process it was sharply divided. Harkishen Singh Surjeet and Basu lost by four votes in the Central Committee of the party, forcing Basu to decline the offer.

"For a while, the 'third force' unsuccessfully chased the elusive V.P. Singh who was unacceptable to leaders of his own party. Ultimately, the choice fell on Deve Gowda. He was elected not by members of Parliament of the parties belonging to the 'third force' but by the ever-squabbling leaders of these parties. No meeting of MPs belonging to 'third force' has been held to date. This much for their commitment to democracy.

"Those who fault the President forget that the head of the State cannot ignore the circus the NF-LF was enacting to grab power. The alliance had won only 111 seats in the 545-member Lok Sabha. Regional satraps of the TDP, DMK, TMC and AGP as also the likes of Arjun Singh and Madhav Rao Scindia who have one or two MPs behind them could by no stretch of imagination be construed to be a cohesive bloc.

"The leaders of Janata Dal and Samajwadi Party are so scared of their MPs revolting against them and joining hands with the saffron brigade that they have quarantined them in new Bihar Bhavan and Andhra Bhavan. Same is true of newly elected MPs belonging to TDP led by Chandrababu Naidu. They are in no mood to be part of a Government sustained by Congress which is their political adversary in Andhra. These MPs are not allowed to talk to any one or move out of their Bhavans excepting in groups and with the permission of their leaders.

"Janata Dal leaders Ramvilas Paswan and Jaipal Reddy indulged in unwarranted and undignified criticism against the head of the State and virtually shouted at Dr. Sharma. Leaders of the 'third force' committed the unpardonable sin of staging a walk-out from the Rashtrapati Bhavan. Better sense prevailed later and Deve Gowda called on the President to express regrets. But the 'third force' has left no one in doubt that this ramshackle combination is not fit to rule the country.

Congress too is in turmoil. Rajesh Pilot and Karunakaran are all out for supporting the 'third force' to keep the BJP out. They make no secret of their determination to split the party if Narasimha Rao tried to remain neutral or made a bid to resume power after the possible collapse of the BJP Government.

"The BJP has not given up hope of winning over regional parties like the AGP and DMK. Talks are underway through mediators to convince regional parties that they have nothing to fear from BJP and that in the long run their association with the saffron party will benefit both the national party and the regional outfits.

"Vajpayee and L.K. Advani are determined not to resort to horse trading to retain power. Nor is BJP working for the split of any party. It will be demeaning for the saffron party to indulge in this type of petty politics. But it cannot help if parties like the Janata Dal, the Samajwadi Party and the Congress split because of their internal contradictions and self-aggrandisement of their leaders.

"BJP has a strong base in the north and the west. An alliance with regional outfits in the east and the south can give the Government a national representation. But if this does not happen and the Vajpayee government is defeated on the floor of the House, it is bound to generate a strong sympathy wave for the saffron brigade which may enable it to get a clear majority in the 12th Lok Sabha."

Bowing Out in Glory

When Atal Bihari Vajpayee submitted the resignation of his government to the President at the end of the debate on the confidence motion, it was widely perceived not as defeat but victory in defeat, because of the BJP's adherence to principled politics. In an editorial comment captioned 'Stealing the Show', *The Indian Express* said:

"It is not often that a political happening in the Capital is transformed into a national drama with a spectacular finale. But if live television coverage transformed the two-day debate on the vote of confidence into a happening in which every Indian was an active participant, the credit has to go to Atal Bihari Vajpayee. To say that the veteran BJP leader stole the show is an understatement. Using his formidable oratorical skills to the hilt, Vajpayee successfully transformed the dubious reputation of presiding over India's most short-lived government into a political achievement. As he wound up the debate with the dramatic announcement of his resignation, he was not merely achieving political martyrdom. He was elevating himself to the role of a folk hero. For a politician in a country where the people have learnt to be deeply suspicious of those in public life, this was a stupendous feat. Vajpayee always possessed charm; after Tuesday's debate, he has acquired charisma, albeit that of a tragic hero—an attribute that no other member of the political class can boast of. In the parliamentary trial of strength, the BJP lost dismally. In the battle for the hearts and minds of the electorate, Vajpayee has emerged triumphant. He has turned failure on its head and come out of a sordid battle smelling of roses.

"Public memory being woefully short, it is uncertain how long the memory of Vajpayee's great parliamentary performance will endure. But having a leader who is considerably taller than the party is calculated to enhance the prospects of the BJP, even in opposition. This has very little to do with politics. In appealing to the Lok Sabha to overcome party barriers, Vajpayee was positioning himself as a statesman, but a statesman who remains wedded to his party and its controversial parent organisation. He was not diluting the BJP's distinctiveness, but asserting the virtues of pragmatism and compromise in a Parliament which is well and truly hung. He admitted his failure openly, but that admission contained a menacing challenge to the amorphous United Front-Congress combination to either perform or perish. In his moment of defeat, Vajpayee loudly proclaimed the existence of an alternative force which is itching to return to the people for a resounding mandate."

In an article in *The Hindu* of 2nd June 1996, Prem Shankar Jha praised the BJP for its refusal to indulge in horse-trading, thus setting a new standard in political morality. He said:

"The BJP has exercised restraint in another way. Having been called to form the Government when it was some 80 seats short of a majority, it would probably have been forgiven if it had held out inducements of various kinds to other parties to swell the ranks of the coalition it headed. Instead, Mr. Vajpayee himself, and senior BJP leaders on his behalf, made it clear that they would not indulge in horse-trading. Exploratory talks were held with almost all the regional parties, but these apparently stopped well short of an offer of ministerial berth or other inducements for support. As a result, when Mr. Vajpayee resigned on May 28, he left behind him a hard act to follow."

'Secular' Cover for Corruption

The support extended by the Congress to the formation of a United Front government by H.D. Deve Gowda was widely seen by political analysts as a move to avoid prosecution of Congressmen, including P.V. Narasimha Rao, who face charges of corruption.

The Times of India of 20th May 1996 carried a front-page story about informal conditions being set for Congress support. The report quoted a former Union Minister as saying: "The Bofors papers should not reach India. St. Kitts should be dropped for lack of evidence. Decisions such as the recent import of urea from a Turkish company should not be probed."

The same newspaper carried a report the next day which said *inter alia*: "What is causing concern to MPs favouring coalition with the Third Front is their information that Mr. (Narasimha) Rao has tried to impose 'conditions' on Mr. Deve Gowda for extending support. The former Prime Minister has said that there should not be any investigation into the Gold Star case, the Harshad Mehta case, the Sugar Scandal, the Fertiliser Import Scandal, and no action taken against him and his family members. Besides, no action should be taken on the Action Taken Report of the Joint Parliamentary Committee which probed the multi-crore scam that rocked the nation because of the magnitude of the fraud."

The *Free Press Journal* of 3rd June 1996 carried an article by Virendra Kapoor in the course of which he said:

"The truth is that the Vajpayee Government bowed before the superior numbers of an all-embracing gang-up which became a reality only when the Congress Party with its 136 members threw its weight behind the Front. Had the Congress decided to stay neutral or, alternatively, given notice of its own intention to stake its claim to form a Government, the outcome of the trust vote last Tuesday in all probability would have been quite different. For the chances are that many in the Front who now strut the political stage as all-conquering warriors of secularism would have been partaking from the feast of Hindutva...

"The company that Gowda, Yadav and other leaders of the Front keep has fuelled fears that Gowda's will be a cash-and-carry government... In this hung parliament itself, Vajpayee could truly get lucky second time."

Towards a Decisive Mandate

Criminalisation of politics is an ugly process which has been under way in some parts of the country like Bihar. This found dramatic expression when, in the early days of the Deve Gowda regime, Mohammad Taslimuddin of the Janata Dal, who had been inducted as Minister of State for Home Affairs, had to resign following the disclosure that many criminal cases were pending against him. With almost every day bringing to light personality clashes and differences on economic policy within the Janata Dal and between constituents of the motley Front, and many aspirants pressing for entry into an already large Council of Ministers, a question that is widely debated in the Press and by the public is how long the Deve Gowda government will last.

A related question is whether, when—rather than if—the United Front government comes down under the weight of its internal contradictions, there will be a realignment of political parties within the present Lok Sabha or there will be fresh elections. Regional parties like the DMK, TDP and AGP may come to the conclusion that they have nothing to gain through another round of elections. These parties apparently preferred coalition with a weak Janata Dal nucleus in the expectation that they would be able to exert greater pressure on it, but if the nucleus does not hold?

In any event, the BJP seems well set to form a government again, perhaps within the duration of the eleventh Lok Sabha. When the next elections come, five years hence or earlier, there is likelihood of the BJP securing a decisive mandate. It can become a certainty if the BJP is able to establish its credentials as a party with a difference: one whose members are dignified and disciplined in their conduct—within the party, in the legislatures and in public. Instead of competing with legislators belonging to other parties in exercise of lung power and paralysing proceedings, they can take initiatives such as Ram Naik, to his credit, did in the tenth Lok Sabha when he raised the subject of 'Vande Mataram'. There is great scope for promoting public good by constantly drawing attention to issues like finding resources to implement Article 45 of the Constitution by scaling down the state subsidy of higher education for students from well-to-do homes; promoting inter-religious ecumenism by such symbolic acts as the long overdue renaming of the Babar and Aurangzeb roads in the capital for Sarmad the Sufi martyr and Dara Shikoh who translated the Vedanta into Persian; helping to restore national self-respect by removing to a museum—along with other relics of a dubious past—the statue of V.K. Krishna Menon which stands before Sena Bhawan; the need to curb the accelerating tendency towards vulgarity and commercialism in the mass media; and the need to make education value-oriented.

On the subject of education the BJP will do well to reconsider its stand on the three-language formula which it has pledged, in the 1996 manifesto, to "strictly enforce in schools". It is true that this formula is not one-sided, like the imposition of Russian which was a potent factor in the disintegration of the Union of Soviet Socialist Republics. The Moscow-based dictatorship of the Russian-dominated CPSU (B) did not stipulate the learning of a non-Russian language of the USSR by students in the Russian Republic. However, with education now in the Concurrent List, opponents of the BJP can conjure up the spectre of Hindi being forced on non-Hindi speakers in terms of Article 343 regarding the official language of the Union and Article 351 which calls for development of Hindi "as a medium of expression for all the elements of the composite culture of India". Moreover, with the explosive growth of knowledge in various fields in recent decades all over the world, our need in India today is to promote subject-matter expertise rather than proficiency in more languages.

If it is important to be mindful of regional susceptibilities in the matter of language, it is equally important that the BJP should refrain from engaging in competitive parochialism in matters like inter-State sharing of river waters. It is vital, above all, that the BJP is seen to place principles above the securing or retention of power whether at the Centre or in this State or that, and that it is free of the corruption and criminalisation that have overtaken most other political parties.

All this amounts to a tall order. But if the BJP can rise to the challenge at the close of an unhappy millenium of subjection to foreign rule, culminating in partition and a half-century of misrule by Congressmen and ex-Congressmen, the party can lead India into a happier millennium. It can launch a new era in the polity by completing the process of recovery of national identity, and can help to fulfil the destiny of the world's largest democracy which is home to the oldest living civilisation.

APPENDICES

APPENDIX I

A.B. Vajpayee: A Life Sketch

(This life sketch was brought out as a leaflet by the Janata Party on the eve of the post-Emergency elections to the Lok Sabha held in March 1977, in which Shri Vajpayee won from the New Delhi constituency. This was the fourth occasion on which he was elected to the Lok Sabha. Subsequently he was elected for the fifth time in 1980, the sixth time in 1991 and the seventh time in 1996. Shri Vajpayee has also served in the Rajya Sabha, having been elected to that House in 1962 and again in 1986.)

Born: December 25, 1926.

Education: Passed B.A. from Victoria College Gwalior; recipient of government scholarship for M.A. and Law; passed M.A. in Political Science in the First Division; left his study of Law incomplete due to mental anguish at the partition of the country.

Interest in Public Life: Interested in public life right from childhood; joined Arya Kumar Sabha; came in touch with RSS; fond of writing, public speaking and writing poetry; won many prizes in poetical symposiums and debates. In this connection, an incident at the University of Allahabad is worth mentioning. When he reached there from Gwalior to participate in a debate, it had been declared closed and the result was about to be announced. The well-known Hindi poet Prof. Harivansh Rai Bachchan was one of the judges. Shri Vajpayee was allowed to speak and he won a prize.

He became active in the student movement when he was in

college. He was elected secretary of the Debating Society and later elected Prime Minister and Vice President of the Victoria College Union—in those days a professor used to be the President of the Union.

As a Journalist: Shri Vajpayee entered the field of journalism in 1947. He was appointed editor of the monthly journal *Rashtradharma* published from Lucknow and made it popular among the intelligentsia. This was followed by his appointment as chief editor of the weekly *Panchjanya*. His poems and articles of those days are still read with great interest. He also edited for some time the daily and the weekly *Vir Arjun*, published from New Delhi.

Political Life: He jumped into active political life to fulfil the mission of the founder-president of the Jana Sangh Dr. Syama Prasad Mookerji. Dr. Mookerji's death in mysterious circumstances while under detention agitated him deeply. He had already come in touch with Dr. Mookerji and had toured many parts of the country as special representative of Dr. Mookerji. The martyrdom of Dr. Mookerji made him give up literature and journalism and take to the path of political struggle. He was President of the Bharatiya Jana Sangh and Leader of its parliamentary wing for many years.

In Parliament: Shri Vajpayee has been working strenuously towards the making of a great and prosperous India. He was first elected to the Lok Sabha in 1957. His very first speech on foreign policy was widely acclaimed. It was due to Shri Vajpayee's efforts that facts about the Chinese aggression on the northern borders were brought to light. While the Government was trying to suppress the truth, Shri Vajpayee, by getting the demand for publishing a White Paper accepted, forced it to admit that Chinese infiltration had been going on for many years and that the Government had been guilty of keeping the Indian people in the dark.

At the time of the Chinese aggression in 1962, Shri Vajpayee played an important role in keeping the public morale high and arousing national feeling for extending full support to the armed forces.

During the Indo-Pak War of 1965, he extended full cooperation to the Government, putting aside all political differences, and this was appreciated by the late Shri Lal Bahadur Shastri.

Because of Shri Vajpayee's political perspicacity and gift of oratory, Shri Lal Bahadur Shastri selected him to explain the Kashmir policy of the Government of India to the African countries. For this purpose, Shri Vajpayee visited Kenya, Uganda, Tanzania and Malawi as a member of a parliamentary delegation. His speeches created a stir in these countries. The Pakistani diplomatic missions could not hide the fact that their country had committed aggression in Kashmir.

Constructive Role: In 1962 Shri Vajpayee was elected to the Rajya Sabha. It had only two Jana Sangh members in those days. Even so the Chairman of the House, Dr. Radhakrishnan, allotted him a seat on the front benches and he soon emerged as the main opposition speaker. He carved out a special position for himself in the parliamentary life of the country by the sharp wit, cogent arguments, incontrovertible facts and constructive suggestions. He never hit below the belt, nor did he allow personal bitterness to be generated. His speech in the Rajya Sabha at Pandit Nehru's death and his speech at a public meeting in New Delhi's Ram Lila Maidan to mourn the death of Shri Lal Bahadur Shastri, are models of the noblest of political traditions and also belong to our cherished literary heritage.

Shri Vajpayee does not believe in opposition for opposition's sake, nor is he ever a party to character assassination. His opposition has been based on principles and policies. The Press referred to his speech in the Lok Sabha on the Pondicherry Licence Scandal as the best speech of his parliamentary career. But there was not a single bitter word against the late Lalit Narayan Mishra. His speeches during the Bangladesh War were acclaimed as historic by even his opponents. It was due to his nationalist viewpoint that Pandit Nehru nominated him to the National Integration Council in 1962. He was also included in the reconstituted Integration Council in 1968.

Shri Vajpayee earned the goodwill of both the ruling party and the opposition as chairman of the Assurances Committee and of the Public Accounts Committee of Parliament. The esteem in which he is held can be judged from the fact that once on a trip to Yugoslavia, the then Lok Sabha Speaker Dr. G.S. Dhillon nominated him as the acting leader of the Indian Parliamentary

Delegation in his absence. The communist hosts were amazed to see an opposition member leading the delegation. This was something unthinkable for them.

Visits Abroad: Shri Vajpayee has participated in many international conferences as member of Indian Parliamentary Delegations. He left a deep impression on the delegates with his speech at the British Commonwealth Conference in Canada in 1966. He had then warned that if the majority rule was not established soon in Rhodesia, there would be armed conflict and the White man's dominance would come to an end. This has come true.

Shri Vajpayee's three speeches at the Inter-parliamentary World Conference at Tokyo in 1974, to which he was a delegate from India, were greatly appreciated. Many African delegates praised his speech against apartheid. His statement that the super powers should keep their hands off the non-aligned countries got full support from the Third World. Shri Vajpayee was also elected to the National Committee of the World Parliamentary Union and represented India at Colombo along with the Minister of State for Home Affairs, Shri Om Mehta, in May 1975.

In the Forefront of Struggles: During the 1942 freedom struggle Shri Vajpayee was an Intermediate student at Gwalior. He was under police watch for active participation in processions and meetings. His father, who was in government service, sent him along with his elder brother to Bateshwar, their ancestral village. But the fire of the struggle had reached there also Shri Vajpayee was involved in it and he was arrested. The police said that he had come to the village with a set design and that he had a hand in instigating the people against the government. On the other hand, Shri Vajpayee's opponents have alleged that he had been sent by the RSS to sabotage the freedom struggle. It is needless to dilate on the absurdity of the charge. If Shri Vajpayee had wanted to oppose the movement as the communists were doing at the time, he need not have left Gwalior. Only a fool or a knave can level the charge that Shri Vajpayee had been sent to a small village like Bateshwar for sabotaging the freedom movement. But it is usual to spread such false allegations during the days of elections.

Shri Vajpayee had to go to jail in free India many times. He has been in the forefront of struggles, whether it is the question of

Kashmir or Kutch, demand for recognition of Bangladesh or fight against injustices in Uttar Pradesh.

On the declaration of emergency, Shri Vajpayee was detained in Bangalore on June 25, 1975. On July 13, he had fever and stomach-ache. He was sent from jail to the public hospital and operated for removing appendix. Later on it was discovered by the doctors that removal of the appendix was not necessary. But the wound got septic and there were complications. The temperature was rising. So he was transferred to the All India Medical Institute at New Delhi in an Air Force plane.

Shri Vajpayee had been an old patient of the Medical Institute. Investigations by medical experts here showed that he was suffering from typhoid and an operation in such condition could be dangerous. In the meantime his backache, which had flared up in Bangalore jail, became acute. X-ray showed that he had prolapse disc which made movement painful. But the doctors wanted to avoid a major operation. At first they tried to set the disc through electric fomentation and traction. When even prolonged treatment of this type failed to yield any result it was decided to remove the disc, because otherwise there was the danger of an attack of paralysis. The operation was successful but Shri Vajpayee remained bed-ridden for weeks. He could not be sent to jail in such a condition, therefore arrangements were made for detaining him at his house. Later on he was released on parole on health grounds as his backache did not subside fully and he had frequent fits of giddiness.

Despite ill health, Shri Vajpayee's will power is strong as ever. He is contesting this election in order to challenge the enemies of democracy.

APPENDIX II

Supreme Court Vindicates Hindutva

(Following are excerpts from the unanimous judgment of a three-member Bench of the Supreme Court comprising Justices J.S. Verma, N.P. Singh and K. Venkatswami, dated 11th December 1995.)

16. It cannot be doubted that a speech with a secular stance alleging discrimination against any particular religion, and promising removal of the imbalance, cannot be treated as an appeal on the ground of religion as its thrust is for promoting secularism. Instances given in the speech of discrimination against any religion causing the imbalance in the professed goal of secularism, the allegation being against any individual or any political party, cannot be called an appeal on the ground of religion forbidden by sub-section (3). In other words, mention of religion as such in an election speech is not forbidden by sub-section (3) so long as it does not amount to an appeal to vote for a candidate on the ground of his religion or to refrain from voting for any other candidate on the ground of his religion. When it is said that politics and religion do not mix, it merely means that the religion of a candidate cannot be used for gaining political mileage by seeking votes on the ground of the candidate's religion or alienating the electorate against another candidate on the ground of the other candidate's religion. It also means that the State has no religion and the State practises the policy of neutrality in the matter of religion.

17. In *Dr. M. Ismail Faruqui and Others etc. etc. v. Union of India and Others etc.*, (1994) 6 SCC 360 (Ayodhya case), the Constitution Bench, after a detailed discussion, summarised the true concept of secularism under the Indian Constitution as under:

> "It is clear from the constitutional scheme that it guarantees equality in the matter of religion to all individuals and groups irrespective of their faith, emphasising that there is no religion of the State itself. The Preamble of the Constitution read in particular with Articles 25 to 28 emphasises this aspect and indicates that it is in this manner the concept of secularism embodied in the constitutional scheme as a creed adopted by the Indian people has to be understood while examining the constitutional validity of any legislation on the touchstone of the Constitution. The concept of secularism is one facet of the right to equality woven as the central golden thread in the fabric depicting the pattern of the scheme in our Constitution."

18. It cannot be doubted that an election speech made in conformity with the fundamental right to freedom of religion guaranteed under Articles 25 to 30 of the Constitution, cannot be treated as anti-secular to be prohibited by sub-section (3) of Section 123, unless it falls within the narrow net of the prohibition indicated earlier. It is obvious that a speech referring to religion during election campaign with a secular stance in conformity with the fundamental right to freedom of religion can be made, if it does not contain an appeal to vote for any candidate because of his religion or to refrain from voting for any candidate because of his religion. When it is said that politics and religion do not mix, it obviously does not mean that even such permissible political speeches are forbidden. This is the meaning and true scope of sub-section (3) of Section 123 of the Act.

19. We would now consider the meaning of sub-section (3A) of Section 123. This sub-section also was inserted along with the substituted sub-section (3) by Act 40 of 1961 w.e.f. 20.9.1961. The meaning of this sub-section is not much in controversy. Sub-section (3A) is similar to section 153-A of the Indian Penal Code.

In sub-section (3A), the expression used is "the promotion of, or attempt to promote, feelings of enmity or hatred" as against the expression "Whoever .... promotes or attempts to promote..... disharmony or feelings of enmity, hatred or ill-will...."in Section 153-A, I.P.C. The expression feelings of enmity or hatred is common in both the provisions but the additional words in Section 153-A, I.P.C. are 'disharmony ....or ill-will'. The difference in the plain language of the two provisions indicates that mere promotion of disharmony or ill-will between different groups of people is an offence under Section 153-A, I.P.C. while under sub-section (3A) of Section 123 of the R.P. Act, it is only the promotion of or attempt to promote feelings of enmity or hatred, which are stronger words, that is forbidden in the election campaign.

20. The provision is made with the object of curbing the tendency to promote or attempt to promote communal, linguistic or any other factional enmity or hatred to prevent the divisive tendencies. The provision in the I.P.C. as well as in the R.P. Act for this purpose was made by amendment at the same time. The amendment in the R.P. Act followed amendments made in the Indian Penal Code to this effect in a bid to curb any tendency to resort to divisive means to achieve success at the polls on the ground of religion or narrow communal or linguistic affiliations. Any such attempt during the election is viewed with disfavour under the law and is made a corrupt practice under sub-section (3A) of Section 123.

22. The decision in *Ziyauddin Burhanuddin Bukhari* v. *Brijmohan Ramdass Mehra & Ors.* 1975 (Suppl.) SCR 281, lends assurance to the correctness of the construction made by us of these provisions. The returned candidate Bukhari was the candidate of Muslim League while the defeated candidate Shauket Chagla was the Congress candidate at the election. Both were Muslims. The returned candidate Bukhari in his appeal to the voters said that Chagla was not true to his religion while he himself was a true Muslim and that Chagla was neither a good Hindu nor a true Muslim. The clear implication of the appeal was that Chagla was not true to his religion whereas Bukhari was, and, therefore, the voters should prefer Bukhari. In short, the appeal for votes was made on the ground that Bukhari was a staunch believer of the

Muslim religion as against Chagla who was not. It was this clear appeal based on the ground of the candidate's religion which was held to constitute the corrupt practices defined by sub-sections (3) and (3A) of Section 123 of the R.P. Act.

23. The next question now relates to the constitutional validity of these provisions on the meaning ascribed to them.

24. Sub-section (3A) of Section 123 is undoubtedly a provision made in the interests of public order or incitement to an offence because the promotion or attempt to promote feelings of enmity or hatred between different classes of the citizens of India on any of the grounds specified therein, apart from creating divisive tendency, would also be prejudicial to the maintenance of public order and may amount to incitement to commission of offences. The freedom of speech and expression guaranteed to all citizens under Article 19(1)(a), which is the basis of the constitutional challenge to this provision, is subject to clause (2) of Article 19 which permits the making of any law imposing reasonable restrictions on the exercise of this right in the interests of public order or incitement to an offence. For this reason, no further attempt was made to press the argument of challenge to the constitutional validity of sub-section (3A) on the construction we have made of that provision.

25. The question now is of the constitutional validity of sub-section (3) of Section 123. We have already rejected the argument that the element of prejudicial effect on public order is implicit also in sub-section (3) as it is in sub-section (3A). According to Shri Ram Jethmalani, unless this element also is read into sub-section (3), it is violative of Article 19(1)(a) inasmuch as clause (2) of Article 19 does not save its validity under any of the other heads specified therein.

26. We have construed sub-section (3) of Section 123 as a restriction only to the extent that votes cannot be sought for a candidate on the ground of his religion, etc. and similarly there can be no appeal to refrain from voting for any person on the same ground. In other words, an appeal to vote for a candidate or not to vote for him on the ground of his religion, etc. is the restriction imposed by sub-section (3). This restriction is in the law enacted to provide for the conduct of elections, the qualifications and disqualifications for membership of the Houses, the corrupt practices and other offences at or in connection with such elections. The right to contest the election is given by the statute subject to the conditions prescribed therein. The restriction is limited only to the appeal for votes to a candidate during the election period and not to the freedom of speech and expression in general or the freedom to profess, practise and propagate religion unconnected with the election campaign.

27. It is true, as argued by Shri Jethmalani, that the freedom of speech and expression guaranteed to all citizens under Article 19(1)(a) is absolute subject to the reasonable restrictions imposed by any law saved by clause (2) of Article 19, under one of the heads specified therein. The heads specified in clause (2) of Article 19 are, therefore, several and they are intended to cover the entire area with which the absolute freedom to say anything which the speaker may like would not extend, in keeping with the standards of a civilized society, the corresponding rights of others in an orderly society, and the constitutional scheme.

28. The expression "in the interests of" used in clause (2) of Article 19 indicates a wide amplitude of the permissible law which can be enacted to provide for reasonable restrictions on the exercise of this right under one of the heads specified therein, in conformity with the constitutional scheme. Two of the heads mentioned are: decency or morality. Thus any law which imposes reasonable restrictions on the exercise of this right in the interests of decency or morality is also saved by clause (2) of Article 19. Shri Jethmalani contended that the words `decency or morality' relate to sexual morality alone. In view of the expression "in the interests of" and the context of election campaign for a free and fair poll, the right to contest the election being statutory and subject to the provisions of the statute, the words `decency or morality' do not require a narrow or pedantic meaning to be given to these words. The dictionary meaning of `decency' is "correct and tasteful standards of behaviour as generally accepted; conformity with current standards of behaviour or propriety; avoidance of obscenity; and the requirements of correct behaviour" (*The Oxford Encyclopedic English Dictionary*); "conformity to the prevailing standards of propriety, morality, modesty, etc.; and the quality of being decent" (*Collins English Dictionary*).

29. Thus, the ordinary dictionary meaning of 'decency' indicates that the action must be in conformity with the current standards of behaviour or propriety, etc. In a secular polity, the requirement of correct behaviour or propriety is that an appeal for votes should not be made on the ground of the candidate's religion which by itself is no index of the suitability of a candidate for membership of the House.

30. Thus, seeking votes at an election on the ground of the candidate's religion in a secular State, is against the norms of decency and propriety of the society.

31. In our opinion, the saving in clause (2) of Article 19 permits the imposition of reasonable restrictions on the exercise of the right conferred by Article 19(1)(a) by making any law in the interests of decency or morality; and sub-section (3) of Section 123 of the R.P. Act, as construed by us, has the protection of clause (2) of Article 19 under the head 'decency' therein. This conclusion is reached by us even if it is assumed that the provision is not saved merely as a condition subject to which the statutory right of contesting an election is available to the candidate. The fact that the scheme of separate electorates was rejected in framing the Constitution and secularism is the creed adopted in the constitutional scheme, are relevant considerations to treat this as a reasonable restriction on the freedom of speech and expression, for maintaining the standard of behaviour required in conformity with the decency and propriety of the societal norms. Viewed at in any manner, sub-section (3) of Section 123 cannot be held to be unconstitutional. This view is also in accord with the nature of right to contest an election, as understood in *Jamuna Prasad Mukhariya and Others* v. *Lachhi Ram and Others*, 1955 (1) SCR 608.

32. The argument assailing the constitutional validity of sub-sections (3) and/or (3A) of Section 123 is rejected.

Meaning of 'Hindutva' and 'Hinduism'

33. The next contention relates to the meaning of 'Hindutva' and 'Hinduism' and the effect of the use of these expressions in the election speeches.

34. We have already indicated the meaning of sub-section (3) of Section 123 of the R.P. Act and the limit of its operation. It may be said straightaway that any speech wherein these expressions are used, irrespective of their meaning, cannot by itself fall within the ambit of sub-section (3) of Section 123, unless the speech can be construed as an appeal to vote for a candidate on the ground that he is a Hindu or to refrain from voting for a candidate on the ground of his religion, i.e., he not being a Hindu. We have also indicated that mere reference to any religion in an election speech does not bring it within the net of sub-section (3) and/or sub-section (3A) of Section 123, since reference can be made to any religion in the context of secularism or to criticise any political pary for practising discrimination against any religious group or generally for preservation of the Indian culture. In short, mere use of the word 'Hindutva' or 'Hinduism' or mention of any other religion in an election speech does not bring it within the net of sub-section (3) and/or sub-section (3A) of Section 123, unless the further elements indicated are also present in that speech. It is also necessary to see the meaning and purport of the speech and the manner in which it was likely to be understood by the audience to which the speech was addressed. These words are not to be construed in the abstract, when used in an election speech.

35. Both sides referred copiously to the meaning of the words 'Hindutva' and 'Hinduism' with reference to several writings. Shri Jethmalani referred to them for the purpose of indicating the several meanings of these words and to emphasise that the word 'Hindutva' relates to Indian culture based on the geographical division known as Hindustan, i.e., India. On the other hand, Shri Ashok Desai emphasised that the term 'Hindutva' used in election speeches is an emphasis on Hindu religion bearing no relation to the fact that India is also known as Hindustan, and the term can relate to Indian culture.

36. The Constitution Bench in *Sastri Yagnapurushadji and Others* v. *Muldas Bhudardas Vaishya and Another*, 1966 (3) SCR 242 held thus:

> "Who are Hindus and what are the broad features of Hindu religion, that must be the first part of our enquiry in dealing with the present controversy between the parties. The historical and etymological genesis of the word "Hindu" has

given rise to a controversy amongst Indologists; but the view generally accepted by scholars appears to be that the word "Hindu" is derived from the river Sindhu otherwise known as Indus which flows from the Punjab. "That part of the great Aryan race", says Monier Williams, "which immigrated from Central Asia, through the mountain passes into India, settled first in the districts near the river Sindhu (now called the Indus). The Persians pronounced this word Hindu and named their Aryan brethren Hindus. The Greeks, who probably gained their first ideas of India from the Persians, dropped the hard aspirate, and called the Hindus "Indoi" (*Hinduism*, Monier Williams, p. 1.).

The Encyclopedia of Religion and Ethics, Vol. Vl, has described "Hinduism" as the title applied to that form of religion which prevails among the vast majority of the present population of the Indian Empire (p. 686.) As Dr. Radhakrishnan has observed; "The Hindu civilization is so called, since its original founders or earliest followers occupied the territory drained by the Sindhu (the Indus) river system corresponding to the North West Frontier Province and the Punjab. This is recorded in the Rig Veda, the oldest of the Vedas, the Hindu scriptures which give their name to this period Indian history. The people on the Indian side of the Sindhu were called Hindu by the Persian and the later western invaders" (*The Hindu View of Life*, Dr. Radhakrishnan, p. 12). That is the genesis of the word "Hindu."

When we think of the Hindu religion, we find it difficult, if not impossible, to define Hindu religion or even adequately describe it. Unlike other religions in the world, the Hindu religion does not claim any one prophet; it does not worship any one God; it does not subscribe to any one dogma; it does not believe in any one philosophic concept; it does not follow any one set of religious rites or performances; in fact, it does not appear to satisfy the narrow traditional features of any religion or creed. It may broadly be described as a way of life and nothing more.

. . . . The term 'Hindu', according to Dr. Radhakrishnan, had originally a territorial and not a credal significance. It implied residence in a well-defined geographical area. Aboriginal tribes, savage and half-civilized people, the cultured Dravidians and the Vedic Aryans were all Hindus as they were the sons of the same mother. The Hindu thinkers reckoned with the striking fact that the men and women dwelling in India belonged to different communities, worshipped different gods, and practised different rites (*Kurma Purana, ibid,* p. 12). Monier Williams has observed that "it must be borne in mind that Hinduism is far more than a mere form of theism resting on Brahmanism. It presents for our investigation a complex congeries of creeds and doctrines which in its gradual accumulation may be compared to the gathering together of the mighty volume of the Ganges, swollen by a continual influx of tributary rivers and rivulets, spreading itself over an ever-increasing area of country and finally resolving itself into an intricate Delta of tortuous steams and jungly marshes.... The Hindu religion is a reflection of the composite character of the Hindus, who are not one people but many. It is based on the idea of universal receptivity. It has ever aimed at accommodating itself to circumstances, and has carried on the process of adaptation through more than three thousand years. It has first borne with and then, so to speak, swallowed, digested, and assimilated something from all creeds." (*Religious Thought & Life in India,* Monier Williams, p. 57.)

We have already indicated that the usual tests which can be applied in relation to any recognised religion or religious creed in the world turn out to be inadequate in dealing with the problem of Hindu religion. Normally, any recognised religion or religious creed subscribes to a body of set philosophic concepts and theological beliefs. Does this test apply to the Hindu religion? In answering this question, we would base ourselves mainly on the exposition of the problem by Dr. Radhakrishnan in his book on Indian Philosophy. (*Indian Philosophy,* Dr. Radhakrishnan, Vol. I, pp. 22-23). Unlike other countries, India can claim that philosophy in ancient India was not an auxiliary to any other science or art, but always held a prominent position of independence.... "In all the fleeting centuries of history", says Dr. Radhakrishnan, "in all the vicissitudes through which India has passed, a certain marked identity is visible. It has held fast to certain psychological traits which constitute its special heritage, and they will be the characteristic marks of the Indian people so long as they are privileged to have a separate existence." The history of Indian thought emphatically brings out the fact that the development of Hindu religion has always been inspired by an endless quest of the mind for truth based on the consciousness that truth has many facets. Truth is one, but wise men describe it differently. (..) The Indian mind has, consistently through the ages, been exercised over the problem of the nature of godhead, the problem that faces the spirit at the end of life, and the interrelation between the individual and the universal soul. "If we can abstract from the variety of opinion", says Dr. Radhakrishnan, "and observe the general spirit of Indian thought, we shall find that it has a disposition to interpret life and nature in the way of monistic idealism, though this tendency is so plastic, living and manifold that it takes many forms and expresses itself in even mutually hostile teachings". (..)

. . . . Naturally enough, it was realised by Hindu religion from the very beginning of its career that truth was many-sided and different views contained different aspects of truth which no one could fully express. This knowledge inevitably bred a spirit of tolerance and willingness to understand and appreciate the opponent's point of view. That is how "the several views set forth in India in regard to the vital philosophic concepts are considered to be the branches of the self-same tree. The short cuts and blind alleys are somehow reconciled with the main road of advance to the truth." (..) When we consider this broad sweep of the Hindu philosophic concepts, it would be realised that under Hindu philosophy, there is no scope for ex-communicating any notion or principle as heretical and rejecting it as such.

The development of Hindu religion and philosophy shows that from time to time saints and religious reformers attempted to remove from the Hindu thought and practices elements of corruption and superstition and that led to the formation of different sects. Buddha started Buddhism; Mahavir founded Jainism; Basava became the founder of Lingayat religion, Dnyaneshwar and Tukaram initiated the Varakari cult; Guru Nanak inspired Sikhism; Dayananda founded Arya Samaj, and Chaitanya began Bhakti cult; and as a result of the teachings of Ramakrishna and Vivekananda, Hindu religion flowered into its most attractive, progressive and dynamic form. If we study the teachings of these saints and religious reformers, we would notice an amount of divergence in their respective views; but underneath that divergence, there is a kind of subtle indescribable unity which keeps them within the sweep of the broad and progressive Hindu religion.

. . . . It is somewhat remarkable that this broad sweep of Hindu religion has been eloquently described by Toynbee. Says Toynbee: "When we pass from the plane of social practice to the plane of intellectual outlook, Hinduism too comes out well by comparison with the religions and ideologies of the South-West Asian group. In contrast to these Hinduism has the same outlook as the pre-Christian and pre-Muslim religions and philosophies of the Western half of the old world. Like them, Hinduism takes it for granted that there is more than one valid approach to truth and to salvation and that these different approaches are not only compatible with each other, but are complementary" (*The Present-Day Experiment in Western Civilisation*, Toynbee, pp. 48-49).

The Constitution-makers were fully conscious of this broad and comprehensive character of Hindu religion; and so, while guaranteeing the fundamental right to freedom of religion, Explanation II to Art. 25 has made it clear that in sub-clause (b) of clause (2), the reference to Hindus shall be construed as including a reference to persons professing the Sikh, Jaina or Buddhist religion, and the reference to Hindu religious institutions shall be construed accordingly."

(from pp. 259-66)

37. In a later Constitution Bench decision in *Commr. of Wealth Tax, Madras & Ors.* v. *Late R. Sridharan by L. Rs.*, (1976) Supp. SCR

478, the meaning of the term 'Hinduism' as commonly understood is stated thus:

> "... . It is a matter of common knowledge, that Hinduism embraces within self so many diverse forms of beliefs, faiths, practices and worship that it is difficult to define the term 'Hindu' with precision.
>
> The historical and etymological genesis of the word "Hindu" has been succinctly explained by Gajendragadkar, C.J. in *Shastri Yagnapurushdasji & Ors.* v. *Muldas Bhundardas Vaishya & Anr.* (A.I.R. 1966 S.C. 1119).
>
> In Unabridged Edition of Webster's Third New International Dictionary of the English language, the term 'Hinduism' has been defined as meaning "a complex body of social, cultural and religious beliefs and practices evolved in and largely confined to the Indian subcontinent and marked by a caste system, an outlook tending to view all forms and theories as aspects of one eternal being and truth, a belief in ahimsa, karma, dharma, sansara and moksha, and the practice of the way of works, the way of knowledge, or the way of devotion as the means of release from the bound of rebirths; the way of life and form of thought of a Hindu."
>
> In *Encyclopaedia Britannica* (15th Edition), the term 'Hinduism' has been defined as meaning "the civilization of Hindus (originally, the inhabitants of the land of the Indus River). It properly denotes the Indian civilization of approximately the last 2,000 years, which gradually evolved from Vedism, the religion of the ancient Indo-Europeans who settled in India in the last centuries of the 2nd millennium B.C. Because it integrates a large variety of heterogeneous elements, Hinduism constitutes a very complex but largely continuous whole, and since it covers the whole of life, it has religious, social, economic, literary, and artistic aspects. As a religion, Hinduism is an utterly diverse conglomerate of doctrines, cults, and way of life... In principle, Hinduism incorporates all forms of belief and worship without necessitating the selection or elimination of any. The Hindu is inclined to revere the divine in every manifestation, whatever it may be, and is doctrinally tolerant, leaving others—including both Hindus and non-

Hindus—whatever creed and worship practices suit them best. A Hindu may embrace a non-Hindu religion without ceasing to be a Hindu, and since the Hindu is disposed to think synthetically and to regard other forms of worship, strange gods, and divergent doctrines as inadequate rather than wrong or objectionable, he tends to believe that the highest divine powers complement each other for the well-being of the world and mankind. Few religious ideas are considered to be finally irreconcilable. The core of religion does not even depend on the existence or non-existence of God or on whether there is one God or many. Since religious truth is said to transcend all verbal definition, it is not conceived in dogmatic terms. Hinduism is, then, both a civilization and a conglomerate of religions, with neither a beginning, a founder, nor a central authority, hierarchy, or organization. Every attempt at a specific definition of Hinduism has proved unsatisfactory in one way or another, the more so because the finest Indian scholars of Hinduism, including Hindus themselves, have emphasized different aspects of the whole."

In his celebrated treatise *Gitarahasaya*, B.G. Tilak has given the following broad description of the Hindu religion:

"Acceptance of the Vedas with reverence; recognition of the fact that the means or ways of salvation are diverse; and realisation of the truth that the number of gods to be worshipped is large, that indeed is the distinguishing feature of Hindu religion."

In *Bhagwan Koer* v. *J. C. Bose & Ors.*, (1904 ILR 31 Cal. 11), it was held that Hindu religion is marvellously catholic and elastic. Its theology is marked by eclecticism and tolerance and almost unlimited freedom of private worship....

This being the scope and nature of the religion, it is not strange that it holds within its fold men of divergent views and traditions which have very little in common except a vague faith in what may be called the fundamentals of the Hindu religion."

(at pp. 481-82)

38. These Constitution Bench decisions, after a detailed discussion, indicate that no precise meaning can be ascribed to the terms 'Hindu', 'Hindutva' and 'Hinduism'; and no meaning in the abstract can confine it to the narrow limits of religion alone, excluding the content of Indian culture and heritage. It is also indicated that the term 'Hindutva' is related more to the way of life of the people in the sub-continent. It is difficult to appreciate how in the face of these decisions the term 'Hindutva' or 'Hinduism' *per se*, in the abstract, can be assumed to mean and be equated with narrow fundamentalist Hindu religious bigotry, or be construed to fall within the prohibition in sub-sections (3) and/or (3A) of Section 123 of the R.P. Act.

39. Bharucha, J. in *Dr. M. Ismail Faruqui and Ors. etc. etc.* v. *Union of India & Ors. etc.* 1994 (6) SCC 360, (Ayodhya case), in the separate opinion for himself and Ahmadi, J. (as he then was), observed as under:

> "....Hinduism is a tolerant faith. It is that tolerance that has enabled Islam. Christianity, Zoroastrianism, Judaism, Buddhism, Jainism and Sikhism to find shelter and support upon this land......."
>
> (at page 442)

41. In *Kultar Singh* v. *Mukhtiar Singh*, 1964 (7) SCR 790, the Constitution Bench construed the meaning of sub-section (3) of Section 123 prior to its amendment. The question there was whether a poster contained an appeal to voters to vote for the candidate on the ground of his religion; and the meaning of the word 'Panth' in the poster was significant for the purpose. It was held as under:

> "It is true that a corrupt practice under s. 123(3) can be committed by a candidate by appealing to the voters to vote for him on the ground of his religion even though his rival candidate may belong to the same religion. If, for instance, a Sikh candidate were to appeal to the voters to vote for him, because he was a Sikh and add that his rival candidate, though a Sikh in name, was not true to the religious tenets of Sikhism or was a heretic and as such, outside the pale of the Sikh religion, that would amount to a corrupt practice under s. 123(3), and so, we cannot uphold the contention that s. 123(3) is inapplicable because both the appellant and the respondent are Sikhs. . . . The corrupt practice as prescribed by s. 123(3) undoubtedly constitutes a very healthy and salutary provision which is

intended to serve the cause of secular democracy in this country. In order that the democratic process should thrive and succeed, it is of utmost importance that our elections to Parliament and the different legislative bodies must be free from the unhealthy influence of appeals to religion, race, caste, community, or language. If these considerations are allowed any sway in election campaigns, they would vitiate the secular atmosphere of democratic life, and so, s. 123(3) wisely provides a check on this undesirable development by providing that an appeal to any of these factors made in furtherance of the candidature of any candidate as therein prescribed would constitute a corrupt practice and would render the election of the said candidate void.

In considering the question as to whether the distribution of the impugned poster by the appellant constitutes corrupt practice under s. 123(3), there is one point which has to be borne in mind. The appellant had been adopted as its candidate by the Akali Dal Party. This Pary is recognised as a political party by the Election Commission notwithstanding the fact that all of its members are only Sikhs. It is well-known that there are several parties in this country which subscribe to different political and economic ideologies, but the membership of them is either confined to, or predominantly held by, members of particular communities or religions. So long as law does not prohibit the formation of such parties and in fact recognises them for the purpose of election and parliamentary life, it would be necessary to remember that an appeal made by candidates of such parties for votes may, if successful, lead to their election and in an indirect way, may conceivably be influenced by considerations of religion, race, caste, community or language. This infirmity cannot perhaps be avoided so long as parties are allowed to function and are recognised, though their composition may be predominantly based on membership of particular communities or religion. That is why we think, in considering the question as to whether a particular appeal made by a candidate falls within the mischief of s. 123(3) courts should not be astute to read into the words used in the appeal anything more than can be attributed to them on its fair and reasonable construction.

That takes us to the question of construing the impugned poster. The principles which have to be applied in construing such a document are well settled. The document must be read as a whole and its purport and effect determined in a fair, objective and reasonable manner. In reading such documents, it would be unrealistic to ignore the fact that when election meetings are held and appeals are made by candidates of opposing political parties, the atmosphere is usually surcharged with partisan feelings and emotions and the use of hyperboles or exaggerated language, or the adoption of metaphors, and the extravagance of expression in attacking one another, are all a part of the game, and so, when the question about the effect of speeches delivered or pamphlets distributed at election meetings is argued in the cold atmosphere of a judicial chamber, some allowance must be made and the impugned speeches or pamphlets must be construed in that light. In doing so, however, it would be unreasonable to ignore the question as to what the effect of the said speech or pamphlet would be on the mind of the ordinary voter who attends such meetings and reads the pamphlets or hears the speeches. It is in the light of these well-established principles that we must now turn to the impugned pamphlet."

(at pp. 793-95)

42. The test applied in the decision was to construe the meaning of the word 'Panth' not in the abstract but in the context of its use. The conclusion reached was that the word 'Panth' used in the poster did not mean Sikh religion and, therefore, the appeal to the voters was not to vote for the candidate because of his religion. Referring to an earlier decision in *Jagdev Singh Sidhanti* v. *Pratap Singh Daulta and Ors.*, 1964 (6) SCR 750, it was reiterated as under :

". . . . Political issues which form the subject-matter of controversies at election meetings may indirectly and incidentally introduce considerations of language or religion, but in deciding the question as to whether corrupt practice has been committed under s. 123(3), care must be taken to consider the impugned speech or appeal carefully and always in the light of the relevant political controversy. ...."

(at page 799)

43. Thus, it cannot be doubted, particularly in view of the Constitution Bench decisions of this Court that the words 'Hinduism' or 'Hindutva' are not necessarily to be understood and construed narrowly, confined only to the strict Hindu religious practices unrelated to the culture and ethos of the people of India, depicting the way of life of the Indian people. Unless the context of a speech indicates a contrary meaning or use, in the abstract these terms are indicative more of a way of life of the Indian people and are not confined merely to describe persons practising the Hindu religion as a faith.

44. Considering the terms 'Hinduism' or 'Hindutva' *per se* as depicting hostility, enmity or intolerance towards other religious faiths or professing communalism, proceeds from an improper appreciation and perception of the true meaning of these expressions emerging from the detailed discussion in earlier authorities of this Court. Misuse of these expressions to promote communalism cannot alter the true meaning of these terms The mischief resulting from the misuse of the terms by anyone in his speech has to be checked and not its permissible use. It is indeed very unfortunate, if in spite of the liberal and tolerant features of 'Hinduism' recognised in judicial decisions, these terms are misused by anyone during the elections to gain any unfair political advantage. Fundamentalism of any colour or kind must be curbed with a heavy hand to preserve and promote the secular creed of the nation. Any misuse of these terms must, therefore, be dealt with strictly.

45. It is, therefore, a fallacy and an error of law to proceed on the assumption that any reference to Hindutva or Hinduism in a speech makes it automatically a speech based on the Hindu religion as opposed to the other religions or that the use of words 'Hindutva' or 'Hinduism' *per se* depict an attitude hostile to all persons practising any religion other than the Hindu religion. It is the kind of use made of these words and the meaning sought to be conveyed in the speech which has to be seen and unless such a construction leads to the conclusion that these words were used to appeal for votes for a Hindu candidate on the ground that he is a Hindu or not to vote for a candidate because he is not a Hindu, the mere fact that these words are used in the speech would not bring it within the prohibition of sub-section (3) or (3A) of Section 123. It may well be, that these words are used in a speech to promote secularism or to emphasise the way of life of the Indian people and the Indian culture or ethos, or to criticise the policy of any political party as discriminatory or intolerant. The parliamentary debates, including the clarifications made by the Law Minister quoted earlier, also bring out this difference between the prohibited and permissible speech in this context. Whether a particular speech in which reference is made to Hindutva and/or Hinduism falls within the prohibition under sub-section (3) or (3A) of Section 123 is, therefore, a question of fact in each case.

46. This is the correct premise in our view on which all such matters are to be examined. The fallacy is in the assumption that a speech in which reference is made to Hindutva or Hinduism must be a speech on the ground of Hindu religion so that if the candidate for whom the speech is made happens to be a Hindu, it must necessarily amount to a corrupt practice under sub-section (3) and/or sub-section (3A) of Section 123 of the R.P. Act. As indicated, there is no such presumption permissible in law contrary to the several Constitution Bench decisions referred herein.

APPENDIX III

BJP's Manifesto, 1996

(The manifesto drawn up by the Bharatiya Janata Party for the elections to the eleventh Lok Sabha sets out in detail its programme for launching India on a new course. It deals comprehensively with the moral, political, social and economic challenges that face the country at the threshold of the 21st century. Given here are excerpts from the manifesto)

OUR VISION, OUR COMMITMENT

Destined Vehicle of Change

Even as this century draws to a close and the millennium turns, India stands at a critical crossroad of history. Centuries old hopes and aspirations of our people yearn for a true expression. The destiny of our land and its people cries for fulfilment. At such crucial turns historical choices are made and instruments of change adopted. That destined vehicle of change is the Bharatiya Janata Party.

Never before in the long history of our land has the country been governed by such a morally rudderless and financially corrupt regime. Seldom have our trusting people been duped by a baser band. With the people's hopes belied and their aspirations thwarted, our ancient land stands today face to face with the option of a real change, a chance for a true departure from the last 50 years of Congress misrule, an alternative and an option: the Bharatiya Janata Party.

Our people are looking towards the BJP to become just this instrument of change. The party is ready to shoulder this great duty and responsibility. The task is nothing short of rekindling the lamp of our eternal *Dharma*, that *Sanatan* thought which our sages bequeathed to mankind—a social system based on compassion, cooperation, justice, freedom, equality and tolerance.

To realise this goal, the BJP will launch a new social, economic and political order. It will strive to transform the existing system of governance, to make it responsive and answerable to the concerns of our citizens. It will strive to make the economy cater to the largest demands of the largest number. The party will endeavour to place in the service of the nation a political organisation that is conscientous and clean. Above all, the BJP will secure for India a place in the comity of nations which befits its vast cultural, intellectual, economic, scientific and human wealth.

We realise that correcting the mistakes of the last 50 years of Congress misrule, of piecing together the shattered dreams of our citizens, of restructuring our polity which has been delivered a body blow by the present regime, of restoring the state's authority and reviving faith in the Government, is by no means an easy task. But we also realise that only the BJP has the ideological commitment, moral conviction and political courage to shoulder this task and gently guide our nation into the next millennium. The present millennium began with the subjugation of our ancient land; let a reinvigorated, proud, prosperous and strong India herald the next millennium.

In this noble mission, we shall be guided by our Manifesto—it contains our commitments to the nation and its citizens. Our State Governments in Uttar Pradesh, Himachal Pradesh, Madhya Pradesh, Maharashtra, Rajasthan, Gujarat and Delhi have demonstrated that for the BJP, these commitments constitute a sacred covenant with the people. We do what we say. This Manifesto shall be the covenant of a BJP Government at the Centre. Hindutva, or cultural nationalism, shall be the rainbow which will bridge our present to our glorious past and pave the way for an equally glorious future: the building of a prosperous and strong India, a country where every citizen regards this land of ours, this Bharatbhoomi, that stretches from the Indus to the seas, as his sacred motherland.

The BJP believes in one nation, one people, one culture. We are, therefore, committed to promoting social reconciliation rather than conflict. We are resolved to put an end to the politics of competitive communalism, of appeasement, and of casteism. The politics of pitting caste against caste, community against community and class against class has torn asunder our social fabric. The BJP will reweave this fabric into a harmonious pattern.

To translate this Manifesto into reality, to fulfil our destined role of leading India into the next millennium, the Bharatiya Janata Party seeks the support and cooperation of all our citizens.

A New Direction, A New Dispensation

Nearly half a century of Congress misrule has all but shattered the internal polity of the country. There is not one institution of the Republic left that can be said now to be in a state of total health. The Legislature, the Executive, unfortunately the Judiciary and even the media have been afflicted by the mindlessness of the Congress' exploitation and loot of our country.

The Bharatiya Janata Party well recognises that to correct this great wrong of the past five decades requires the skill and commitment of a Vishwakarma. With humility, we address ourselves to this task.

The first is to restore to our State its authority. Perhaps never since the scourge of the Pindaries has the writ of our State been as enfeebled as by Congress misrule. The primary task, therefore, is to restore to the State, and to governance, its honour and its prestige—*izzat* and *iqbal*. For this the BJP will institute a set of measures. This is a challenge that is principally moral and only then functional. The BJP commits itself, therefore, to:

1. Addressing purposefully the many challenges being posed to us in Jammu & Kashmir and in the north-east of India. We are of the view that in both these strategically important border regions of the country, misgovernance, neglect and emotional separation from India lie at the root of the problems. Terrorism and challenges to the State will be met forthrightly; changes in law where warranted will be brought about expeditiously; the approach will be firm but always fair.

2. Launching a major nationwide drive to identify influx of illicit arms and their possession. Proliferation of small arms affects directly the law and order in the country as also the security of the nation. We recognise that narcotics smuggling and narco-terrorism are linked. The country must be rid of both. The law in this regard will be made more effective and implemented.
3. Toning up the administration (as enumerated subsequently) and reforming its functioning, accountability and responsiveness.
4. Rationalising the number, structure, composition and role of paramilitary forces, including recent initiatives like National Security Guard (NSG), Rapid Action Force (RAF) and Special Protection Group (SPG). We will review the personal security arrangements: We believe that the security of the high dignitaries of the country is the responsibility of the State. This security, however, should neither be exaggerated nor intrusive. It should not ever be at the cost of the collective convenience of the citizens of the country. The BJP will reform this.

AN AGENDA FOR CHANGE

Constitutional Reforms

The BJP believes that Centre-State relations, which have been on a downslide for the past 50 years, need to be improved. We also believe that reforms are needed for a stronger Union and equal rights for all citizens.

1. The BJP will implement the main recommendations of the Sarkaria Commission, such as:
   (a) Restoring the balance of resources in favour of the States;
   (b) Ending the misuse of Art. 356 to dismiss State Governments and dissolve State Assemblies. We will explore the possibility of making it mandatory for the Union Government to seek Parliament's approval by two-thirds majority for dismissal of State Governments; and,
   (c) Consulting State Governments before appointing Governors.

2. We promise to carve out Uttaranchal, Vananchal, Vidarbha and Chattisgarh and give them full Statehood. We will further consider setting up a Commission to examine the formation of smaller States. Delhi will be given full Statehood.
3. The BJP will provide Jammu, Kashmir and Ladakh in J & K State with regional development councils.
4. We will abrogate Article 370 of the Constitution, which puts Jammu & Kashmir on a separate and separatist pedestal, for the State's full and final integration with the Union.
5. We will set up an inter-State council under Article 263 of the Constitution to settle all inter-State and Centre-State disputes to avoid ad hoc responses to issues like that of Cauvery waters.
6. The BJP is committed to Article 44 of the Constitution. We will adopt a Uniform Civil Code which will be applicable to every community and foster a common Bharatiya identity, apart from ensuring gender equality. Regressive personal laws will cease to have legal validity.
7. The manner of appointment of Constitutional functionaries will be reviewed.
8. We will maintain a national register of citizens and introduce a multi-purpose identity card.

Electoral Reforms

The BJP carries a conviction that amongst the many causes that have brought the State of our polity to its present plight, a major factor is faulty elections. We will, therefore, immediately on assuming office, implement various electoral reforms. For free, fair and fearless elections, the BJP will:

1. Update and adopt the Goswami Committee report;
2. Grant statutory status to the Code of Conduct drawn up by the Election Commission and give it teeth;
3. Introduce a scheme of State-funding of candidates to all legislatures;
4. Provide suitable incentives for open, official corporate funding to all recognised political parties;
5. Undertake fresh delimitation of Lok Sabha and Assembly constituencies on the basis of the 1991 Census;

6. Make it mandatory for political parties to submit audited accounts for public scrutiny annually;
7. Examine the feasibility of introducing the list system;
8. Expedite the process of issuing identity cards to all voters and make it a mandatory requirement for voting;
9. Scrutinise all voters' lists to ensure that no legitimate voter is excluded;
10. Take steps to curb expenditure on elections by imposing a ban on advertisements, cutouts, etc;
11. Introduce electronic voting machines to hasten the process of counting;
12. Examine the possibility of simultaneous elections to Parliament, State Assemblies and Panchayats;
13. Ensure speedy and exemplary punishment for those who indulge in booth-capturing;
14. Officials found guilty of involvement in poll rigging will be given exemplary punishment;
15. Amend the anti-defection law whereby a member of any Legislature who changes parties will lose his or her membership of the House; and,
16. Prevent the misuse of Doordarshan and A.I.R. by the ruling party.

Corruption and its Cure

The BJP treats this affliction as the single greatest wrong that the Congress misrule of the past 50 years has brought about on our land. The corruption that now corrodes our country is of the spirit, it is moral, and it is also financial. The challenge thus to governance is principally of setting an example—of impeccable probity and unimpeccable accountability of all public men and women. This must not cover simply the elected representatives of the people but also the executive, the police and, indeed, even the judiciary, where the touch of corruption can already be felt. The BJP will address itself to this challenge and task, by adopting measures that are mentioned hereunder. We do not claim that this is either the ultimate blueprint for the reduction of corruption or the last word on it. It is an expression of our commitment; a first step to setting right a very great wrong of many years' malignancy; a beginning and that, too, with ourselves. For a clean public life in which morality and ethics find due recognition, the BJP will:

1. Make it obligatory on every elected representative to make public his entire income and wealth within 90 days of election;
2. Introduce extensive regulations and requirements upon those who hold public office so that no conflict of interest in ever permitted to influence a proper discharge of their duties;
3. Appoint a Lok Pal to entertain complaints of corruption against anybody holding public office, including the Prime Minister;
4. Take measures to modify and reform the methodology of Government approval for contracts, schemes and large money value agreements so as to make them more transparent. The powers of patronage, the right to say 'Yes' or 'No' to simple daily requirements of the citizens will be reduced drastically. A Government that intrudes the least, we hold, governs the best. We will endeavour to combine this with open and transparent governance;
5. Expeditiously deal with cases of corruption unresolved and in which no action has been taken in the past 10 years;
6. Take steps to ensure that investigative and intelligence agencies like RAW, IB and CBI are not used to subserve the political designs of the ruling party.

Judicial Reforms

For speedy, fair and inexpensive justice, the BJP will:

1. Appoint special judges to clear the huge arrears at all levels of the judiciary;
2. Fill the vacancies in the High Courts and the Supreme Court without any further delay;
3. Legislate to the effect that courts do not give unending adjournments and complete cases within one year;
4. Constantly review the salaries and pension benefits of all judges so as to attract the best legal talent to the Judiciary;
5. Expand and strengthen the existing legal aid facilities for economically weaker sections of society; and,
6. Set up a National Judicial Commission which will be responsible for making judicial appointments in the High Courts and the Supreme Court.

Panchayati Raj

For better local self-governance at the village-level, the BJP will:

1. In the light of recent experience, make changes in the Constitution 73rd and 74th amendments to further strengthen the Panchayati Raj system; and,
2. Endeavour to make the panchayats financially self-sufficient.

Administrative Reforms

For a caring, just and accountable administration, to provide high quality services the citizens value, and for a new paradigm in public administration, the BJP will:

1. Make the district administration accountable for any outbreak of violence; institute a time-bound inquiry; publish the findings; punish the guilty; and, compensate the victims;
2. Update and implement the National Police Commission report in a time bound manner;
3. Ask each Ministry/ Department to set clear performance standards, including cost consciousness, in quantifiable terms and monitor the adherence to these standards;
4. Introduce a scheme of fixed minimum tenure for some identified posts at higher ranks, e.g. Chief Secretaries, Secretaries to Government, DGPs, etc;
5. Disfavour extensions to bureaucrats and police officers;
6. Institute an annual Sardar Patel award for the best three district officers, as a beginning;
7. Ensure uniform housing and other related facilities for officers in the same grade and in the same station. The system of allotment of houses will be made transparent;
8. Introduce a system of allowing lateral entry of personnel; from the private sector, NGOs, educational/research institutes into Government;
9. Identify areas from which Government must withdraw so that departments can be wound up in a phased manner;
10. Strengthen the department of administrative reforms at the Centre and in the States; and,
11. Give the citizens what is their due. A huge divide today separates the citizen, the society and the State. This is prin-

cipally on account of the State not treating the rights of the citizens as sacrosanct; not fulfilling its obligations towards the citizens sincerely; and, not providing to the citizens the services that are its bounden duty. The BJP will, therefore, identify such areas as warrant immediate correction, as they affect the daily life of the ordinary citizen, and implement reforms in them within a given timeframe.

Shri Rama Mandir at Ayodhya

The BJP is committed to the concept of one nation, one people, one culture—our nationalist vision is not merely bound by the geographical or political identity of India, but defined by our ancient cultural heritage. From this belief flows our faith in 'Cultural Nationalism' which is the core of Hindutva. That, we believe, is the identity of our ancient nation—Bharatvarsha.

Hindutva is a unifying principle which alone can preserve the unity and integrity of our nation. It is a collective endeavour to protect and re-energise the soul of India, to take us into the next millennium as a strong and prosperous nation. Hindutva is also the antidote to the shameful efforts of any section to benefit at the expense of others.

We hold that only by recognising the limitless strength of cultural nationalism, can the nation be moulded. When the BJP joined the movement for the construction of the Shri Rama Mandir at Ayodhya, it was to strengthen just these foundations.

On coming to power, the BJP Government will facilitate the construction of a magnificent Shri Rama Mandir at Janmasthan in Ayodhya which will be a tribute to Bharat Mata. This dream moves millions of people in our land; the concept of Rama lies at the core of their consciousness.

OUR ECONOMY AND DIRECTION

Economic Growth and Employment Through Swadeshi

Four decades of Congress misrule have ruined the economic creativity of our country; these decades failed to place the country on a sound economic footing, befitting India's stature as the largest democracy in the world. The experiments of the Congress, with vastly divergent models, have brought the country, from time to time, to the brink of crisis. The passive victim of all these experiments has been the long suffering citizens of our country; even as under-nourishment, malnutrition, illiteracy and deprivation afflict a large percentage of them; even as the quality of life gets fractured between India and Bharat.

We commit ourselves to bringing certainty in economic policy. The Bharatiya Janata Party is proud of India's heritage and has an abiding faith in the creative genius of every Indian. We are committed to an economy that enables India to achieve its destiny in the forefront of the nations of the world.

In 1991, the present Government claimed that it inherited an economy which had slender foreign exchange reserves. Accepting IMF conditionalities, it initiated a programme of deregulation of Industry, trade and exchange rate policies, a radically different approach to foreign investment. The consequential foreign exchange reserves that it will be leaving, as a legacy to the successor government, are, however, fragile, being composed mainly of quick-sand components of foreign institutional investments and FCNR deposits. Foreign direct investment (FDI) is only a minor component of them. An enormous $ 7 billion becomes ripe for debt servicing in 1996-97 itself. In its zeal to contain fiscal deficit--a task in which it failed, the fiscal deficit continuing around 7% of GDP—it pruned developmental expenditure beyond acceptable limits, in consequence constraining growth.

Despite the proclaimed deregulation, over the past five years, all earlier structures and institutions of the License-Quota-Permit Raj remain intact. Social infrastructure has been neglected and the lot of the poor and deprived has further deteriorated. The country's defence requirements were also neglected, thereby putting the nations' security in jeopardy.

The neglect of infrastructure by this Government has left a legacy of a fractured physical infrastructure—roads, railways, post, power, telecom—are grinding to near immobility, in the process constraining growth elsewhere in the economy. In its methodology for containing the budget through limits on monetisation of the deficit, this Government has compulsorily resorted to heavy borrowings, which in turn has resulted in illiquidity to the rest of the economy and a heating up of the interest rates. Our domestic industry, starved of liquidity, is in danger of slipping into recession.

In totality, this Government will leave an economy more fragile and shattered than what it inherited in 1991. The challenges thus, to us in our bid at governance, are formidable.

Our Economic Thought

In outlining our strategy, we recognise that the post-Cold War world has adopted the market place for fast economic growth. However, our thought is defined by the following:

(i) Market may ensure growth, but it cannot ensure redistributive equity and justice. The state continues to have a role to play;

(ii) The poor and deprived have, therefore, to be helped by the State to cross the poverty line and to attain a sustainable minimum quality of life;

(iii) On the economic front, the old order, based on comparative advantage of labour or resources, is giving way to a new order built on the basis of human resources, skills and technology. A proper policy can make it India's strength; and,

(iv) A society such as ours has to innovate its own strategy, to adapt itself to the high-tech challenges of a supposedly borderless world, without the attendant social stresses, economic instability and the abandonment either of its identity or of its own socio-cultural ethos. This is the essence of our Swadeshi approach: A self-reliant India, asserting its national economic interests, not as autarchy, but as a pre-requisite to meeting the challenge of globalisation; of preserving our identity without compromising our sovereignty or self-respect. We reject unbridled consumerism and believe in adherance to sustainable consumption and growth.

Foreign investment will be required and encouraged for world class technology. But when foreign savings have to supplement and assist the economy in circumstances where domestic savings are inadequate, we compromise with the nation's long term interests. While many countries which started late but arrived much earlier than India, managed their growth on savings levels around 35-40% of GDP, the Indian domestic savings rate has steadily declined to a low level of 20% of GDP during Congress rule. This is grossly inadequate for even the current level of investment, let alone the levels required for a faster growth of the economy. Not only have private savings declined, more worrisomely, governmental savings are now virtually nil.

We recognise two immediate priorities—first, providing the physical and economic infrastructure that is appropriate for the stipulated growth in our GDP; second, providing the required social infrastructure for a minimum sustainable quality of life.

To attain these and yet contain fiscal deficit requires a different approach. The BJP will work towards pruning non-developmental expenditure; minimise the commercial activities of Government; severely cutting back on bureaucracy; shedding the structures of controls and regulation; and re-equipping itself for its new role of providing a framework for free market operations for growth, accentuating programmes for poverty eradication and social infrastructure.

Fiscal Reform and Taxation

We believe that taxation alone cannot be the base for revenue. A stable and fast growth is possible only through a high order of investment matched by an appropriate level of domestic savings. The present Government has done a great disservice by encouraging avoidable consumerism and diverting the depleted savings into speculative rather than safe and productive channels.

- We will structure our fiscal reforms so that savings and contracted savings are augmented to levels that will take care of a higher order of investment needed for faster growth.
- In taxation, we will ensure that not only levels and rates of taxation are such that growth is not constrained, but that the burden-sharing of taxes is equitably distributed among all affluent sections of society. We will mitigate the undue rigours of indirect taxes—today indirect taxes constitute 71% of tax revenue-so that productivity and growth are not hampered.
- We will devise a suitably structured valued added tax (VAT)

so as to ensure better burden-sharing among goods and services that contribute to value addition.

- In tariffs we will ensure that the domestic sector gets a level playing field, and does not become uncompetitive.
- We will also strive to lighten the debt burden on the nation. This in turn will contribute to interest rate stabilisation.
- We will not hike Excise Duties on items of mass consumption.
- We will examine the aspect of sales tax reform and equalisation.
- We will ensure operational autonomy of the RBI.
- We will adopt firm measures to prevent the generation of black money.
- We will rationalise and simplify the present tax structure and raise the Income Tax exemption limit to Rs. 60,000.
- We will provide weighted deductions taking number of dependents on earning member.
- We will exempt all investments in approved organisations, private or public, from the levy of Wealth Tax.
- We will give tax reliefs to employment-oriented industries in non-municipal areas.
- We will ensure minimum contribution to Government exchequer by all profit-earning business units. The concept of "zero business units" will be done away with.
- We will give special tax concessions to writers, artists, academics and others engaged in intellectual and cultural pursuits.

Price Stability and Consumer Protection

It is our firm belief that the price level can be controlled only through maximisation of production and a minimisation of costs of production. This is to be achieved through technology upgradation, economics of scale and free competition. Towards this end, the BJP will:

- Ensure an efficient, low-cost, corruption-free Public Distribution System (PDS), so that there is a regular, assured, timely and adequate supply of commodities to the consumers in the rural, tribal, remote and backward areas of our country;

- Supply better quality foodgrains through the PDS by enhancing the quality standards rather than easing them as has been done by the Congress.
- Make pulses, cooking oil and soap also available through PDS, in addition to foodgrains, sugar and kerosene;
- Improve the Consumer Protection Act of 1986, and ensure its application; and,
- Encourage consumer movements.

Black Money and Corruption

Starting from its Jana Sangh days, the BJP has been waging a relentless battle against the twin evils of corruption and black money. We are committed to rooting out corruption, thus also the malignancy of black money.

- We will encourage capital creation through funds from such a parallel economy, retaining the right of Government to tax the revenue flows from created capital so created.
- The BJP will open up sectors such as social forestry, wasteland development and housing for rural and urban poor.
- We will also review, in this context, the rationale of the Urban Land Ceiling Act.

Infrastructure

We hold that power, telecommunications, transport (surface, sea and air) constitute the basic building blocks of our development. With hardly 50% of the roads surfaced, about 40% of the traffic volume is handled by the National Highway System (NHS) which constitutes hardly 2% of the road network.

- Our Railway network has grown by only 16% over five decades. The ports have become the greatest constraint on our world trade. The power and telecommunications situation cripple development.
- We need to actively develop a National Waterways network.
- To meet our minimum needs, a staggering 10,000 MW have to be added annually for the next 15 years. Irrigation needs press upon our resources. All these call for large investments.
- We propose, therefore, to lay the foundations of a strong bond market in the country which can take care of the mas-

sive financial requirements. We invite foreign capital in the field of infrastructure.

- We will initiate a framework which will facilitate quick redressal of the acute infrastructure crisis based on international co-operation and partnership.
- We will strive to confine the role of the state to that of a facilitator, withdrawing in favour of suitably structured independent regulatory authorities.

Public Sector

Currently the policy relating to public sector is in disarray.

- The BJP believes in confining the public sector to sensitive areas where the nation's security is involved and to areas where the presence of public sector is necessary for providing a moderating or counter-poising role to the ill effects, if any, of an unchecked private sector.
- Public sector presence will continue in areas furthering social objectives.
- The public sector will be managed with the least interference by Government.

A Disinvestment Commission will be constituted for disinvestment from ailing, non-profitable or sick public sector undertakings.

- While disinvesting, care will be taken so that the workers' interests are not harmed.
- The National Renewal Fund will be realigned to take care of the constant requirements of retraining and redeployment of workers that may be necessary in a fast growing economy.
- Sales proceeds from PSU disinvestment will be utilised only for capital expenditure.

Foreign Trade and Capital

Foreign Trade Policy has degenerated into one of providing palliatives. It is now necessary to strengthen the interface between industry and foreign trade.

- We will select core industries and a system of destinations and initiate production planning for export with selective intervention so that this sector, so vital to the economy, acquires dynamism.

- We will also strive to forge such alliances with or membership of regional trading blocs as will give further impetus to our exports.

The BJP welcomes foreign investment, because we hold that it supplies knowledge, technology and know-how and sharpens the quality and competitive edge of our economy.

- We will, however, strive to minimise our dependence on foreign savings.
- We will prioritise foreign investment in sectors that will promote exports in preference to sectors that will cater solely or exclusively to the domestic market.
- Keeping in view that dissemination of world class technology is an objective of foreign investment, we will give preference to overseas investors who have domestic partners.
- We will encourage foreign investment in infrastructure, areas of high technology and R & D within India.
- As for MNCs in consumer non-durables, we do not consider them as areas of priority.

Industrial Policy

Industry in India has to be enabled to become more productive, more innovative. Only then will it fulfil its main role: enhance the national wealth, provide greater employment in ever increasing numbers and thus assist the growth of other sectors, including agriculture. We recognise this inseparable interdependence. Our exports must compete with the best in the world, add to our resources and fiscal health, and thus enable India to achieve the status that we believe is its destiny. The BJP assures all about creating a healthy investment and industrial environment.

The BJP believes in the continued role and relevance of the small-scale sector. This important segment of our national economy, which has been entirely ignored by the Congress and whose very existence is threatened by the present policy of economic liberalisation, will receive all encouragement and help from a BJP Government.

The following principles will guide the industrial policy of the BJP:

A. Economic Sovereignty

The party regards the preservation of the nation's economic interests as a component of our external economic relations. Globalisation, to us, is not a synonym for the obliteration of national economic interests. Indeed, in the ensuing global competition we need to be constantly mindful of preserving them.

B. Modernisation

BJP stands for a modern and progressive India, open to new ideas, new technology and fresh capital. A modern India to the BJP is not a Westernised India; a pale copy of the Western economic models.

C. Decentralisation

We stand for a decentralised economic order. The BJP stands for political as well as economic democracy. The role of the Government must change from the restrictive to the supportive and encouraging.

The BJP will therefore:

- Debureaucratise industrial approvals and cut down the plethora of restrictive controls. Industrial Development and Regulations Act will be replaced by Industrial Development Act;
- Encourage research and development as part of the process of industrial growth and over-all modernisation;
- Hazardous industries will be permitted only in specified areas. Separate industrial satellites will be set up exclusively for such units;
- Small-scale sector will be given all importance and encouragement. We will establish agencies to help the small-scale sector in purchasing, marketing and selling their products; and,
- Ensure a healthy capital market.

OUR CONCEPT OF EMPLOYMENT AND LABOUR'S ROLE

Creating Jobs and Opportunities

Apart from employment which will be created in the normal course by the growth of the economy, special employment schemes will be undertaken by the Bharatiya Janata Party to eradicate unemployment.

The BJP proposes to introduce a scheme of voluntary National Service to undertake the task of national reconstruction and also in order to instill a sense of discipline and nationalism among the youth of the country. This service will aim at reclaiming waste land for commercial use—for instance, after reclaiming the waste land, it will be used for horticulture, social forestry or any other purpose that will provide the youth involved in the reclamation with continued income. Similarly, the National Service will be used for river management schemes.

Apart from this, the BJP proposes to:

1. Increase employment opportunities in all sectors of the organised economy;
2. Introduce policies and programmes to:
   (i) Develop agriculture, particularly in regions which are at present less developed and backward.
   (ii) Promote industrial growth with special attention to village, cottage and small-scale sectors. Special emphasis will be laid on agro-industry.
   (iii) Undertake large-scale housing activity that will generate both jobs and additional shelter in both rural and urban areas.
   (iv) Provide transport facilities with special emphasis in improving availability of transport in rural areas.
   (v) Augment employment opportunities in villages through schemes like Antyodaya, Gokul Gram, Gopal Gram, Saraswati Yojana as already being implemented by BJP governments in Rajasthan and Gujarat.
   (vi) Provide and improve infrastructure, especially in rural areas, such as roads, small dams and water conservation projects.
   (vii) Promote vocational training.

Labour

BJP believes in healthy trade unionism. It will:

1. Rationalise and simplify Labour Laws;
2. Recognise unions on the basis of secret ballot and have provisions for comprehensive bargaining;

3. Introduce worker participation from the shop floor to the board room in all public sector projects, public limited companies and foreign companies operating in India;
4. Protect workers against inflation;
5. Evolve an effective mechanism and ensure better implementation of laws to protect labour from occupational health hazards arising from industries like asbestos, cement, slate, mica, chemicals, textiles, etc. The workers will have the right to be informed about the possible health hazards they could be exposed to on the shop floor; and,
6. Not allow an exit policy without fulfilling corresponding obligations towards labour.

Government Employees

BJP will set up a permanent Employees Welfare Board with a view to resolving the long-standing problems related to:

1. Time scale promotion;
2. Revision of pay scales and award of bonus;
3. Implementation of awards;
4. Housing; and,
5. Social welfare measures and travel concession for retired personnel.

OUR SCIENTIFIC TALENT, OUR TECHNOLOGY

Harnessing Nature for Human Welfare

The BJP believes that science and technology must play its due role in transforming India into a prosperous and strong country. The BJP will apply appropriate scientific and technological methods for increasing productivity, eradicating poverty, hunger and disease and providing meaningful employment along with the basic amenities of life. We believe that science and technology need to be harnessed to improve the lot of the vast section of our population living below the poverty line. We hold that science is not merely harnessing nature for material wealth but is as well for liberating and enriching the mind and enlarging the human spirit. The BJP will use science in the service of the poor and develop technology that has a humane face. Towards this end, we will:

1. Foster a scientific temper among the people;
2. Use science and technology for increasing productivity and generating employment;
3. Implement a vigorous programme of science education and research for improving quality of life;
4. Establish a network of centres for application of science and technology to rural areas, implement "lab-to-land" programmes and develop a strong low-cost agro-industrial base;
5. Put new life into National Laboratories to develop them as centres of excellence in applied research;
6. Direct these laboratories to evolve appropriate technology for Indian needs;
7. Accelerate the production of scientific literature in regional languages and evolve a national terminology for science and technology;
8. Create the right working conditions for our best brains to remain in India and serve the country and not migrate to other lands;
9. Make a systematised effort to bring national laboratories and industry together by setting up Technology Parks to be patronised by industry. This will promote cooperation between industry's resources and talent in laboratory;
10. Safeguard national interests and our intellectual property rights by encouraging research and development;
11. Undertake research in the field of drugs, micro-biology, biotechnology, bio-fertilisers etc.; and,
12. Strengthen research in indigenous systems of medicine.

OUR FOREIGN POLICY

India, the New Millennium, the World

In a post-Cold War world India will be confronted by many new challenges and opportunities. To meet them, to benefit from the opportunities, mindful of the existing global disequilibrium and in consonance with India's national interests, our foreign policy in the emerging decades will be based on the human values of peace, equality and cooperation.

The BJP holds that as a departure from the recent past, Indian diplomacy should be conducted in tune with India's position as a strong power and a major player in the world arena. A billion people who do not depend upon anyone for feeding or clothing themselves are a power which cannot be ignored. Our nation needs to regain its lost pride and the BJP alone can undertake this task. While we believe in partnership with everyone, we reject the very thought of patronage by anybody. The BJP's foreign policy will be guided by the following agenda:

1. Sovereign equality amongst nations; a rejection of political or economic hegemonism.
2. Promotion of Asian solidarity; development of South Asian Regional Cooperation; and, emphasis on improved relations with neighbouring countries. The BJP does not accept outside interference in this region as being beneficial for it.
3. Pakistan continues to follow a policy of fomenting insurgency, seeking to create instability and unrest in India. The BJP stands committed to thwarting all these attempts. In this context, we state:
   (a) The BJP affirms unequivocally India's sovereignty over the whole of Jammu & Kashmir, including Pakistan-Occupied Kashmir; and,
   (b) The BJP declares that it will not accept any interference in our country's internal affairs.
4. Our relations with the USA will be based on mutual respect and a congruence of interests. We note, however, that US policy for this region continues to suffer from lack of vision and that it disregards India's political and security interests.
5. India and Russia have a long tradition of good relations and have much to gain from the compatibility of their geo-political interests in Asia. The BJP will endeavour to further explore the avenues of bilateral cooperation in this direction.
6. Our relations with the People's Republic of China offer an opportunity to put them now on a footing of friendship and cooperation. For this we need to resolve the border question in a fair and equitable manner. It cannot, however, be ignored that the People's Republic of China continues to support Pakistan militarily and otherwise.

7. The BJP greatly regrets the continuing bloodshed in Sri Lanka, particularly as India all through its history has had warm fraternal ties with all sections of the population in that country. The BJP is confident that within a united Sri Lanka it should be possible to fulfil the aspirations of the Tamil people.
8. The BJP pledges to maintain warm and friendly relations with Nepal, with which India has the closest cultural, religious and historical ties. The BJP will work actively for resolving all outstanding issues. We welcome the restoration of democracy in Nepal.
9. The BJP views with great sympathy the struggle for restoration of democracy in Myanmar. It extends its support to the task of reconciliation and reconstruction in that country with which India has a long border and age-old religious, cultural and historical ties.
10. The BJP will try to consolidate further the close and friendly ties between India and Bhutan.
11. In our relations with Bangladesh, illegal immigration into India from that country has proved a major irritant. This issue has cast its shadow on our bilateral ties and needs to be resolved early.
12. Millions of sons and daughters of Mother India, settled abroad as Overseas Indians, are considered by the BJP as an asset to the country. Their emotional attachment to the motherland is still deep. This must find due expression. Schemes will be drawn up to attract substantial investments by non-resident Indians. They will be welcome to set up industrial units and industrial parks, and invest in the infrastructure. The BJP will examine afresh the issue of dual citizenship.
13. The BJP will launch a vigorous campaign for a permanent membership for India in the UN Security Council.

The BJP stands committed to peace amongst all nations; prosperity for all the peoples of the world; and, an international role for India that befits this great and ancient nation.

OUR NATION'S SECURITY

Protecting Our Country

The BJP accords the highest importance to the security of our nation, our society and our citizens. We charge the present Government with imperilling our security, internal and external, as never before.

Our defence expenditure has been cut steadily in real terms during the Narasimha Rao regime. This has seriously compromised our combat effectiveness. The present Congress Government has been functioning without a full-time Defence Minister for over three years, and this negligence of India's sword arm has begun to effect the morale of our gallant forces.

The BJP will correct this damaging imbalance. We will accord due importance to all security-related issues—the emerging global realities and regional complexities demand this as the very minimum response from our Government.

Internal Security

The nature of the state and its relationship with society has a direct bearing on the level of the citizens' national commitment. An insensitive and uncaring state erodes the citizens' allegiance to the nation. The BJP will restore national commitment to its rightful place by establishing a harmonious relationship between State and society. We will:

1. Defuse tension in long-festering trouble spots;
2. Ensure protection of life and property from insurgents and foreign mercenaries;
3. Provide our security apparatus with a free hand to deal with terrorism;
4. Revitalise and reinforce law and order machinery;
5. Institute police reforms and upgrade the capability of the force; and,
6. Legislate tough deterrent laws against terrorist and disruptive activities (TADA was repealed to pander to vote bank politics) while safeguarding democratic rights.

Jammu & Kashmir

The absence of political far-sightedness and clarity of national objectives has resulted in our nation continuing to have to pay a price even 50 years after Jammu & Kashmir became a part of the Republic. The failure of successive Congress Governments to formulate a Jammu & Kashmir policy that takes into account the State's internal problems has led to a situation where this strategic border State has emerged as the principal challenge to Indian nationhood. The BJP realises the magnitude of the challenge and dedicates itself to the task of not only solving the internal problems of the State but also reclaiming the portion of our territory which has been illegally held by Pakistan for nearly five decades. Without repeating the mistakes of yester-years and merely reacting to Pakistan's moves, we will:

1. Immediately strengthen the civil administration by inducting able and honest administrators;
2. Provide a free hand to our security forces to deal with the menace of terrorism and induction of men and arms from Pakistan, while ensuring that democratic rights are not violated;
3. Cleanse the local police and administration of malcontents who have aligned themselves with the terrorists or are pro-Pakistan;
4. Declare Doda a disturbed area and invoke the Armed Forces (Special Powers) Act to prevent this district from becoming a haven for mercenaries and terrorists;
5. Launch a massive welfare programme for all regions of the State and ensure there is no seepage;
6. Hold free and fair elections in the State after terrorism has been brought under control and every person, including the Pandits who have been forced out of the Valley, is provided with an opportunity to participate in the polls;
7. Rehabilitate all persons displaced from terrorism-afflicted areas of Jammu & Kashmir; and,
8. Set up regional councils for Kashmir, Jammu and Ladakh.

North-East

The north-eastern States of our country continue to suffer from the violence perpetrated by insurgency and ethnic strife. Poor governance, a callous administration, seepage of development funds, and Congress' politics of manipulation have contributed to the alienation of the people and the growth of insurgency. In Assam, ULFA and Bodo militants have begun to strike with regularity; in Nagaland and Manipur the NSCN continues with its depredation; and, in Tripura, militant tribal outfits have once again reared their ugly heads. The tide of illegal immigration from Bangladesh has only worsened the situation. The BJP will address itself to the problems of our north-eastern States and institute a grievance redressal system monitored from Delhi. It will also take the following steps to restore the rule of law in the troubled States:

1. Check the inflow of foreign arms and terrorists from training camps across the border;
2. Strengthen the security apparatus and intelligence network;
3. Provide all citizens with identity cards on a priority basis;
4. Check the narcotics trade and attendant ills in the region; and,
5. Plan and execute an integrated and accelerated economic development programme.

Himalayas

Over the past five decades, our Himalayan bastions have been strategically pierced. Despite that, the attitude of successive Congress governments has remained unchanged: Strategically, the Government has failed to restore a balance there, leave alone regain the initiative. In the process, we have also lost large national territories to the People's Republic of China, demonstrating an absence of strategic thought about our Himalayan bastions. The BJP will evolve a security policy for the Himalayas so that India's national interests are fully safeguarded.

External Security

We believe that pro-active diplomacy, especially defence diplomacy, coupled with adequate preparedness of our armed forces, is the key to securing our frontiers against aggression. This requires both strategy and tactics. The BJP will:

1. Set up a National Security Council;
2. Re-evaluate the country's nuclear policy and exercise the option to induct nuclear weapons;
3. Though the BJP stands committed to a nuclear-free world, we cannot accept a world of nuclear apartheid.

(i) The BJP will thus not agree to the Comprehensive Test Ban Treaty (CTBT) unless there is a simultaneous agreement for a time-bound global elimination of nuclear weapons in their entirety.

(ii) The BJP will not agree to the Fissile Material Control Regime (FMCR).

(iii) The BJP will not agree to the Missile Technology Control Regime (MTCR).

4. Expedite the serial production of Prithvi and make Agni I operational for the deployment of these missiles. In addition, hasten the development of Agni II;
5. Immediately upgrade conventional weapons and weapons systems of the armed forces;
6. Strengthen the intelligence-gathering system, inclusive of all intelligence agencies, initiate a Centre-State initiative on intelligence gathering and sharing, step up air surveillance of our territory, and acquire state-of-the-art electronic equipment;
7. Strengthen the Air Force fleet with new generation aircraft;
8. Make a qualitative and quantitative improvement in our naval capabilities;
9. Invest in R & D in areas of defence and missile technology so that we become increasingly self-reliant;
10. Peg defence-related expenditure to real requirements; and,
11. Re-examine the role, structure and composition of the numerous para-military forces and reorganise and reform them.

Jai Jawan

The BJP is rightly proud of our valiant soldiers who have dedicated their lives to defend our nation from external aggressors and internal subversives. We believe it is our duty to take care of our serving jawans and look after those who have retired from service, as well as their families. To fulfil this duty, the BJP will adopt the following programmes and policies:

1. The terms of service, including pay and allowance, housing, education for children and pension, of all ranks will be improved so as to attract men and women of high calibre. The present shortage of men and officers does not have to be met by lowering standards of entry;

2. Widows and dependents of jawans who die in action will receive higher benefits and compensation;
3. Pension disparities will be levelised and anomalies sorted out expeditiously;
4. Hospitals for veterans will be set up throughout the country so that no ex-serviceman, irrespective of his rank, is denied medical care;
5. Ex-servicemen's welfare will be included in the concurrent list;
6. The services of our retired soldiers will be used to the maximum extent possible, especially in insurgency-affected areas. Wherever there is a stipulated percentage for employing ex-servicemen, it will be fulfilled;
7. Necessary changes will be made in agricultural and urban tenancy laws to secure the proprietary rights of servicemen; and,
8. District Sainik Boards will be strengthened.

Illegal Immigration: A Threat to Our Security

We believe that illegal immigration from our neighbouring countries, especially Bangladesh, has a direct impact on our nation's security and has an unsettling effect on our demography. Given the sheer dimension of numbers—there are as many as 1.7 crore illegal immigrants, the bulk of them Bangladeshis, living in various parts of the country—illegal immigration is not only transforming the geography, but the sociology, the economy, indeed even the politics of this country. India is facing an explosive issue. If our demographic balance is allowed to be disturbed by inept policies and political considerations, various demographic entities are bound to come in conflict, thus adversely affecting our security environment. The invasion of illegal immigrants from Bangladesh has led to an alarming growth in a section of the population in our North-East, in Assam, in West Bengal, parts of Bihar and Delhi. In certain areas, a section of the population has grown by almost 100 per cent.

The BJP proposes to :

1. Complete barbed wire fencing along the India-Bangladesh border, beginning with the plains, to prevent infiltration;

2. Detect illegal immigrants, delete their names from voters' lists and arrange for their deportation without any further delay;
3. Declare all property deals between Indians and illegal immigrants as null and void;
4. Amend immigration rules and other laws to impose stringent checks on illegal entry into India; and,
5. Expedite the issuance of identity cards to all citizens of the country.

OUR VILLAGES, OUR FARMERS, OUR POOR

Towards a Revitalised Rural Economy

Our country has an abundance of natural resources—fertile lands, flowing rivers, rich mineral deposits and verdant forests. More than anything else, we have a large army of farmers that shoulders the onerous task of feeding our people. But the wrong priorities of the last 50 years of Congress misrule and the lopsided model of development pursued by policy-makers have impoverished vast sections of our farmers, rendering agriculture economically non-viable. Worse, bulk of the monies earmarked for infrastructural development, health, education and civic amenities has been canalised to the urban areas despite the fact that the majority of the population lives in villages.

Less than a quarter of the country's population, 23.31 per cent, lives in urban areas, compared to the overwhelming 76.69 per cent which lives in villages. As many as 71.4 per cent of our people are economically dependent on agriculture: This sector of our economy, therefore, generates the highest employment as well as provides the biggest market. Yet, this sector continues to be neglected by Congress policy-makers.

The Bharatiya Janata Party believes that India cannot emerge as a powerful nation until the lot of our farmers is improved, adequate attention paid to the agricultural sector, an all-out war launched against poverty, and investments are made in agro-industry as well as small-scale and cottage industry catering to the requirements of our villages. Our country's progress is linked to the well-being of our villages, our farmers and our poor.

Congress' Policy: Not to have a Policy on Agriculture

In the absence of any well thought out agricultural policy focussing on rural development and reconstruction, agriculture is fast becoming a losing proposition for our farmers. While fixing agricultural prices, successive Congress Governments have not taken into account the expenses incurred by our farmers on seeds, fertiliser, power, water, pesticides, machinery and labour. No effort has ever been made to bring about parity in the prices of industrial and agricultural produce.

As a result, our farmers are forced to sell the fruit of their labour at low prices even while they have to pay ever-increasing prices for the necessary inputs. Not surprisingly, this has contributed to the impoverishment and indebtedness of our farmers, pushing vast sections of them dangerously close to or even below the Poverty Line. According to the Planning Commission's own estimates, almost 42 per cent of our rural population lives below the Poverty Line.

No less alarming is the fact that the number of our villagers dependent on per acre of land has been steadily increasing, compared to other countries where this dependency has dramatically decreased with governments investing in agro-industry which offers alternative sources of employment. No effort has been made to set up an adequate number of small-scale and cottage industries in our rural areas to absorb idle hands. This has also contributed in no small measure to the impoverishment of our farmers. In 1950-51, the ratio of the disparity between the per capita income in rural and urban areas was 1:2, in 1995-96 it stood at 1:4. Similarly, while per family income has risen by 52 per cent in urban areas since 1952, it has increased by a mere 7.8 per cent in rural areas.

Ironically, these neglected villages form a vast market—and from this market, as much as Rs. 48,000 crore flow to our urban areas every year. By killing our villages, we will be destroying this market. Conversely, by developing our villages, we will be strengthening this market, which in turn will benefit our urban areas. In other words, urban India cannot survive without rural India.

But this simple truth has been ignored for the last 50 years.

Today, three out of every four Indians live in villages, condemned to a life of exploitation and increasing social, political and economic marginalisation.

BJP's AGENDA FOR OUR FARMERS, OUR POOR

We pledge to reverse this trend of social, political and economic marginalisation of our rural population and empower our farmers. We are committed to restoring agriculture to its rightful place and thus steering our people into an era of prosperity and social equality by the opening decade of the new century.

No country can be great if its people remain poor. The first task for us will be to wipe out the dark curse of poverty. We will allocate greater resources for effective poverty alleviation programmes; we will invest in agriculture and small-scale industry; we will build from the bottom up, for that is the only way we can build an enduring edifice of development.

To Develop Rural India, the BJP will :

1. Allocate 60 per cent of Plan funds for agricultural and rural development;
2. Treat villages as the basic unit of development and provide each village with basic facilities like roads, irrigation, drinking water, education, health and sanitation;
3. Provide shelter to the homeless in our villages;
4. Develop agriculture, enhance production and improve living standards in our villages by—
   (a) Fixing agricultural prices after taking into account all expenses incurred by farmers;
   (b) Reducing the per acre cost of production;
   (c) Increasing the average per acre production;
   (d) Reducing the overall dependence on agriculture;
   (e) Providing alternative employment to displaced farmers;
5. Give agriculture the same benefits as industry;
6. Set up an Agricultural Costs and Prices Commission in which farmers and agricultural specialists will together comprise two-thirds of the members. The Commission will be autonomous and its recommendations will be binding.

7. Announce the total cost of inputs, the total expenditure incurred by farmers, and thereafter announce the support prices;
8. Link support prices to the price index;
9. Ensure parity between agricultural and industrial products in respect of pricing;
10. Conduct extensive research to evolve methods of dryland farming;
11. Give priority to the farmers' interests while determining the exim policy for agricultural produce;
12. Enforce prompt payment for agricultural produce. There will be automatic interest addition to payments delayed beyond two weeks;
13. Extend crop and animal insurance to all agricultural produce. Insurance schemes will also cover natural calamities;
14. Establish a chain of warehouses with facilities for grant of advance payments of up to 80 per cent of the agricultural produce deposited;
15. Encourage the use of fruit juice in the production of all beverages;
16. Allow free movement of foodgrains throughout the country;
17. Free sugar industry from licensing, and production of molasses from all restrictions on production and movement, as well as ensure that farmers receive an adequate share of the total prices;
18. Maintain the subsidy on fertilisers;
19. Improve the Public Distribution System;
20. Establish farmers' service centres;
21. Give comprehensive documents to farmers which cover land records, ownership and all other relevant papers;
22. Reform land acquisition laws and ensure that agricultural land acquired for any purpose receives prompt and full compensation at market rates;
23. Free bonded labour and rehabilitate them; and,
24. Launch employment guarantee schemes in rural India that will cover the largest possible number of people.

To Revive Village Industry, the BJP will :

1. Establish an extensive chain of tiny and small-scale industrial units;

2. Give the greatest impetus to this sector. To make agriculture sustainable, the BJP will sharpen the edge of agro-based rural industries and food-processing;
3. Provide all facilities, including easy access to credit and marketing to rural artisans and craftsmen;
4. Set up a National Artisan Development Bank;
5. Set up special institutes for skill upgradation; and,
6. Give a thrust to wasteland development, social forestry and horticulture.

To Provide Irrigation Facilities, the BJP will:

1. Launch time-bound irrigation projects and complete ongoing projects;
2. Give priority to small and minor irrigation projects;
3. Remove disparities between districts within States;
4. Encourage the use of alternative sources of irrigation through incentives and better water management;
5. Ensure that farmers are made to pay only for the water they consume; and,
6. Draw up a master plan for flood control and harnessing of flood waters for irrigation. Offer prompt compensation for crops lost in floods.

To Provide Power for Agriculture, the BJP will:

1. Encourage rapid electrification of our villages so that no village is left without power by the turn of the century;
2. Ensure adequate supply of power for agricultural activity;
3. Set up small power stations and sub-stations in rural areas for supplying power exclusively to villages; and,
4. Electricity Boards will be made to pay compensation to farmers if they fail to supply assured quantity of power. Similarly, farmers will be required to pay their power bill on time.

To Strengthen the Cooperative Movement, the BJP will:

1. Free cooperatives from political interference;
2. Prevent the intrusion of vested interests;
3. Simplify rules and regulations governing the functioning of cooperative societies;

4. Make entry in passbooks mandatory for all money deposits;
5. Only those entirely dependent on agriculture will be allowed to become members of farmers cooperative societies; and,
6. Ensure free and timely elections to cooperative bodies.

To Implement Land Reforms, the BJP will:

1. Enforce the implementation of Land Ceiling Laws in all States;
2. Set up designated courts to expeditiously deal with all land ceiling disputes and monitor enforcement of verdicts;
3. Expedite distribution of ceiling surplus land among landless farmers;
4. Monitor the use of distributed land and prevent its alienation from beneficiaries;
5. Reclaim cultivable land lying fallow;
6. Time-bound registration of all lands; and,
7. Decide ownership rights at the level of Gram Panchayats without any delay.

To Alleviate Poverty, the BJP will:

1. Enhance public outlays for poverty alleviation and social infrastructure;
2. Restructure the PDS, confining it only to the poor and the needy. Burgeoning food stocks with a vastly reduced off take and a decline in the per capita consumption of cereals from PDS are powerful indicators of poverty rather than the misleading inflation indices. PDS prices and the regulated intervals of offtake will be suitably adjusted so that the scheme becomes meaningful for fighting hunger and malnutrition. PDS will also be dovetailed to provide 'Food for Work' in employment programmes linked with poverty eradication;
3. Identify poverty through indexation reflecting not only the level of consumption of calories but also the minimal social infrastructure status such as literacy, housing, drinking water, health and sanitation;
4. Implement 'Antyodaya' schemes throughout the country because we hold that sustainable employment is at the core of

poverty eradication. These Antyodaya schemes will be targeted at the poorest of the poor: Five crore families will be selected for immediate relief;

5. Allocate more resources for food-for-work programmes so that they can be implemented round the year, as well as monitor their implementation; and,
6. Introduce Langar Yojana and Annadan Yojana to ensure that no man, woman or child goes hungry.

To Ensure Cow Protection, the BJP will:

1. Impose a total ban on the slaughter of cows and cow progeny by amending Article 48 of the Constitution to cover bulls and bullocks, and prohibit all trading (State as well as private) in the slaughter of cows and cow progeny;
2. Implement a policy for improved cattle-breeding; and,
3. Provide tax exemption to the income of Goshalas and Pinjrapoles.

The BJP recognises the fact that from times immemorial, cow-protection has remained one of the basics of Indian culture and Indian agriculture, and it is on the patient back of the cow and its progeny that the entire structure of Indian agriculture rests. Over 70 million animals are employed in farming operations in Indian villages, more than 80% rural transport needs are met by the bullock-cart. Our livestock is also an effective protection against environmental degradation.

The BJP regretfully observes that millions of cows and cow progeny are slaughtered every year, most of them for export.

OUR HUMAN WEALTH

Literacy and Health for All

The Bharatiya Janata Party is committed to the creation of a Bharat whose citizens will not suffer from the dual affliction of illiteracy and malnutrition. We believe that the State should invest in developing every citizen's potential to contribute to the regeneration of our country. To achieve that, we will stress on health and education, both of which are challenges that have to be met by the first decade of the 21st century. India has to emerge as a powerful, self-reliant and proud nation. True development will be possible only when we draw sustenance from our citizens; they are our true wealth.

Education

The past five years have witnessed this core area of human resource development being increasingly deprived of State support. As a result, quality education is fast becoming the preserve of the social and economic elite of the country. The vast multitudes, who have been victims of inequity, continue to be denied the cherished ideal of literacy. The BJP will stress on providing equal opportunity of education, literacy and information. Towards this end, we will:

1. Increase state spending on education progressively to at least six per cent of our Gross National Product;
2. Spend more on primary education and enrol the help of non-government organisations in this area;
3. Provide free education in order to universalise access to primary education;
4. Offer incentives in the form of free textbooks, nutrition programmes and stipends to check dropout rate so that at least 80 per cent children, both boys and girls, who enrol complete primary school education;
5. Reduce learning period and introduce self-employment oriented vocational training programmes at high school level;
6. Introduce an anti-cheating law which will be applicable to all States and whose abuse will be prevented through adequate safeguards;
7. Launch community-level adult education programmes to provide functional literacy to at least 90 per cent of our adult illiterates in both villages and the cities;
8. Set up a special monitoring authority to scrutinise the quality of education and remove gender disparity;
9. Ensure autonomy to universities, encourage them to mobilise resources for research and higher education, and provide academic freedom to our scholars, especially in the social sciences;
10. Improve the pay and emoluments of teachers at all levels

and remove anomalies in college/university promotion rules;

11. Enrol industry's help to set up more technical and agro-industrial institutions that will provide affordable education;
12. Abolish the system of capitation fees and monitor the functioning of private engineering and medical institutions;
13. Launch a scheme for low interest bank loans for meritorious students who want to go in for higher education; and,
14. Thwart attempts by foreign universities, colleges and institutes of dubious reputation to open branches in India and prevent the outflow of foreign exchange on studies abroad unless the course is relevant to our needs and requirements.

Health

We believe in increasing State investment in health and nutrition programmes because this is the only path to the creation of a productive workforce by the beginning of the next century. Our goal will be health for all. Towards this end, we will strive for:

1. Ending the scourge of malnutrition;
2. Drastically reducing our infant mortality rate and under-five mortality rate by spending more on pre-natal and post-natal health care programmes;
3. Immunising every child against killer diseases;
4. Providing every panchayat with a free primary health care centre with facilities for mother and child care, as well as access to these centres;
5. Canalising a substantial portion of the health care allocation on preventive rather than curative aspects;
6. Promoting awareness on cleanliness and disease prevention;
7. Re-evaluating existing programmes to tackle sexually-transmitted diseases, with special focus on AIDS;
8. Making the screening of blood at blood banks mandatory and provide for punitive punishment for any violation;
9. Holding doctors, para-medical and non-medical staff at Government hospitals and health care centres accountable and instituting a mechanism for swift disposal of all complaints;
10. Revising pay and emoluments of staff at Government hospitals and health care centre to attract the best talent;

11. Promoting alternative medical sciences with special emphasis on Ayurveda and Unani systems;
12. Protecting traditional medicinal plants, trees and cures;
13. Preventing drug prices from escalating to a point where they become non-affordable for the masses;
14. Introducing health insurance schemes at a minimal cost to the subscriber; and,
15. Instituting a mechanism to monitor and collate health-related information.

OUR AGENDA FOR WOMEN

Nari Shakti: Towards Empowerment

We hold that 'Nari Shakti' is not merely a phrase, it is the enunciation of our approach. Towards this end, the BJP will empower women, ensure that their dignity and rights are not trampled upon and help develop their full potential. We are also committed to protecting the rights of the girl child. The BJP will:

1. End discrimination in any form against women and encourage gender sensitivity. All national policies will be subjected to gender analysis;
2. Reserve 33 per cent seats in all elected bodies, including State Assemblies and Parliament, to make women real participants in a resurgent India of the 21st century;
3. Actively promote the legal and economic rights of women which must be equal to those of men and not subject to the debilitating clauses of personal laws;
4. Introduce a Uniform Civil Code that will:
   (i) Give women property rights;
   (ii) Ensure women's right to adopt;
   (iii) Guarantee women equal guardianship rights;
   (iv) Remove discriminatory clauses in divorce laws; and,
   (v) Put an end to polygamy;
5. Create conditions in society and workplace to ensure equal opportunities in employment and promotion, and end sexual harassment;
6. Enforce the principle of equal wages for equal work whether in the organised or unorganised sector;

7. Evolve a scheme for part-time jobs for women;
8. Promote a health care system that will focus on the non-reproductive health needs of women, especially in rural areas;
9. Provide state support for single and working mothers through grants and subsidy, and formulate a forward looking housing policy to help women;
10. Make women partners in the management of community assets and properties;
11. Enrol the help of local self-governments to set up latrines for women in the rural areas;
12. Set up a micro-credit system with the help of a national corpus to which both the Union and State governments, apart from banks, will contribute;
13. Encourage the setting up of cooperative societies in rural areas to be managed by women and to benefit women entrepreneurs;
14. Introduce skill-based training programmes and employment schemes which are area-specific;
15. Design a special programme to provide women who were denied education with functional literacy;
16. Amend laws that deal with molestation, rape and dowry to provide for in-camera trial, swift justice and tough deterrent punishment as well as rehabilitation of the victims of these crimes;
17. Amend the Prevention of Immoral Traffic Act to make clients as culpable as commercial sex workers;
18. Rehabilitate commercial sex workers and set up a special fund to provide health care and education to their children;
19. Enact a law that will make registration of marriages with foreigners mandatory;
20. Make it compulsory for the mother's name also to be mentioned in all Government and non-Government records, starting from a child's birth certificate to a person's death certificate.
21. Set up designated courts in every district for expeditious trial of civil and criminal complaints relating to women;
22. Rapidly induct more women in the police force and appoint them in senior positions as well as set up a 'Crimes Against Women Cell' in every police station;

23. Enact a special law to deal with the crime of domestic violence against women;
24. Promote a social agenda designed to discourage negative influences and end discrimination against the girl child in any form;
25. Ruthlessly punish those who indulge in unethical practices like prenatal sex-determination test and female foeticide and infanticide;
26. Invest in the girl child's health, nutrition and education, from infancy through adolescence;
27. Universalise primary and secondary education to narrow the gender gap and offer incentives for the girl child's education in the form of free uniforms and books;
28. Strictly enforce age of consent laws and end child prostitution; and,
29. Have a fresh look at the UN convention for the elimination of discrimination against women (CEDAW) to determine whether the reservations expressed by the Government of India are justified.

OUR POPULATION POLICY

Towards a Sustainable and Balanced Growth

Our people are our primary concern—their basic needs of health, education and employment must precede everything else. To ensure an equitable disbursement of resources so that the largest number of our people benefit from development policies, we must arrest the country's runaway population growth. An increasing population can only mean a decreasing share of the fruits of development. Successive Congress Governments have ignored this crucial area of development planning, often for petty political motives. This has resulted in a steep rise in population and severe demographic imbalances. The Bharatiya Janata Party believes that children are born—and have the right—to be happy, and not merely for existence. We will, therefore, put population-related issues, especially family planning, firmly back on the national agenda, and launch a people's movement against the impending population explosion through persuasive policies. The BJP proposes to:

1. Act on the reports of the National Development Council and the Swaminathan Committee to formulate a National Population Policy that will stabilise the population growth by the first decade of the new century;
2. Enact a law that will debar those with more than two children from holding elected office, with 1996 as the cut-off year;
3. Provide incentives to those among the economically weaker sections who opt for the "two-child" norm in the form of special facilities for health, education, nutrition and employment opportunities. At the same time, the BJP will also introduce disincentives like limiting subsidised ration and maternity benefits to two children with 1996 as the cut-off year. These disincentives will apply to all sections of society, irrespective of their social, economic or religious status to discourage large, unsustainable families;
4. Ensure universal access to family planning information and quality facilities by involving non-government organisations, and promote awareness among the people, especially women, through counselling and educational programmes;
5. Introduce family planning methods and facilities that will allow women greater freedom of choice without imperilling their health;
6. Launch a special campaign to educate local communities about negative practices and encourage women to seek reproductive health services;
7. Offer a special incentive in the form of a fixed deposit that will mature in 21 years for those couples who have only a girl child or those who adopt a girl child under a "Dattak Putri Yojana".
8. Make family planning an integral part of our development policies to ensure widest applicability of these incentives and disincentives.

OUR ENVIRONMENT

Only One Earth

The BJP holds as a firm conviction that our "only one Earth" is the endower of all our wealth and natural resources. This, however, is not for endless exploitation. Our environment has to be protected, not only to prevent the sanctity of Mother Earth from being profaned but also because our forests, our rivers and our skies sustain a multitude of lives. No less important is the crucial role that environment plays in our nation's security. Environment must be protected by subscribing to the concept of `sustainable development', a philosophical tenet that is integral to our civilisational and cultural consciousness.

OUR SOCIAL PHILOSOPHY

Harmony and Equality Through Integral Humanism

The Bharatiya Janata Party's social philosophy, which is the bedrock of its social agenda, is rooted in integral humanism. It rules out contradictions between society and its various components, as also between society and the individual, or, for that matter, between the family, the basic building brick of our social structure, and the individual. From this stems the BJP's commitment to the eradication of social and economic disparities that have prevented India from emerging as a modern, dynamic nation; to the creation of a socially integrated Bharatiya society which can proudly enter the new century. The BJP will help all socially and economically weak and backward sections of society, through special welfare and other schemes, to reach their full potential. For us, it is a historic task which we are resolved to fulfil.

Equity and Equality

1. The BJP will adhere, through its policies and programmes, to the ideals, principles and goals of equity and equality as enshrined in our country's Constitution.
2. The BJP will promote a casteless socio-economic order which will effectively provide access to equal opportunities to all citizens, irrespective of their caste, creed, religion or gender.
3. The BJP will ensure that the place of an individual in society will not be determined on the basis of his birth.
4. The BJP will dismantle practices, customs, beliefs, usages and institutions which are divisive and discriminatory, and which in any manner hurt the dignity of the individual.

Untouchability

1. The BJP condemns unequivocally the practice of untouchability which is not only against the law of the land but runs counter to the very concept of integral humanism. Not surprisingly, the first brick of the Ram temple at Ayodhya was laid by a member of the Scheduled Castes, Kameshwar Chaupal.
2. The BJP will endeavour to create an ethos of equality in social and inter-personal relationships.

Weaker Sections

1. The BJP will make the existing institutions and Constitutional safeguards for Scheduled Castes and Scheduled Tribes operationally more effective.
2. The BJP views the provision of special facilities and special opportunities, including reservations, in the Constitution as practical steps to advance the deprived and under-privileged sections of society. The BJP will continue with the existing policy on reservations till social and economic equity is achieved.

Our Socially and Educationally Backwards

The BJP is committed to providing both social and economic justice to the socially and educationally backward classes (Other Backward Classes) through the instrument of reservations. At the same time, we hold that the path to progress of all sections of our people lies not through social divisions brought about by casteist politics but through social harmony. The BJP advocates:

1. Continuation of reservations for the Other Backward Classes till they are socially and educationally integrated with the rest of society;
2. Uniform criteria for demarcating the 'creamy layer';
3. Flow of reservation benefits in an ascending order so that the most backward sections of the OBCs get them first;
4. Ten per cent reservation on the basis of economic criteria to all economically weaker sections of society, apart from the Scheduled Castes/Scheduled Tribes and the Other Backward Classes; and,

5. Special programmes to provide education and vocational training as well as awareness campaigns.

Our Minorities

Wherever and whenever the Bharatiya Janata Party has been in power, it has ensured peace and security for all sections of society, irrespective of their religious identity. The BJP is committed to further strengthen this achievement. This is in stark contrast to the insecurity faced by minority communities under Congress rule. We have been steadfastly opposed to appeasement as state policy since it benefits only those sections which profess regressive and retrograde social norms in the guise of protecting their religious beliefs. The BJP will be guided by its policy of "justice for all, appeasement of none". A resurgent India will enter the 21st century with the resolve of one nation, one people and one culture. To achieve this goal, we will:

1. Guarantee all minority communities equal opportunity for economic development;
2. Lay stress on education and vocational training;
3. Provide incentives to those who are self-employed, especially artisans, and those who want to set up their own business enterprise;
4. Launch community programmes to create awareness among women members of minority communities;
5. Ensure equality for all and discrimination against none on grounds of religion in matters of education by amending Article 30;
6. Disband the Minorities Commission and entrust its responsibilities to the National Human Rights Commission;
7. Set up special courts for speedy trial of those accused of participating in communal riots;
8. Protect wakf property from being usurped and misused by unscrupulous individuals and organisations and help wakf boards to become self-sustaining bodies so that they do not have to be dependent on Government doles;
9. Set up trusts along the line of the Tirupati Temple Trust with official nominees for managing the affairs of dargahs;
10. Ensure that no religious property is misused or usurped;

11. Ban all foreign funds irrespective of the organisation which is the recipient;
12. Make fraudulent conversions, including those done by holding out the promise of economic or social benefits, a punishable offence and introduce a system of registering all conversions;
13. Ban the publication of job advertisements that mention religious identity as a criterion; and,
14. Set up a Commission of Inquiry (similar to the Neogi Commission) to inquire into the activities of foreign missionaries and other organisations that have been receiving foreign funds.

Human Rights

The BJP subscribes to the view that human dignity, justice for all and protection of the individual from the tyranny of the State are among the basic tenets of Hindutva. We are committed to upholding the human, democratic and civil rights of every individual, irrespective of the person's caste, creed, religion or gender. But we will not allow this commitment to be used as a shield by those who commit inhuman atrocities and thus forsake their claim to human rights. The BJP believes that the State should be fair to all citizens, but firm while dealing with those who militate against civil society. The BJP will not allow any foreign interference in our country's internal affairs on the pretext of monitoring human rights violations. We will:

1. Strengthen the existing National Human Rights Commission through more powers, additional resources and better infrastructural support;
2. Disband the Minorities Commission, which has only succeeded in feeding separatist sentiments and giving rise to imagined grievances, and entrust its responsibilities to the National Human Rights Commission;
3. Take swift action on the basis of the Commission's findings and punish the guilty; and,
4. Include the study of human, democratic and civil rights in school curricula.

Displaced Communities: Protecting their Rights

Separatist violence and Islamic fundamentalism/terrorism in Jammu and Kashmir has forced more than 300,000 people, including 250,000 Kashmiri Pandits and Punjabi and Dogra Hindus, apart from thousands of Sikhs and even some Muslims, to flee their homes and hearths. Most of the displaced Pandits are living in abysmal conditions in refugee camps in Jammu and some other places. Together, they perhaps form the largest internally-displaced community in the world, forced to live as refugees in their own motherland, condemned to the mercy of an uncaring and callous Congress Government at the Centre and its puppet administration in Jammu and Kashmir. The Bharatiya Janata Party has mobilised its own resources, men and material to provide succour to these unfortunate victims of Government apathy and terrorist violence. But a lot more needs to be done.

Similarly, thousands of Buddhist Chakmas have fled the Chittagong Hill Tracts in Bangladesh in the face of persecution by Muslim settlers from the plains and the Bangladesh Rifles. Most of them are at present living in camps in Tripura. Regardless of the grim future that awaits them back home, the Government of India has shown unnecessary haste in trying to repatriate them—an action that is largely motivated by the petty politics of the Congress. The BJP is opposed to such forced repatriation in the absence of foolproof security guarantees from the Government of Bangladesh.

The escalating conflict in Sri Lanka between Sinhalese and Tamils is posing a demographic threat to South India with a large number of Tamil refugees beginning to pour into this region. Such a movement is bound to increase the influence of the LTTE which may in turn promote separatist tendencies.

We must also address ourselves to the concerns of non-resident Indians, especially those who had settled in Hong Kong and now find the future uncertain with Britain handing over this territory to China in 1997.

The BJP Proposes:

For Kashmiri Pandits

1. As urged by them for social cohesion and cultural preservation, designate the Pandits who have been forced out of

Kashmir Valley as an internally displaced community.

2. Provide adequate financial relief, proper health, housing, education and employment facilities on a priority basis to all displaced families.
3. Take adequate steps to protect their assets and properties in Kashmir Valley till such time they are able to return home.
4. Elections in the Valley should be held only after the displaced people are able to return to their homes.
5. Ensure proper documentation of the displaced Pandits and their assets.

For Chakma Refugees

1. Resettle Chakma refugees, the bulk of whom are at present in Tripura, in camps in other contiguous States and provide financial support to their governments so that they do not have to take on the economic burden.
2. Provide full citizenship to those Chakmas who do not want to return to Bangladesh and whose children were born in India.
3. Negotiate with Bangladesh for the phased repatriation of those Chakmas who want to return, provided Dhaka guarantees their safety and well-being.
4. Ensure full security for the Chakmas who live in refugee camps so that they are not harassed or threatened.
5. Maintain an official register of Chakma refugees and their whereabouts.

For Sri Lankan Tamil Refugees

1. House them in refugee camps and monitor their movements.
2. Prevent their association with local organisations or opening local chapters of Sri Lankan organisations.
3. Screen the antecedents of the Tamil refugees and disallow asylum to those who have or had links with Tamil terrorists.
4. Maintain a register of all such refugees.
5. Repatriate Tamil refugees as soon as the situation is conducive for their safe-being.

For non-resident Indians

1. Provide citizenship to those Hong Kong Indians who wish to return to their motherland.

2. Help rehabilitate the returning Hong Kong Indians.
3. Examine afresh difficulties in granting dual citizenship to non-resident Indians all over the world.

OUR IDENTITY, OUR CULTURE

The Cornerstone of Bharatiyata

The Bharatiya Janata Party believes that modernisation does not mean the mechanical imitation of a particular way of life. It will redefine the concept of development to accommodate the Bharatiya way of living, belief system and values to reach the ultimate goal of Bharatiyata. We hold that it is necessary to emphasise the linkage of development elements to cultural elements, including local relevance, relevance to geographical and environmental factors, historical traditions, traditional knowledge and skills. We believe that cultural factors play an important role in energising a nation. For a resurgent India whose people can proudly flaunt their Bharatiyata, the BJP will:

1. Strengthen and revitalise our cultural institutions;
2. Revive and rejuvenate our positive cultural traditions and values;
3. Include Indian cultural studies and 'Naitik Siksha' as part of school curriculum;
4. Establish a Bharatiya Sanskriti Kendra in each district;
5. Declare all places of pilgrimage as national heritage centres;
6. Encourage the study of Sanskrit and strictly enforce the three-language formula in schools;
7. Promote Bharatiya classical music and performing arts through State support; and,
8. Discourage indecent representation of women in advertisements and publications.

Media and Publishing

The BJP believes that a free press is a sine qua non for a democracy. At the same time, we also hold that this freedom should not be misused to defame or malign any individual, organisation or institution.

For a free, fair and fearless media, the BJP will:

1. Expedite the recommendations and implementation of the

wage-board set up for journalists and non-journalists as well as evolve a mechanism for the automatic institution of a wage-board for journalists every five years;
2. Free All India Radio and Doordarshan from Government control and implement the Prasar Bharati Act;
3. Ensure that no book or publication is banned without proper scrutiny;
4. Disallow foreign print media to launch Indian editions;
5. Evolve a comprehensive visual media policy for uplinking facilities and transmission via our satellite transponders;
6. Review the difficulties of small and medium newspapers;
7. Review the practice of contracted jobs in newspapers;
8. Strengthen the Press Council for speedy and fair disposal of complaints; and,
9. Consider the legislation of a 'Right to Reply' law which will enable any person who has been unfairly villified to publish his or her version.

Cinema

Popular cinema has played an important role in promoting social harmony and nationalism, apart from providing inexpensive entertainment to the masses. But in recent years, popular cinema, increasingly funded by the underworld, has had a negative impact on society, especially impressionable young minds. Sex and violence on the silver screen are beginning to gnaw at the moorings of our cultural ethos. To check this abuse of popular cinema, the BJP will :

1. Provide film-making the status of industry so that producers can be made accountable for their resources and expenses;
2. Enable film-makers through suitable provisions in law to raise resources from financial institutions to curb the influence of underworld financiers and mafia dons;
3. Analogous to the concept of the Customs 'green channel', provide automatic certification for films which do not contain explicit scenes and dialogues of violence and sex-producers and exhibitors of such films will not have to wait in the queue for Censor Board clearance. Deterrent punishment will be meted out to any producer who abuses the

facility; theatre owners who screen such films will also be penalised;

4. Exempt quality films, which will be certified as 'Q' from entertainment tax;
5. Encourage viewers to form local Darshak Sanghs—on the lines of consumer organisations—to monitor the quality of films being screened in their area;
6. Set up special theatres at district headquarters and metropolitan cities for screening art and quality films;
7. Appoint 50 per cent women on the Censor Board and Censor Panels;
8. Create a special fund for promoting regional cinema; and,
9. Introduce legislation to ensure minimum wages and retirement benefits for film extras and crew members.

OUR YOUTH—OUR FUTURE

In the Vanguard of Change

Our youth form the backbone of our vibrant nation and they alone can shape the destiny of this country. The BJP has a tryst with the youth of India and will harness their creative energy for bringing about social, cultural and political change. We will aim at transforming Yuva Sankalpa into Yuva Shakti, which, in turn, will be the catalyst for reinvigorating India.

We will inculcate in the country's youth a sense of pride in our ancient traditions and heritage. We will instil in them a sense of self-confidence so that they can take their rightful place in the vanguard of change.

Towards this end, through its policies and programmes, the BJP will:

1. Inculcate in the youth a sense of being indebted to society at large and thus prepare them to repay this debt by involving themselves in development programmes and social, cultural and economic activities;
2. Initiate schemes both at Government and non-Government levels to achieve overall development of young talent;
3. Mobilise the youth to fight regressive and retrograde social practices and customs by making community service a

compulsory and integral component of college and university curricula;

4. Set up a National Youth Commission and a Youth Development Bank to design and implement comprehensive employment oriented education policies as well channelise youth power for the purpose of nation-building;
5. Encourage the youth to form 'Yuva Sena' and 'Dharti Raksha Vahini' for voluntary community service with the ultimate aim of generating employment;
6. Launch a massive self-enterprise programme to provide employment opportunities to the educated unemployed;
7. Allocate adequate time for youth programmes on Doordarshan;
8. Promote sports through enhanced expenditure on training sportsmen and their rehabilitation after they retire from the field;
9. Establish a network of youth hostels throughout the country and provide travel concessions; and,
10. Encourage the study of yoga and promote our cultural heritage by incorporating them in educational curriculum.

LET'S COMMENCE A NEW CHAPTER

This then is the blueprint which the Bharatiya Janata Party will implement on coming to power. The task will be undertaken by the party's inspiring team of leaders, each one of whom has an unblemished record of selfless service to the nation. It is through this blueprint that the BJP will bring about radical change in the country's polity, society and economy. It is this blueprint which will be the bedrock of a new India where every citizen shall be free from fear, hunger and discrimination. This blueprint will pave the way to the next century and the new millennium.

But to implement our commitments we need your support. The sweeping change that has become so necessary to save the nation can be brought about only with your help. To begin with, you have to change the leadership at the helm of the country's affairs and vote out the Congress. The time has arrived for a nationalist Government which will lead India from the dark curse of poverty to prosperity; which will free the administration from the clutches of criminals and restore probity in public life; which will reinvest the state with authority and strengthen our security forces; and, which will secure our country's frontiers so that we do not have to suffer once again the humiliations of this millennium. Such a Government can be provided only by the BJP.

The past five decades have been a tragic story of missed opportunities and self-serving opportunist politics. The Congress has abused power and authority for the benefit of few and to the detriment of millions of Indians. The leaders of the Janata Dal have demonstrated their inability to think beyond themselves. The Left parties, orphaned by the passing away of Communism all over the world, are struggling to come to terms with an ideological vacuum. None of these parties can boast of ideological commitment, moral courage and political conviction. On the other hand, the BJP has emerged as the only national alternative, a party that stands apart for its ideology, commitment and courage.

We are standing at an important crossroad of our nation's history. The BJP appeals to all patriotic Indians to join the noble mission of national reconstruction, the task of creating a strong and prosperous India. Let us be partners in a new era of equality, peace and progress.

Vande Mataram!

is not only to prosperity which will free the [illegible] the clutches of criminals and [illegible] which [illegible] so that we do not have to suffer [illegible] Army which a Government [illegible] provided only by the BJP.

The past five decades have been a [illegible] Congress [illegible] and to the [illegible] Janata Dal [illegible] themselves. The [illegible] Communist [illegible] On the other hand, the BJP [illegible] a party that [illegible] country.

We are [illegible] vision of the BJP [illegible] the next [illegible] and prosperity [illegible] country, peace and progress.

Vande Mataram

Index